This Terrible Ordeal

*Manx letters, diaries and
memories of the Great War*

At the present time Manx hearts are especially drawn together in the thought of the gallantry of all the fine Manxmen who are fighting for us by land & sea. May all ... come safely through this terrible ordeal, & may Peace soon bless us.

Sophia Morrison 25 March 1915
(Manx National Heritage MS 09495)

This Terrible Ordeal

Manx letters, diaries and memories of the Great War

MATTHEW RICHARDSON

First published in the Isle of Man in 2013 by

Manx National Heritage
Kingswood Grove
Douglas
Isle of Man
British Isles
IM1 3LY

Copyright © Manx National Heritage

ISBN 978-0-901106-67-4

A CIP catalogue record for this book is available from the British Library

The right of Matthew Richardson to be identified as the author of this work has been asserted in accordance with the Copyright Act 1991.

Cover Illustration: Private Matthew McCauley, and Mary Brew, a munitions worker, both of Douglas (PG 13708-2 and PG 7058-9)

Contents

Douglas War Memorial
(John Caley, Manx National Heritage)

Foreword

1913 had been the busiest year for the Isle of Man, and 1914 promised to break all records. The summer weather was kind, and Douglas harbour was black with the smoke of fifteen Steam Packet ships. Just before Tynwald Day, an event happened in faraway Bosnia that triggered the worst calamity in modern history. By early August, the peoples of Europe were at war. Here in the Island, the season came to an abrupt halt, as visitors went home, local men enlisted and ships were requisitioned for a conflict the scale of which no one could imagine. It was a war that shaped the century and transformed the lives of generations. Decimation is an over-used word, but it accurately describes the terrible loss of Manx lives: of the young men who left the Island in uniform, one in ten did not return.

Matthew Richardson has a talent for communicating deep scholarship in a most accessible and readable form. Here he links world events with the personal testimony of individuals serving abroad on land and sea, their families at home and of the unwilling 'visitors' interned here through the exigencies of war. Apart from the tragedy and heroism, he describes the social changes ushered in by the war: the role of women outside the home, the pressure for greater democracy, equality and political independence. When the guns fell silent in 1918, the scene was set for the world in which we now live.

This is an epic story well told....

Tony Pass
Chairman, Manx National Heritage

Acknowledgements

This book grew out of a day school entitled *The Isle of Man and the First World War: Aspects and Insights* which I taught at the Centre for Manx Studies in 2010. The preparation for this surprised me, in as much as it made me realise how wide the gaps in my knowledge about the First World War in the Isle of Man really were. Overall, it has taken me more than ten years even to reach the stage where I feel that I am beginning to get to grips with a subject as broad as this.

Most people with a knowledge of Manx history are aware of the Island's role in the First World War as an internment centre, but the more I looked into this era, the more I realised that there were aspects of this period of history, such as crime during the war, and conscientious objection, which up to that point had never really been investigated. This book is the result of my attempt to fill some of those gaps; I hope that you the reader will agree that I have covered some aspects of the Isle of Man's experience in the First World War which are completely new, and offered fresh insights into others which are already well known.

A number of people deserve acknowledgement for their assistance and advice over the years. Dean Johnson has had a long term interest in Manx soldiers of the First World War and has readily shared his material. Likewise Barry Bridson has long had an interest in Manxmen who served in the war, and was more than willing to loan valuable documents. Barry Quilliam with an interest in the Manx Service Company was equally generous. Andrew Scarffe has published his research on the Great Laxey Mine to much acclaim, and has always answered my many questions about that subject. Ivor Ramsden at MAPS is also deserving of my thanks. My colleague Yvonne Cresswell is a noted authority on internment on the Isle of Man and I am grateful to her for her help. Wendy Thirkettle and Alan Franklin in the Manx National Heritage Library and Archive introduced me to a number of new sources. Roy Baker at the Leece Museum was more than willing to share material under his control. Alan Kelly of Mannin Collections generously provided a number of photographs, whilst Frances Coakley, creator of the *Manx Notebook* website (www.isle-of-man.com/manxnotebook/) allowed me to quote from the Rudolf Hartmann papers.

Adrian Corkill is a noted authority on shipwrecks around the coast of the Island, and I would like to acknowledge his research in particular in relation to Chapter Two. Alexander McKinnion and Martin Mosse provided valuable material, and I thank them both warmly. Likewise Tom and Rob Lilley provided important information and photographs. Audrey Mansell was a great help with family photographs and memories, as was Edwyn Green. Others who I wish to thank for allowing me to use family material include Ruth Bannon, Marie Radcliffe,

David Quayle, Christa Bedford, Elizabeth Harrison, Alison Graham, Sue Rimmer, Jane Coomer, Jennifer Corlett, Stuart Kelly, Sue King, Julie Quine, Voirrey Johnson, Mrs E.L.Hogg, Adrian Cain and Gary Corlett.

Peter Elliott at the RAF Museum provided assistance, as did Andrew Dawrant at the Royal Aero Club and Caroline Rhodes at Hull Museums. Brian Roberts at the Isle of Man Public Record Office and Sarah Christian helped to guide me towards internment related material which I might otherwise have missed. Dr Breesha Maddrell and Dr Fenella Bazin provided advice and information relating to Mona Douglas. Tony Thompson at Manchester City Council was most helpful in sourcing photographs. Sue Hill at Southampton City Archives likewise deserves credit.Manx National Heritage images are shown with their respective accession numbers. Other sources of illustrations are as credited.

I would like to thank Laura Wehr upon whose work Chapter Three draws. Her research into internment camp magazines (and translations) reveals a great deal about the mood within those camps, and deserves recognition. Likewise Professor Bill Niven was a great help with translation work and internment sources in general. Jennifer Kewley-Draskau was also generous in sharing her work in this area. Cem Fakir in Turkey was instrumental in obtaining material from the Ottoman archives in Istanbul, whilst Terry Cringle in the Isle of Man offered tremendous support for this book and its associated museum exhibition through his *Times Past* newspaper column. The Trustees and Friends of Manx National Heritage are worthy of special mention in connection with their support for the iMuseum project; this marvellous research facility is indeed the bedrock upon which the book is based.

Finally my thanks go to Kirsty Neate for once again supporting me in obtaining resources for publishing my research, likewise to the Trustees of Manx National Heritage for again making available financial assistance, and to Tony Pass, Chairman of Trustees, for providing the foreword of the book.

Matthew Richardson
Douglas 2013

Figure i
A map showing the major theatres of
conflict during the First World War.

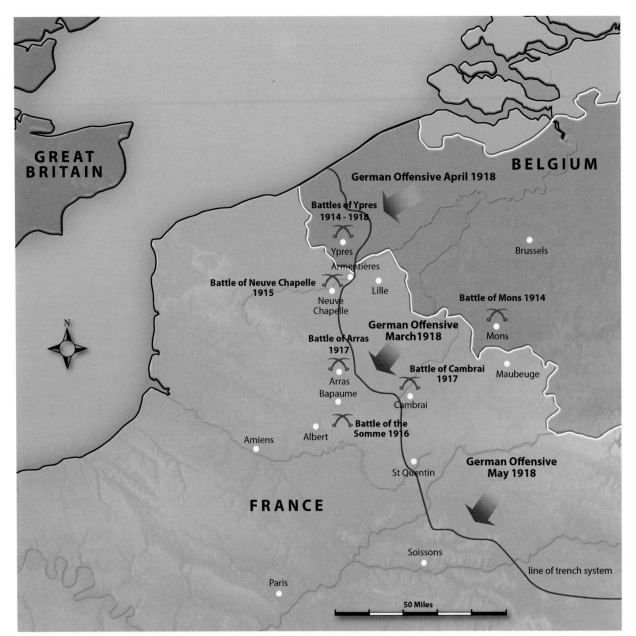

Figure ii
A map showing the Western Front and the major engagements, 1914-1918.

GREAT BRITAIN

BELGIUM

German Offensive April 1918

Battles of Ypres 1914 - 1918

Ypres

Armentières

Brussels

Battle of Neuve Chapelle 1915

Neuve Chapelle

Lille

Battle of Mons 1914

German Offensive March 1918

Mons

N

Battle of Arras 1917

Battle of Cambrai 1917

Maubeuge

Arras

Bapaume

Cambrai

Battle of the Somme 1916

Amiens

Albert

German Offensive May 1918

St Quentin

FRANCE

Soissons

line of trench system

Paris

50 Miles

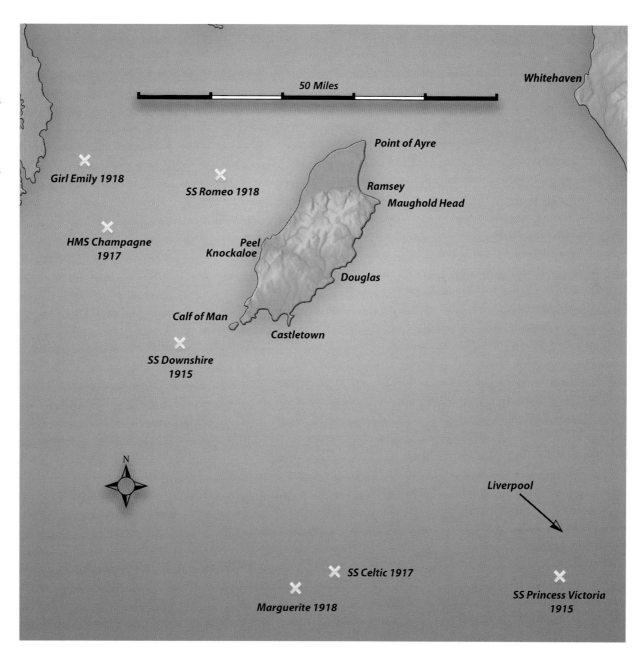

Figure iii
A map showing the Isle of Man and the surrounding Irish Sea area, with some of the First World War U-boat attacks on shipping marked.

50 Miles

Whitehaven

Point of Ayre

Girl Emily 1918

SS Romeo 1918

Ramsey

Maughold Head

HMS Champagne 1917

Peel
Knockaloe

Douglas

Calf of Man

Castletown

SS Downshire 1915

N

Liverpool

SS Celtic 1917

Marguerite 1918

SS Princess Victoria 1915

Introduction

The First World War, known at the time and in the years immediately after as the Great War, was a cataclysmic event. It marked the ending of the world of our grand-parents and great grand-parents, and the beginning of the world which we know today. It was a true watershed, which signalled the close of the long Victorian age, the ideas, values and aspirations of which did not die suddenly with Queen Victoria in 1901, and the real beginning of the twentieth century. Twentieth century ideas about the relationship between the individual and the state, the relationships between social classes, national self-determination, and political concepts such as Fascism, Nazism and Marxist-Leninism, were all born on its battlefields or in its factories.

During the First World War, the nature of the world as it would be throughout much of the twentieth century began to take shape. When Britain declared war on Germany on 4 August 1914, Europe and Asia were dominated by five powerful empires: the British Empire, that of the Tsars in Russia, the Austro-Hungarian (Hapsburg) Empire, the German (Hohenzollern) Empire and the Ottoman Empire in Turkey. When the war ended, four of the five were in ruins, broken into myriad nation states. Even though it reached its greatest geographical expanse in the years immediately after the Great War, as an idea and as a philosophical concept, the British Empire also began its decline during the conflict. The rise in India of national self-awareness, together with the ideal that Britain was fighting for the rights of small nations for self-determination, would fatally undermine it. At the same time, the war saw the first awakenings of the colossus in the west, the United States, and that in the east, the USSR, which emerged from the wreckage of the Russian Empire. In Britain, the legacies of the Great War are still discernable today, in things like British Summer Time, pub licensing hours, regulations concerning the strength of alcoholic drinks, the long-term eclipse of the Liberal Party by the Labour Party, nationalised industries, sexual equality and what some might call the permissive society.

In spite of the massive changes which swept the British Isles in those years, the effects of the Great War were surprisingly localised in their nature, and varied from region to region. This book examines the Isle of Man's response to this monumental event, and to some extent attempts to compare this with what was happening across the British Isles as a whole, in order to try to understand in what ways if any the experience of the Isle of Man was unique. It also assesses the scale and depth of the impact of that war on Manx society, political institutions and culture, and argues that the legacy of those events can still be traced today. This book is not about strategy or the higher direction of the war, but instead examines how the war was experienced by ordinary people of the Isle of Man, in the Isle of Man, and in Manx ships, be they soldiers, sailors, airmen, prisoners or civilians. As far as is possible, it allows the participants themselves to describe the events, and to express their feelings and reactions to them. Above all, it seeks to show that even in so small a community as the Isle of Man there was no single 'war experience'; even in the close confines of an internment camp, it is difficult to argue that there was a single homogenous outlook or perspective. For the Manx, this war was encountered in innumerable ways according to gender, class, nationality and, not least, personal outlook.

The political turmoil in far away Austria-Hungary, and the assassination of the Austrian archduke at Sarajevo which sparked the conflict, must have barely entered the consciousness of most Manx people in 1914. Their island home was in the midst of a tourist boom which saw thousands of visitors come flocking to the Isle of Man each summer. The trade had brought great prosperity to some, but not to all, and there were already worrying divisions within Manx society. Politically and constitutionally, the Isle of Man lay outside of the United Kingdom of Great Britain and Ireland. At the same time as a sense of a separate and distinctive Manx identity was growing and taking root, the Island was controlled by a Lieutenant-Governor appointed from London, whose autocratic methods aroused the ire of its people. If anything, that summer the concern of most was over the dubious benefits of Manx 'home rule'. Whilst it had allowed the Island the freedom to stage the TT races which the Westminster government disavowed, the anomalous position of the Isle of Man also meant that it had not shared in the raft of social legislation sweeping the United Kingdom in the Edwardian era. None the less when war broke out and the call of the British Empire came, the 'little Manx nation' stood ready to play its part ...

British soldiers in action in France in 1914, before the Western Front settled into static trench warfare. (Author's collection)

Chapter One

Show that you are Manxmen

When the First World War began, the first British soldiers to set foot in France were members of the British Expeditionary Force (BEF). They were almost all Regular soldiers, or reservists who had completed their Regular service but could still be called up in an emergency. The 1914 campaign began in the heat of summer amid fields of swaying wheat and corn, and came to a close with the frosty chill of Christmas. Just as dramatic as that change in climate was the shift in tactics in just five months, from the almost Napoleonic - with heroic cavalry charges, gaudy uniforms, and field guns firing at massed bodies of infantry as they moved across country - to twentieth century industrialised warfare, dominated by the machine-gun and other weapons of the modern age. By that first Christmas, the protagonists had literally 'gone to earth', and the network of trenches which they dug for protection would not move to any great extent until 1918.

From a Manx perspective, this early period of the war is particularly interesting. Although there had been Volunteer soldiers in the Isle of Man for many years, and they were affiliated to the King's Liverpool Regiment, the Island was not officially part of the recruiting area of any particular regiment. Hence Manx soldiers prior to 1914 had enlisted into a wide variety of units, cavalry and infantry, English, Scottish and Irish. These men came from right across the Island, and they occupied positions at almost every level of society, from Government House, to the back streets of Douglas. Their letters and reports from the early days of the war provide a remarkably complete record of the ebb and flow of battle in those turbulent times.

One of the first men to see action was Private James Comaish, the son of Mr Walter Comaish, a farmer of Maughold. At the outbreak of war he was living at Wesley Terrace, Douglas. He was not the stereotypical enthusiastic volunteer, responding to the call of King and Country or Lord Kitchener's famous poster with outstretched finger, which many people associate with the First World War. Instead, he was a reservist who had already spent nine years in the army, eight of them in India, with the 1st Battalion of the King's Liverpool Regiment. Having completed his military service, for the two years prior to the war he had been a driver on the Manx Electric Railway. Upon the outbreak of war on 4 August 1914, he was recalled to the Colours by a telegram, instructing him to rejoin his old regiment at Aldershot without delay.

On 12 August 1914 Comaish and his battalion arrived in France, and began the journey in railway cattle trucks towards the concentration area of the BEF, which was at Maubeuge on the Franco-Belgian border. The British under their commander Field Marshal Sir John French were numerically far smaller than their French allies or their German foes, and so the plan initially was for the BEF to form up close to the Fôret de Mormal, and then take its place on the left flank of the French Army.

To understand what happened next, one must examine the nature of the enemy that the BEF was facing. Germany in 1914 was nothing short of a military superpower. By calling up her reservists, she could rapidly put some six million men into the field. Britain by contrast relied on naval firepower for protection. Her army in 1914 was little more than a colonial police force. The Kaiser's comment that the British possessed a "Contemptible Little Army" is well known. Less well known is his joke to his generals that if the British sent an army to attack him, he would simply have the police arrest them!

The German army had long been faced with the prospect of war on two fronts simultaneously, with the Russians in the east and with their French allies in the west, and had devised the Schlieffen Plan in response. German High Command reasoned that the enormous Russian army would take longer to mobilize than the British and French, and they planned to deal the French a knockout blow, before the Russian threat could fully materialise. Accordingly, that summer the German armies swung like a great arc through Belgium and on into northern France, aiming simultaneously to capture Paris and smash the Franco-British armies in their path.

The northern end of this arc was now moving faster and in greater strength than anyone had dared to imagine, Maubeuge was in danger of being overrun and the BEF swept aside before it could even gather its strength. On 23 August its First Corps under General Sir Douglas Haig advanced to meet the foe near the Belgian town of Mons. Private James Comaish recounts the movements of his battalion as they went forward to take their position on the right of the BEF's line:

> On Sunday August 23rd we made a forced march of 19 miles starting at three o'clock in the morning. Our packs, with rifle and ammunition, weighed close on 100 lbs. When we got to Mons, our regiment was quartered in a farmyard. Our artillery commenced firing over our heads and we got orders to leave the yard. Just as we got out, the German artillery found the range and four shells dropped into the yard, which we had only just left. We advanced into the firing line, and took up a position after digging trenches. Each man carries a pick and shovel, and we usually dig the trench four feet deep, and if we have time, with a sheltering ledge to escape the shell fire. At dark we left the position, and retired some three miles where we again dug trenches. [1]

The trenches which Comaish mentions here should not be confused with those which came later when the Western Front had stagnated. At this early stage these would have been mere foxholes or rifle pits, large enough to accommodate just one or two men. Dawn on 24 August found the 1st Liverpools near the village of Harmignies:

> We just got nearly finished digging when just before daybreak a further retreat was ordered. We went back about another mile, where we were supplied with some biscuits and tea, and "bully". As we were eating the Germans commenced to shell the trenches we had left. They kept bombarding the empty trenches for six hours, while we lay out behind them in extended order. After the bombardment, the German infantry charged, and we let them get nearly up to the empty trenches, when our artillery and infantry went for them. The Germans charged in close order and we cut them up terribly and

drove them back. They did not seem to care for the loss of life, and as soon as a gap was made others filled it. The fighting continued all the Monday and we gradually retired. During the fight word came that the Germans were advancing in very strong force over a hill right in front of our position and soon after they came in swarms. When they got well into our view our artillery got at them, and we could see from where we were lying heads and legs flying in all directions. It was awful. Large gaps were torn in the German ranks, but on they came. I noticed that the German officers never lead their men like ours do, but keep at the back. [2]

The Germans had been given a bloody nose, but were now threatening to overwhelm the BEF by sheer weight of numbers. Secretary of State for War Lord Kitchener's parting words must have been ringing in the ears of Sir John French - his duty was to cooperate with the French army, but above all else he must not allow his force to be destroyed. With this in mind he ordered the fighting withdrawal that became known as the Retreat from Mons. The Liverpools duly retreated to the south of the Fôret de Mormal, following the road from La Longueville to Berlaimont, and thence to Landrecies where they spent a sleepless night repulsing German incursions. James Comaish and his comrades provided the rearguard, and in addition to German attacks, the heat, dust and lack of sleep took a heavy toll on the retreating British infantry. Comaish remembered:

We kept on retiring for six days, walking 172 miles with only ten hours solid sleep. Sometimes we were falling asleep on the march if the Germans would let us. When

we did settle down, it was not the bugle which woke us, but German shells ... At Landrecies we had a very stiff fight on, I think the 26th but we forgot days. We had just got into the town when we heard the Germans were coming through the forest, and we had to turn out ... We were fighting in the streets all night, and some of the regiments lost heavily, but we did not do badly. We were lying in extended order in the streets, and the losses of the Germans were very great, so heavy indeed that when we got the order to charge with the bayonet, we could hardly get at them for dead bodies. We did get at some of them at the finish. [3]

For Comaish the retreat ended when he was hit in the arm by a shell splinter, other fragments from the same explosion having killed the men to the left and right of him. He concluded his account with his opinions as to the fighting qualities of the German soldier:

The week's fighting and marching was awful heavy. The German infantry are not good shots, but their artillery is very good. They can't stand our charges, and they are very funny when they charge. Before they commence, a side drum goes for about five minutes, an officer steps in front, and calls out something, and then gets behind, and the men charge, making an awful row with something like a child's penny trumpet in their mouths. We could not make out what the row was at first, but got used to it. We would let them get quite close (about 100 yards) before opening on them with our rifles, and they never got a charge home. When we get among them with the bayonet, they squeal like pigs. They are very treacherous, and fire on Red Cross men and the ambulance. [4]

The British regular soldier possessed a quiet self-confidence born of years of training, and a simple faith in his officers. Lance Corporal Charles Sladen of the Black Watch, whose home was at Laxey, gave an account of his experiences in 1914 which illustrates this. He tells us:

> ... on the Tuesday morning we retired from Mons. We found the packs we had to carry, especially with the extra ammunition, far too heavy, indeed, after a long march our arms were numbed and at last we got orders that we could take from the pack our greatcoats. The retreat went on, and we fought a rearguard action all the way. We could not make out the reason for the retreat, but we all felt that the German Generals were not as good as our own, and we knew that our officers were all right, and knew what they were doing, so we just kept on fighting, and retreating. There was no difficulty about food, as our kitchens travel with us on wheels, and can cook on the march, while there are always plenty of vegetables. [5]

As battalions of infantry began to straggle on the road south from Mons there was a danger of them losing contact with each other and with their brigade and divisional headquarters. Among the Royal Engineers motorcycle dispatch riders who maintained communications during the Retreat was a Manxman, Corporal Douggie Brown, who had, prior to the war, ridden in the TT races; Brown was competing in a race at Brooklands on the day war was declared, and he immediately volunteered to serve as a dispatch rider. He went to France in August 1914, and was soon under fire. He wrote to his parents in Douglas on numerous occasions. One of his letters, written from France, states:

> I am very well and comfortable, considering all things, but the only thing that we do require are cigarettes and matches, especially in tins of 50. We are kept very busy riding day and night. The French roads in the country districts are good, but in the towns and villages, or rather what the Germans have left of them, are really vile. I have had to give up my Rover bicycle, and now ride a Douglas. All the riders in our company have to ride the same machine, so as to solve the 'spare part question'; and then, again, the Douglas being very light, we can carry it over potholes and other places. Of course it is slow, especially after the Rover, which I left at the base. [6]

Brown added in another letter that his party consisted of eight riders, of whom two were former TT competitors: Davis of the Sunbeam team and Boyton who had ridden for Triumph. Corporal Eric Williams meanwhile had actually won the 1914 Junior TT race, before enlisting as a dispatch rider upon the outbreak of the war. Motorcyclists however were not exempt from danger. Lance Corporal Fred Hetherington of Castletown was serving with the Northumberland Fusiliers, and later recounted an incident which occurred in France in 1914:

> It was here that I saw perhaps the most terrible sight of my lifetime. A motor cyclist, one of our brave dispatch riders - had been captured. His machine was standing by the roadside, where he had probably been taken prisoner. His body was on the road where he had been 'done in' with the butt end of a rifle. One side of his face was bashed completely round, so that it was at the other side. [7]

A Manx dispatch rider: Douggie Brown seen before the First World War with his motorcycle (PG 13502)

Accounts of German atrocities at this time are controversial. For many years they were dismissed as propaganda; research from German sources however has produced strong evidence for these crimes. Certainly, British soldiers in their letters and recollections are remarkably consistent in their accounts of atrocities committed by the German army in France and Belgium in 1914. These range from firing on red cross flags and advancing under the cover of a white flag of truce, to the murder of civilians and the murder of prisoners of war.

During the 200 mile Retreat from Mons the 'bogey man' of the BEF had been the German General von Kluck. The tommies had derived a great deal of enjoyment from devising obscene ditties incorporating his name, but the fact remained that he and his First Army had been a sword in the back of the BEF. On 5 September 1914 however the tables were turned. The Schlieffen Plan had called for the wheeling German armies to pass around the top of Paris and down the western side in order to encircle the city. Instead, the Germans suffered a crisis of confidence and feared that if they did this they would be cut off. Instead they turned to pass down the eastern side of Paris. As they did so, they were simultaneously attacked by French formations from the west and from the east. The Battle of the Marne had begun.

The German First and Second Armies parted to meet the twin assaults, and the men of the BEF advanced into the gap. Their nemesis von Kluck had now thrust his head into a giant bag, and in order not to be cut off and surrounded by the British and French, was obliged to retire. The 'miracle of the Marne' had not only saved Paris but in the opinion of Winston Churchill at any rate, probably cost the Germans the war.

The BEF followed up the retreating Germans. A Manx officer in action here was Lieutenant W.A.W.Crellin of the 2nd Battalion Sherwood Foresters. He was the son of the late Mr J.C.Crellin JP of Ballachurry, Andreas and was also an old boy of King William's College. A Regular officer, Crellin had been commissioned from Sandhurst in 1912. His battalion had embarked at Southampton for St Nazaire on 8 September 1914, and at Coulommiers they began to follow the line of retreat taken by the Germans from the Marne. Signs of caddish Hun behaviour were everywhere:

The interiors of the houses had all been wrecked, furniture had been destroyed, pictures knocked down, tapestries cut and so on, and the place was full of empty wine bottles. The Germans had evidently been enjoying themselves there. One could not always describe damage to the actual structure of a house as being sheer uncivilised vandalism, for if soldiers were shelling a bridge and a house happened to be in the way of a shell then so much the worse for you, but this wholesale smashing of furniture and similar household accessories was nothing but wanton destruction. [8]

Among those wounded near here was another soldier from the north of the Island, Sergeant Charles Christian, of the 5th Dragoon Guards. He regarded his experiences of the war up to that point (which had included taking part in a bayonet charge and having his horse shot from under him) as fascinating rather more than enjoyable, and wrote of the incident on 12 September which occurred whilst clearing Germans from a farm yard:

I was shot down through both legs, and since that moment it has been my fate to see some of the worst sides of the war. I lay in a ditch for an hour with rain falling until the fight finished... After the fight we were taken in hand by the RAMC [Royal Army Medical Corps] and after our wounds were dressed we were carried to an improvised hospital in a church. I was hit in the left calf and right ankle. The calf wound was a nice clean hole, and it is nearly healed, but that in the ankle is more serious.[9]

He went on to describe how the doctors' struggle to save his foot from amputation had not been helped by delays and difficulties in getting the wounded away by train.

The Germans now dug themselves in on the north bank of the River Aisne. The weather had broken, and the Battle of the Aisne which followed is chiefly remembered by those who took part in it for the torrential September rain which followed. Having blown up the main bridges across it, the Germans made the river, now swollen by the heavy rains, into a formidable obstacle. To cross it under fire would be a major undertaking but this the British set themselves to do, and on 12 September the battle began to dislodge the Germans, who had entrenched themselves on the heights of the Chemin des Dames ridge. This chalky plateau was home to the first properly constructed trenches of the First World War, and for almost a fortnight battalion after battalion of British soldiers hurled themselves at them without significant gain. In fact, the Germans would not finally be turned from these positions for another four years. Fred Hetherington describes how he and his comrades now

Sergeant Charles Christian of the 5th Dragoon Guards, wounded in action in France in 1914. (PG 13746)

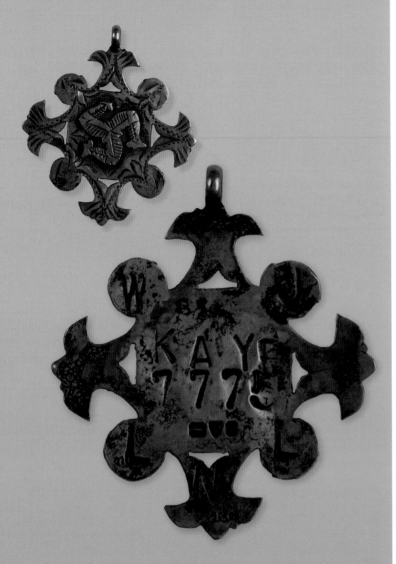

This personalised identity tag belonged to Private William Kaye, Loyal North Lancashire Regiment, of Douglas. He was killed on the Aisne on 14 September 1914, and the tag was found many years later in a French bric-a-brac shop, suggesting that Kaye gave it away before he died. (2011-0090)

took part in a bayonet charge against German positions on the banks of the Aisne, on 14 September:

We were so near the German trenches that we got the order to charge. When they saw the steel glittering on our rifles they squealed like rats and bolted from the trenches. To escape us they had to get over other trenches behind and some of them were not quick enough. One fellow scrambled out just in front of me. He may have had a mother living, a wife, children, a sweetheart. I cannot say: I did not stop to think of that, but while I ran blindly towards their fire, I just thought of our fellows lying dead and wounded in the trenches. As I struck, I tripped and fell right over him. By the time I had picked myself up, the charge was practically over. They opened fire on us from the trenches behind, and we had to fall back. We were about 300 yards from shelter. I think I did that 300 yards in shorter time than it would take me to do 100 at another time. They trained a couple of machine-guns on us, and then all they had to do was to move it from side to side, while it went 'b-r-r-r-r' just like a motor cycle with its engine racing. Every inch we ran the bullets were spitting all around us. Every step we took we were saying to ourselves "The next one is mine, the next one is mine, the next one -hah" then a man would drop, but still we ran on in the hail of bullets. Out of the 200 of us that went out in the charge, forty answered the roll! When we reached shelter and looked behind we could see wounded crawling, inch by inch, to our lines. Then one of them would give a spasmodic jump, and we would know that he could crawl no further. [10]

It was here that Hetherington received the injury which was to bring him back from France. Hit in the foot by a German bullet, which had passed through his boot from one side to the other, he lay in a field dressing station for several hours under German fire before it was safe for him to be moved. To the residents of Castletown he must have cut rather a strange figure, back home and walking around in the late summer sun, wearing an army ammunition boot on one foot and a lady's old carpet slipper on the other.

On the day that Hetherington was wounded, in another dressing station not far away lay Lieutenant the Honourable Nigel Somerset, of the 1st Battalion Gloucestershire Regiment. Somerset was the son of the Lieutenant Governor of the Isle of Man, Lord Raglan. He had been hit by a piece of shrapnel behind the right ear whilst advancing in action on the Chemin des Dames, also on 14 September. After launching an attack on the enemy trenches, men of the Cameron Highlanders and Black Watch were heavily counter-attacked by several times their number of Germans, and two companies of Gloucesters (one of which was under the command of Lieutenant Somerset) were sent forward to cover their retreat. He told his story to a Manx journalist, whilst recuperating in London:

I was told to get in touch with Company B and for that purpose I extended my company of forty men through the wood, which was very thick and dense, making the extension most difficult. The other ten of my platoon had been killed or injured by this time ... I told my men to keep cover, and just at that moment there was an explosion and I was struck at the side of the head by something, and

I was knocked down. I expect it was a splinter from a shrapnel shell but I was exceedingly lucky to get off with so slight a wound, as the same shell not only killed two of my men but injured several others. [11]

Days later on 20 September Lieutenant Crellin's battalion was rushed forward to plug a gap in the line, and was heavily engaged. A French Moroccan battalion under pressure of a German attack had fallen back, leaving the flank of the 1st Battalion West Yorkshire Regiment exposed. In a furious assault, the Germans overwhelmed first one then two other companies of the West Yorkshires. Crellin witnessed this incident and states that the Germans advanced under a white flag before opening fire, but be that as it may his own battalion was ordered forward to prevent a rout. Whilst using a pair of binoculars to direct the fire of his men on to a party of Germans taking cover in a turnip field, a machine-gun bullet passed through his left sleeve and left hand, and on through the palm of his right hand. Bleeding profusely, he was evacuated by horse ambulance to a hospital on the French coast and subsequently to Torquay for recuperation. Crellin eventually returned to France and rose to command a battalion of his regiment. He was amongst the most highly decorated Manx soldiers of the war, being mentioned in dispatches three times and receiving the Distinguished Service Order twice, before he was killed in 1918, but like the best British officers he was fiercely proud of his men and spoke in the highest terms of their conduct in 1914:

They were as cheery as paint, and never showed any signs of funk, but were dying to get at the enemy. [12]

Between Sladen's simple but honest faith in his officers, and the respect which officers like Crellin clearly held for the men under their command, one begins to see something of the glue which bound the British Expeditionary Force together throughout the bitter fighting on the Western Front, and the suffering which it endured.

Both sides were now temporarily exhausted, and as the fighting on the Aisne died away there came a brief lull, before what was to become known as the race to the sea. Anticipating a German flanking movement towards the coast, the BEF handed over the Aisne positions to the French, and moved north by train in order to protect the Channel ports which were so vital for its supplies. A series of clashes would follow in the countryside west of Lille, known as the battles of Armentières and La Bassée. The terrain was open and flat, with tree lined roads, and small villages containing factories and breweries, the chimneys of which provided excellent vantage points for German snipers. With one of the formations in action here, the 1st Battalion Cheshire Regiment, was a private soldier from the Isle of Man named Robert Oates. Oates was born at 6 Drury Lane, Douglas and had joined the army in 1900, seeing service at the end of the Boer War. He was recalled to rejoin his regiment in 1914, and writing to his brother he recounted:

> I have been up at Lille and La Bassée. Oh it is terrible to see the houses that are destroyed ... Well I have had my share of fighting for a bit. We have been taking position after position, just a little at a time, and it has been awful, I can tell you. Their big guns, with their shrapnel, are terrible, and if it gets anywhere near us it means at least a dozen men [dead] ... One afternoon, about five o'clock we got an order to advance. We had to take a factory in the village, which the Germans had occupied, and had a Maxim gun there, which was doing a lot of damage. We were told to take it at all costs. I was in the first company to advance, and we got about 150 yards off them, and then it was like hell - bullets flying all over us, so we had to take cover, and the Germans had men on the tops of houses and in trees, sniping at us ... I got hit when taking cover. I had to run across an open space, and while crossing this space one of the German snipers got me in the leg and smashed two bones. I think it was a dum-dum bullet; it made such a terrible hole where it came out. I have a compound fracture of the leg between the knee and ankle, and it will be some time before it is alright. It was awful lying there wounded with shells flying all around. The agony was terrible. The stretcher bearers could not get near me - the fire was too heavy.[13]

In fact Oates' injury was so severe that it necessitated the amputation of the lower part of his leg. He was subsequently discharged from the army as 'no longer fit for war service'. Here at La Bassée the fighting perhaps first took on the nature of a gruesome slogging match, for which the First World War has become infamous. Troops of both sides advanced with little protection against withering small arms and shell fire, and were shot down as they did so. Yet with indomitable and as some today might say incomprehensible courage, the survivors rallied and charged again and again.

By late October the fighting had shifted further north still, to the Belgian city of Ypres. The countryside around here was low-lying and wet, and characteristically for the

Flanders plain was exceedingly flat. Save for the rather ambitiously named Mount Kemmel, there was scarcely any landscape feature with height. As a consequence, a church spire or any building above two storeys offered advantages in terms of observation. The Germans claimed the British were using the medieval Cloth Hall as an observation post, and proceeded to shell it. The British denied this, but the Cloth Hall was systematically reduced to rubble anyway. The semicircular network of trenches in the fields around the city now formed part of a continuous trench system that would stifle attempts at movement for the next four years.

The battles of 1914 were now about to enter their most critical phase. If the Germans had broken through in Flanders, they would quickly have reached the channel coast, and thus cut the BEF off from its supplies and reinforcements. The almost fanatical German efforts to break the British line here were matched only by the grim determination of the men of the BEF to hang on, and the name of Ypres was to be remembered in hallowed terms for many years afterwards as the graveyard of the British regular army. The Germans threw in one after another of their newly raised student battalions. Singing patriotic songs like *Deutschland über Alles* and *Die Wacht Am Rhein* they marched into the withering rifle fire of the British tommies and were cut down. The British for their part clung grimly to their trenches and ditches as a hurricane of shells preceded each new attack.

Today the accepted 'canon' of First World War literature as taught in schools and colleges consists almost exclusively of the work of Public School educated officers such as Robert Graves and Siegfried Sassoon, but ordinary board school educated private soldiers were just as capable of articulating their experiences in gripping prose. One example comes from Private William McLean, a reservist who before the war had worked at the Sheffield Hotel in Douglas. Writing to a member of his family about the fighting east of Ypres he stated:

Now and again we would sing or tell tales. It was on Sunday, October 26th, just before the Germans made their final attack, much laughter was caused as we lay in the bottom of our trench by a fellow named Kirkpatrick, from Kendal, Cumberland. He kept us laughing all the afternoon telling us tales and things he had done while in civil life, but all that laughter stopped and our faces grew stern, and lips tight, our hand gripping our rifles with bayonets fixed, ready for the worst. How we longed to meet them face to face. For eight days they had kept under cover, but at last it came. It was just about 6pm, on Sunday October 26th, when it came, and we emptied our rifles into them time after time. They replied with shell, rifle and Maxim gun, but we held on to our trenches. [14]

McLean served with the 2nd Battalion Border Regiment, and Private Thomas Cain was a fellow Manxman in the same formation. He grew up on Hatfield Grove in Douglas, and was the son of a joiner. His letter written on 26 October 1914 and also published in the *Isle of Man Times* is a document equal in value to that of McLean. He writes:

Just these few lines to let you know that I am still alright, but I have had an awful time. I am sure there are grey hairs in my head. We have been up in the trenches for eight days, just a few thousand of us keeping back about 100,000 Germans ... it was terrible; they kept on shelling us. They blew the trenches to pieces three times, but we fixed them up as soon as it got dark. Then their infantry would charge and it was slaughter. They would get to about fifty yards of us and they would lie down and would not come any further or go back. We could hear them moaning with fear, so we stopped firing. Then their officers got up and started shouting, but they would not come, so they started shooting their own men with revolvers. When we saw them doing that, we shot their officers, and then they stopped yelling and we let them sneak away. Out of our platoon of 56 men, there are 19 left. We have about two captains and about four lieutenants left. Our colonel and adjutant are both dead. Two majors were killed and one badly wounded out of A Company, and there are about 12 men and a lieutenant left out of 250 men ... Nearly all were killed by the shells in the trenches ... My nerves are shattered with the terrible noise that has been going on. We are now in a big town trying to get the pieces sorted out. Nearly all my mates are dead. The last time we met in this house, about ten days ago, there were 12 of us, now there are only five. If I get home you will not believe me if I told you what has happened to me... [15]

As autumn gave way to winter the trenches around Ypres and elsewhere began to turn into slippery morasses as seasonal rain set in. The battle against the enemy gave way to the battle to stay warm and dry, and by late November both sides were more concerned with the effects of the weather than each other. Hostile activity was reduced to localised sniping and shelling. By this stage of the

campaign, the first Territorial units began to arrive in France to bolster the depleted Regulars. One of these was the Liverpool Scottish, in which a number of Manxmen were serving including two brothers from Port St Mary, Cunningham and William Rae. Cunningham wrote to his relatives of his experiences in the line in late 1914:

You will be surprised to hear that I am in hospital. I have had my feet frostbitten and they are swollen up in a fearful state. I cannot get my socks or boots on. We were up to our knees in water the last time we were in the trenches and we were very lucky to come out of it alive. I owe my life to two of my pals. They got me out of a hole, where I had been under fire for goodness knows how long, and was almost up to my neck in water ... I can assure you I have no wish to get into such a tight corner again. [16]

The year ended with another extraordinary event, which has been depicted in film and other media many times since: the Christmas Truce, when along a roughly twenty mile stretch of front line, the erstwhile protagonists met and fraternised. A remarkable first hand account of this event exists in the form of a letter from a Douglas soldier serving with the 1st Battalion Royal Fusiliers to his sister. Tantalisingly the soldier is identified only as Ted, but his letter reads:

On Christmas Eve, the Germans stopped firing, and our chaps did the same. No firing was done that night, and on Xmas Day our chaps, ready for sport, went over to the Germans and shook hands with them. We exchanged beer and cigarettes for wine and cigars, and one of the Germans cut off all his buttons and gave them to one of our men in exchange for a pair of puttees. Then we took a football over, and we were just going to play them a match when along came one of their fussy officers, three parts drunk, and raised Cain. He went off shocking, and ordered them back again, so we played ourselves, and they watched us and cheered. This is the truth, but as soon as 12 o'clock came, we started to fight again. [17]

The spring of 1915 found the British Expeditionary Force holding its ground from Ypres southwards towards Armentières and La Bassée. The early part of that year witnessed a number of offensives on the part of the BEF, with varying degrees of success. The first major battle of 1915 was at Neuve Chapelle. Two Manx brothers, Harry and Norman Green of Derby Square, Douglas, were serving together here in the 1st/4th Battalion Seaforth Highlanders and penned a joint letter to their younger brother at home:

In front of us 150 or 200 yards away, was a trench held by some Gurkhas and we had to get there to support them. Unfortunately it was broad daylight and the enemy broad awake. However, led by our old Major, we sprang like lightning over the parapet and ran down the field like hares. I pitched headfirst into a disused trench half full of mud and water. When I had recovered my breath I looked round for the others and there were Clayton and Norman grinning close by. From there it was a matter of 10 yards which we did on our stomachs ...we three went out with stretcher parties and Sandy and I had the bad luck to be left behind for a further spell after the battalion moved off ... what a march. We had put off all our equipment to carry more easily and

with it all our food. Our last meal was a slice of bread and marmalade in the front line trench the previous evening ... we did look sketches yesterday. We had a 5 day's beard and no toilet outfit to help us out of the difficulty. Norman was fully equipped and Sandy had a greatcoat, but I hadn't a stitch except my tunic and kilt. Rifle, pack, equipment, bonnet – all lost ... Don't suppose though Ken, that war is anything but inexcusably damnable. When it was over we cried like a couple of babies, and we were not the only ones ... there is no glory in war, only inexpressible sorrow and untold suffering. [18]

In all, six sons of the Green family would see active service during the war, a remarkable record which was acknowledged by His Majesty King George V in a letter from Buckingham Palace. Back on the Western Front however, the Germans at the Second Battle of Ypres were to introduce a new element to warfare, with their use of poison gas for the first time. Private Joseph Killey of the 2nd Battalion Lancashire Fusiliers was among those involved. He was the son of Mrs Killey, a widow living on Tower Road, Ramsey, and had been an agricultural labourer before joining the army at the age of eighteen, around 1910. He wrote from a convalescent camp on 11 May 1915 to his brother in England:

I am suffering from pains in my chest caused by the poisonous gases and my wind is very short and to tell you the truth I don't think I will last much longer than a couple of months ... the reason why I am telling you this is so as you know if ever you get out here what you will have to go through. But all the same I hope and pray to God that I will be able to do my best and come through safely as I have gone

Privates Harry and Norman Green of Douglas, with their brother Edwyn in France in 1915. A further three brothers would see active service during the war. (PG 13716)

7 months and only got my first souvenir and I am thankful to [sic]. Well Ned I suppose you are wondering where I am. Well I can't tell you but I am wear [sic] the heavy fighting is and as for the name I daren't tell you as it is worth more than my life is to me. But some days I hope to tell you all as I am going to start a book of my adventures... [19]

Sadly, Killey's prediction was accurate and he was killed just two months later. Despite repeated enquiries to the Imperial War Graves Commission from his brother after the war, and in spite of the fact that former comrades asserted it was close to Hill 60, Killey's grave was never located and he was commemorated on the Menin Gate memorial at Ypres.

Other Manxmen served with formations of the British army in all theatres of the war. Writing to his former schoolmaster, Private Amos Collister of Port Erin, serving with the Royal Inniskilling Fusiliers, described his part in the second phase of the Gallipoli campaign:

We arrived on Saturday morning 8th August. Suvla Bay presented a sight one can hardly describe – battleships, torpedo destroyers, hospital ships, and transports, all marshalled out and anchored as if for a grand review. Lying on the deck of our ship we could see regiment after regiment landing and moving off in extended order, just as though they were practising manoeuvres at home. Rifle, machine-gun, and shell fire was the music that greeted the dawn of that beautiful day. The determination of our attack forced the Turks to retire over seven miles, and the landing was successful. On Sunday 15th August, my regiment was ordered to attack a position where the enemy was heavily entrenched. This was at a place named Kidney Hill. Our job was to straighten the line, a task we accomplished. For over 300 yards we advanced in extended order without firing a shot, though subjected to rifle, machine-gun and shrapnel fire all the time. When about 900 yards off the enemy we lay down and opened fire, and then the fun started in deadly earnest. We determined to win, and for six hours the enemy got a taste of Irish 'potheen.' Not being able to stand it any longer, the Turks fled, and their positions became ours. Many a brave soul went down, and after the battle, of all our officers but two survived. We lost over two-thirds of our men, and it was a host of weary broken men who answered 'roll call' the following day. On 20th August we attacked a place called Chocolate Hill ... we then occupied some trenches evacuated by the enemy. We made ourselves quite at home here, and began naming the various trenches. One that the Turks were always shelling we called Sydney Street. Then there was Hyde Park corner, where rations were drawn. We left the Peninsula on [censored] and went to the base, where we were re-clothed and equipped, and proceeded against the new foe. On Gallipoli we complained about the heat; here it is the reverse, and frostbite is a factor to be reckoned with. However, in spite of Kaiser Bill's boast and ridicule of Kitchener's Army, they have proved themselves better soldiers and cleaner fighters than the German bullies, and in the words of our officers, 'We have nothing to be ashamed of.' [20]

The Manx Service Company would also see service in the eastern Mediterranean in 1916. The company had been formed in March 1915, drawn from members of the Isle of Man Volunteers. Although the Volunteers had been mobilised by the Lieutenant Governor in August 1914, they had been retained on the Island to guard internment camps and vital points. However, such was the eagerness of many members for overseas service, that problems arose with men deserting to join English regiments. Thus the Manx Service Company, with its own insignia and identity, was formed. It was eventually posted overseas to the 2nd Battalion Cheshire Regiment, fighting against the German and Bulgarian Armies at Salonika. In many ways this was the Manx equivalent of the Pals battalions raised in other parts of the British Isles – friends and workmates from the same locality serving together and with a ready-made esprit de corps.

However, a second service company, raised shortly afterwards, was less fortunate, in that the army chose instead to break it up and use it piecemeal. Most of its members went to the Western Front, and where a few members did remain together there was comfort to be drawn from the presence of fellow Manxmen. In May 1916, Lance Corporal Lewis Merrifield, formerly of the 2nd Manx Service Company and now serving with the 1st Battalion Cheshire Regiment, wrote home to inform friends of the death of a comrade, Private Harold Russell of Kewaigue:

> *It has been a great blow to the Manx boys who came out with him ... I was in the firing line the night he was killed, but I did not hear of his death until four days after ... Little did we think that we were to lose one of our little Manx section so soon, and we all feel this blow*

very much. I knew Harold quite a long time, and we all liked him; no matter what he had to do he never grumbled. [21]

The year 1916 on the Western Front was dominated by the Battle of the Somme, and soldiers from the Isle of Man played a full part in this campaign also. The first day of the Battle of the Somme is remembered as the darkest one in the history of the British army, with over 60,000 casualties, of whom some 20,000 were killed. The reasons for the disastrous failure are well documented. Sir Douglas Haig, though commander in chief, deferred too much in the planning to the Fourth Army commander, Sir Henry Rawlinson. The preparations for the attack were so obvious that the Germans considered them to be a deliberate feint, and the timetable went rigidly forward regardless of evidence on the ground that the British preparatory bombardment was not cutting enough of the German wire. None the less the overwhelming majority of British soldiers were resolved to do their duty. By 1916 the reality of warfare on the Western Front was clearly apparent, yet one young Manx officer in late June wrote to his parents:

> *Within the next day or so it is possible – indeed probable – that I shall die while attacking the Germans. If I do, then know that I have died happy, having done my duty. Grieve not for*

Corporal Lewis J. Merrifield, of the 2nd Manx Service Company. In 1916 he was serving in France with the 1st Battalion Cheshire Regiment. (PG 7870-38211-1) *me Mother mine, but rather rejoice that you were able to give a son for our noble cause. I shall do my duty – never fear ... I am glad now that I live in these present times so that I am and have been able to take part in this, the greatest ... of all wars.* [22]

Second Lieutenant Ashley McGain, this young officer from Port Erin who so clearly identified with his cause, was in fact to lose his life on the opening day of the battle, serving with the 11th Battalion Suffolk Regiment. Among the other attacking formations which went over the top that morning was the 2nd Battalion Seaforth Highlanders. With them was Second Lieutenant James Harvey. Harvey was born in Scotland in around 1892, the third of four sons born to James and Jessie Harvey. The family moved to the Isle of Man whilst he was a young child and they lived at 47 Palatine Road, Douglas, a comfortable middle class home.

James Harvey volunteered for service through the recruiting office above Parr's Bank in Douglas in September 1914, initially joining the 1st Dragoon Guards. He arrived in France in June 1915, and rose to the position of Lance Corporal before being commissioned as a Second Lieutenant in the Seaforth Highlanders on 19 March 1916, shortly before the Somme offensive opened. He arrived with the 2nd Battalion on 26 March, straight from Cadet School, and was assigned to serve with D Company.

On the morning of 1 July 1916, James, along with just over nine hundred men from his battalion, found himself

Second Lieutenant Ashley McGain, of the Suffolk Regiment, who was to lose his life on the first day of the Battle of the Somme. (PG 13704/2)

climbing out of the assault trench parapet, into no-man's land to face a lethal hail of fire emanating from the German lines in the area of Beaumont Hamel. James died leading his men into action, along with twelve brother officers, almost certainly within the first two hours of the battle. He was twenty-five years old. In total, the battalion lost 394 men of all ranks, killed, missing or wounded on 1 July 1916 – almost half of its strength.

On 10 July, his oldest brother, Charles, who ran an ironmongery in Douglas, received a telegram at his place of work, informing the family of the tragic news of the death of James. The next day, James Harvey Senior, received a letter dated 4 July from Major Percy Carr, 2nd Battalion Seaforth Highlanders. Sadly it was only one of thousands of such letters written in the aftermath of the horrendous losses suffered on the opening day of the Somme offensive. The letter read:

It is with the very greatest regret and sorrow that I write to tell you that your son was killed whilst leading his men with the utmost gallantry in the attack in which the battalion took part on 1st July. Nothing could possibly have exceeded his coolness and devotion to duty, and in dying such a heroic and splendid death he in every way proved himself entirely worthy of the traditions and record of the 2nd Seaforth Highlanders, and you will, I feel sure, understand that one could not possibly say more than this. Everyone – other regiments included – is talking of how splendidly the "Jocks" fought and we have already received the special thanks of the Corps, Divisional and Brigade Commanders. In conclusion, I must repeat on behalf of our Commanding Officer that your son has met his death in the most splendid and gallant way, and we are all more proud of him than we can ever say, and we all sympathise with you most profoundly in your irreparable loss and sorrow. Your son died almost at once, and could have suffered little, if any, pain. [23]

James Harvey has no known grave but is remembered on the Thiepval Memorial. His award of a Mention in Dispatches, most likely for actions on 1 July, was confirmed several months later. Sadly, his story was not unique and more and more Manx homes would be shrouded by the black shutters of mourning as the Battle of the Somme progressed. Perhaps his grief contributed to James Harvey Senior's premature death within a couple of years of that of his son.

The Battle of the Somme ground on through the summer of 1916; the capture of the Bazentin Ridge to the south of the battlefield in mid July swung the direction of the offensive in a north-easterly direction, along the axis of the Albert-Bapaume road. The next key objective was the hamlet of Pozières, situated on gently rising ground and guarded by a mighty block house on either side of the village. The Australian and New Zealand divisions were heavily committed to the battle here from 22 July onwards – indeed Australia's official historian stated afterwards that her dead lay thicker on the Pozières ridge than any other battlefield on earth.

Such was the Manx diaspora around the world prior to the First World War that Manxmen were to be found serving in the armies of Canada, South Africa, Australia and New Zealand on the Western Front in 1916. The three Manx-born sons of Mr J.S.Teare of Melbourne all served in the Australian armed forces. Two were commissioned into the Australian Field Artillery and served in France,

Lieutenant J.S. Teare being awarded the Military Cross. Sergeant Phil Faragher, the son of a Manx émigré from Ballachurry, was wounded on the Somme with the Australian infantry, as was Corporal R.E.Kewley of Sulby, for whom it was his third wound, having previously been injured at Gallipoli. Kewley served with the 48th Battalion Australian Imperial Force and wrote home to his sisters:

Woods that were one time are now nothing but skeletons torn up by the roots, and every yard of country for miles was torn up as if by volcanic eruptions. We passed big shell holes, in which a wagon and horses could hide, or a platoon of men. We were told we were passing through the village of Pozières, but not a trace of a village could we see. We moved along a sap, trampling over dead and wounded on our road. We got to a certain point, and we were told to occupy the front trench. We went out over the parapet into the open country, several falling by the way. It is almost inconceivable to believe that humanity could face such an ordeal. The enemy artillery was turned on us, and shells were falling thick and heavy all around, and we had to make short rushes and get into shell holes for safety. Some lay in these shell holes all night. Under cover of the black smoke of bursting shells some of us rushed further forward, but no trench could be found; it was absolutely blown to smithereens by our heavies, so men had to take cover wherever they could. Five men and myself found ourselves in a most advanced position, in a little section of evacuated German trench, and we were safer there than anywhere, so decided to stay the night. Before daybreak next morning we decided to look round under cover of the dense haze that covered the ground. We had just started to move when we

spied a Boche. We covered him with our rifles, and took him prisoner. On turning round, four more Huns were coming scrambling over the debris; we also covered them and took them prisoners. We disarmed them, and handed them over to HQ ... That day we got hell from the enemy guns; in fact our Battalion was nearly annihilated; terrible slaughter. One platoon officer had just buried another when he got killed himself. I had just bandaged the Captain's wounds; he had a hole through his shoulder; and both legs smashed to pulp, and got him away on a stretcher, when I got buried by a shell. I wriggled out and in two minutes I got plugged through the right thigh making a great gash. I crawled on my hands and knees for quite a few hundred yards to the first dressing station. From there I had to be carried on a stretcher. [24]

Meanwhile Private Joseph Clague, originally of Castletown but latterly of New Zealand, was serving with the Wellington Infantry Battalion when he was awarded the Military Medal on the Somme. Also among the Manx-Australians serving here was Corporal John Cowley, 6th Field Company Australian Engineers. A Ramsey man, he had served an apprenticeship at Clague's Foundry in the town before emigrating. He was killed in action on 31 July 1916. Shortly afterwards his mother received a letter from a comrade which read:

It is my painful duty to inform you of the death of your son, John. He was my particular chum in the section, and he asked me to write to you if anything happened to him. He was killed by a shell about 2am ... near the ruins of the village of Pozières. At the time of his death he was the only non-commissioned officer of our section; we having

An impromptu service for burial of British dead, on the Somme battlefield in 1916. (Author's collection)

Sergeant John Cowley of the 6th Field Company Australian Engineers. Cowley, who like so many Manxmen had emigrated prior to the war, was killed in action on 21 July 1916. (M 00237) *suffered rather heavy casualties. Two nights previous to his death he was with us in a bayonet charge, and he among others was complimented on the satisfactory manner in which he carried out his duties. He was a fine man – a pillar of strength to the section – well liked, and greatly respected by all his men. The sympathy of the entire section is with you in your trouble. We feel that our loss is almost as great as yours, but we know that your grief will be lessened by the knowledge of the fact that he died for his country. Many brave lives must be sacrificed in this tremendous struggle, but everyone thus sacrificed brings the hour of victory closer.* [25]

The British army ground its way forward inch by inch that summer, over terrain that was pulverised by artillery, strewn with wrecked barbed wire entanglements and punctuated by the stark stumps of shattered trees. On 8 August, the German stronghold of Guillemont was attacked, and Private Bobby Corlett of Sulby, in peacetime the village postman, was in the line here, serving with the 1st/5th Battalion King's Liverpool Regiment. He remembered:

The trench mortars were terrible things, and you could see them coming over and if there were sparks coming from them they were going up and wouldn't come near where you were, but if there were no sparks they were coming down and then you were for it. [It was] a hot August day and we were in the trench, and there was a man there wounded in the legs, and he was dying, you could see that, and I asked the officer wouldn't it be better to put a steel helmet over his face in case he got a second hit, for his own helmet had rolled off his head and the officer .... got a steel helmet and covered his face with it, and that saved him from the shrapnel, so he could die in peace. I got hit in the leg and was taken to a field dressing station.... [26]

The focus of the offensive now came to rest upon a number of woods which had been heavily fortified by the Germans: High Wood and Delville Wood would be the next objectives, both would hold out stubbornly for over a month. Another Douglas soldier, Private Daniel Faragher, was serving with the Royal Fusiliers on the Somme when his battalion was involved in an attack on Delville Wood on 15 August 1916. Faragher had enlisted with a close friend Private John Quine (also from Douglas). Quine was killed in the attack and lay dead next to Faragher all night, before stretcher bearers arrived on the scene. Because of the delay in reaching hospital Faragher's leg became gangrenous, and it was amputated at the hip.

Aircraft had demonstrated their value in terms of observation and reconnaissance right from the outset of the war, but the Battle of the Somme witnessed the first concerted effort in the history of warfare to use an air arm directly in tactical support of a ground offensive. Sir Hugh Trenchard, commander of the Royal Flying Corps, believed that its role was entirely subordinate to the needs of the ground forces. He knew that it would be costly in terms of aircraft and aircrew lives (and some 400 were to be lost over the Somme) but he intended to dominate the skies that summer through aggressive patrolling, thereby denying the German air force the opportunity to use its own machines to interfere with the advance through aerial observation. Less glamorous than the single seat fighters, but probably of greater importance to the overall campaign were the two seat reconnaissance aircraft. They provided information to the artillery as to German gun positions and troop movements. With aircraft which were invariably slower than the enemy fighters, the work of spotting and photographing German positions was extremely hazardous, particularly at this point in the war, when the Germans had gained a decided advantage with the Fokker Eindecker equipped with forward-firing gun gear.

Just north of the Somme battlefield, No 18 Squadron were engaged on this work equipped with FE2b aircraft. In these machines, the engine was mounted at the back, the pilot in front of it, with the observer/gunner in the forward compartment, armed with a Lewis machine-gun. The observer stood up to fire, his knees level with the sides of the cockpit, no seatbelt to hold him in, and only his grip on the gun standing between him and eternity, should the pilot dive or swoop suddenly. It must have been utterly terrifying! Among their crews was a Manx aviator, Captain Elgie Jefferson of Ballahot, near Ballasalla. He was an officer of the King's Liverpool Regiment, attached to the Royal Flying Corps, and serving now as an observer. In one hair raising incident on 30 August 1916, Jefferson who was in the forward gunner's compartment of an FE2b, clung on helplessly as the machine drifted out of control after it was attacked over enemy lines, and the pilot was wounded. Fortunately the pilot recovered consciousness before the machine struck the ground, and he was able to bring it down in a controlled crash landing at a British aerodrome. Not surprisingly, Jefferson's injuries were not confined to physical bruising. His medical notes mention 'nerve shock', and whilst on convalescent leave after the incident he wrote to his superiors:

I have the honour to apply for 3 weeks leave of absence from my squadron in the field, on medical grounds. I was given special leave which expires on the 19th [September] for medical reasons. My nerves are very strained and I feel very run down and do not feel fit enough to carry out my work as an observer, for the present... [27]

Aged just twenty, Jefferson none the less recovered his nerve, and in a subsequent letter to the authorities expressed his wish to return to flying duties. He later qualified as a pilot. Life expectancy for aircrew on the Western Front was measured in weeks, and for this reason, as well as a glamorous and dashing reputation, they often had a 'live for the moment' attitude. Jefferson was no exception to this rule, and the following year he was treated in hospital for gonorrhoea.

The face of warfare was again changed forever on 15 September 1916, when for the first time tanks were used in action. Cumbersome and unreliable, many of the fearsome beasts broke down before reaching the enemy front line, but reports indicate that those which did succeed in reaching the German positions struck fear into the enemy. A fascinating report survives from a Manx soldier who was present. Private Edgar Robinson, of the Royal Scots, was clearly not yet familiar with the term 'tank', when he wrote:

We had a lot of trouble with the Germans at Contalmaison before we got them out, and then we took a village called Martinpuich, about a mile from our

*firing line, on the 15th September. We went over the top
and it was 'Hell' all the way, but those motor machines
helped us a lot. The Germans were fairly astounded at
them, as they could not damage them, however hard
they tried. They started throwing bombs at them, but
that did not affect them, so they were thrown off their
mark, and we were giving them something for running,
only their machine-guns played on us terribly. But when
we get the Germans from behind they don't half get
along. We had just reached Martinpuich, and were
digging ourselves in for safety, when a machine-gun
turned on us, and as luck would have it I got one just
above the left knee.* [28]

Private Tom Rowell of Onchan also served on the
Somme, with the King's Liverpool Regiment. In a letter
home from hospital after being wounded there, he related
his own experiences in battle and the unexpected
steadiness of his nerves in the situation:

*What surprised me when we went 'over the top' was the
perfect order and coolness. I remember thinking how
straight the lines were as we went across 'No Man's Land,'
and how the officers handed out cigarettes (they did not go
ahead but amongst us) and stopped here and there to light
up. Nearly everyone was smoking, and the three lines of
men went walking across as if it were a 'tea-fight' they were
going to. 'Fritz' let us get 300 yards before he said anything,
then well, I'd rather not think about it ...* [29]

The battle of the Somme ground on into the autumn of
1916. On 21 October another tough German nut was
finally cracked with the capture of Regina Trench by the

Captain Elgie Jefferson of the Royal Flying Corps. Despite a
dramatic crash in 1916, Jefferson returned to aerial combat, but
was killed in a flying accident in 1919.
(Courtesy of the Royal Aero Club)

Canadians. Among them was Private William Callister, of Peel, serving with the 102nd Canadian Infantry, who was understandably jubilant about his battalion's role in the removal of this particular thorn in the allied side. His letter cannot be dismissed purely as bravado, and shows that resolve to carry on the fight remained strong, even as casualties mounted and the autumn weather added to the misery of the men in the front line:

We made our first bayonet charge two days ago, and gained our objective, and hold it still. Everyone is talking of the feat, the trench we took having been taken before by three different divisions, but they were always driven out. So you see the honour it is for our green battalion to take and hold it after standing for 48 hours up to our waists in freezing mud. We were a terrible sight when we came out ... We had a good many casualties, and I certainly never expected to get out of it. I was buried half a dozen times, and three 'whiz bangs' burst over my head in succession, but I was never hit ... I walked on dead men all the way out – men who have fallen through numerous battles in the same place, and it was a horrible sight. But the charge was glorious. All hardships were forgotten when the signal came to get over the top, and we were on the top of Fritz before he realized what was happening ... a chum of mine was killed at my side. He was such a nice fellow, and I felt quite sick when we buried him where he lay. Don't think by what I have written that we are downhearted; in fact it is the other extreme, as we are too proud for our boots now that our blades have been wetted. [30]

One exceptionally well documented pair of brothers, who played more than their fair part in the First World War,

were Roy and Cyril Corlett of Douglas. Roy, who served as a Second Lieutenant with the King's Own Yorkshire Light Infantry, was wounded and captured on the Somme in November 1916. His official statement of the circumstances of his capture, which he was required to make to the War Office upon eventual repatriation, ran as follows:

My unit, the 2nd battalion KOYLI attacked at 6.10 near Serre, on November 18th 1916. My orders were to take the third line of enemy trenches with my platoon. We reached the first line, and proceeded as quickly as possible up a communication trench towards the second line. We cleared this trench. I shot two of the enemy with my revolver; the remainder were disposed of by rifle fire. We sent a few prisoners back to the first line ... This communication trench ended at the second line, so I decided to go over the open to the third line. We came under fire, and a number of us were hit. I was hit by a ricochet rifle bullet in the knee. A corporal put on a tourniquet and bandaged my knee. I tried to proceed with this corporal's help, but found my wounded leg perfectly useless; so I sent him on. I crawled towards the third line, but could only proceed very slowly, as I had to pull myself along with my hands ... before I reached the third line, the enemy ... sent out a party of about twenty under an officer. I was captured by these people, who gave me a German Red Cross man and an English private wounded in the arm to carry me down a dugout. [31]

Earlier, as a prisoner of war, he wrote to his family from Mulheim in the Ruhr region of Germany:

LEFT: Second Lieutenant Roy Corlett in German captivity. He was hit in the leg by bullet during the latter stages of the Somme battle. (MS 10987)

BELOW: Corlett's Prisoner of War armband (identifying him as such when out of the camp on parole), and POW camp identity disc. (2004-0038/2012-0106)

Kriegsgefangen

The doctor did not seem satisfied with my knee and on the 22nd [December] he sent me to a 'kranken haus' (hospital) in the town where they x-rayed my knee. The photographs showed a bullet in the knee. The photographs were taken by two R.C. Sisters of Mercy, they in their black gowns & hoods made I thought rather a striking picture amongst the electric machines and apparatus. They went about things in a very workmanlike manner. The Good Sisters of Mulheim are certainly very up to date in their charity ... Wednesday the 27th I was transferred to the Garrison hospital. Friday 29th they operated on me and extracted the bullet ...I have it now as a souvenir. (32)

Corlett would spend the remainder of the war in German hands, suffering a variety of privations in the process.

Ministering to the spiritual needs of the men in the front line was the responsibility of the Royal Army Chaplains' Department. No clearer account of the nature of this work, and indeed its importance, will probably be found than that given by Captain Harry Maddrell, formerly a Curate at St George's Church in Douglas, and during the Battle of the Somme a padre in a territorial division. As well as providing emotional support and solace to men who were far from home and facing great danger (in order for which they had to gain the confidence of the men) the chaplains also provided practical support in terms of reading or writing letters, or comforting the wounded. Maddrell gave an address to an audience in Douglas in December 1916, in which he said:

I want to tell you something about our work as chaplains, but no one has any right to talk about this war unless he has been 'over the top' in a charge. That is one of the things – the only thing – that we chaplains are not allowed to do. An order is issued to us that, under no circumstances, are we to leave our battle posts, or go over with the men. We observe the letter of the law, but many hundreds do not observe the spirit of it; they do not go over at the minute the men do, but they are very close on their heels, if they have half a chance. In the London Territorials, where I am, there are nine Church of England chaplains, and out of those five have been awarded the military cross, so we feel we are a part of the show ... It is useless to tackle men straight away on spiritual matters. You have to tread lightly and go easily, wait for the opportunity, and grasp the opportunity when it comes. We have to live with the officers and be friends with the men as well as the officers, and it is very hard to do both. All night you sleep in a room with half-a-dozen other fellows, who perhaps, never spoke with a parson above once or twice a year. If they find he is one of themselves, it is alright. You have to show what you are worth before they take you to their hearts. You have to show you are a man the same as they are. They sum you up, and you have to show what you are worth. (33)

April 1917 saw the Battle of Arras, and Roy Corlett's brother Second Lieutenant Cyril Corlett of the Tyneside Scottish was wounded here whilst leading his men forward into an attack. His injuries were so severe that for the next eight months he was to be confined to a spinal carriage. The chaplain of his battalion wrote to his mother:

Your brave boy was wounded on the first day of our great advance ... I happened to be with the doctors when he was brought in and so great was his enthusiasm and so loud his cheerful voice that it was hard to realise he was wounded. He was hit by shrapnel on the arm and side but his first words on seeing us were, "It's worth it. This has been the most glorious day in my life. We laughed like to kill ourselves at the Boche. They ran like rabbits. My men went over like heroes. Topping fellows every one of them. Look here, you write my mother & tell her that I am as fit as a fiddle but can't write on account of my arm." [34]

Cyril was ultimately discharged from the army as a result of these wounds, but the shortage of officers by 1918 was so acute that he felt compelled to offer his services again, and was granted a second commission.

The Battle of Arras was notable for one of the most spectacular pieces of planning and execution, in a war supposedly dominated by blunders and disaster. The capture of Vimy Ridge by the Canadian Corps on Easter Monday, 9 April 1917, has rightly gone down in the folklore of that nation as surely as the Gallipoli campaign entered the national consciousness of Australia and New Zealand. As so often in battles of the First World War, a Manxman Private A.J.McEwan was present and has left a first-hand account. He wrote:

I could not occupy my time better than in giving you a brief account of the taking of Vimy Ridge by the Canadians. I suppose you read all about it in the papers, but to realise it one had to be right there and see it for oneself. I thought I could not go through anything worse than the Somme, but, believe me, this had it beat a thousand ways. We put up, or rather our artillery did, a ten days' bombardment, going continually all the time. Then the night before we had to go over, there was a lull, while we were all packed in what they

Padre Harry Maddrell, a chaplain with a London territorial division. His duties included tending to the wounded and caring for the spiritual needs of the men. (PG 7095/2)

call the assembly trenches. We stayed in these trenches from about 9 o'clock at night until 5.30 in the morning, when the barrage opened up. First, a mine blew up; then the machine-guns got going: and then the roar of the guns for miles and miles around. I thought the bombardment of that ten days was a good one, but it was just nothing one might say, to that which started at 5.30 in the morning between light and dark, which was the hour for us to go over the top. We had not gone many yards when the German machine-guns and snipers got going, and the way those bullets whistled past us and kicked up the mud at our feet was no joke. The man on my left got hit with a bullet, and the fellow on my right got a piece of shrapnel in him; they both went down at the same time. I and three others crawled into a shell hole, and let them have it hot and strong with our rifles. We could see them in their trench about 100 yards or so from us. They did not stay long to face it. The ground we had to go over was terrible – it was just walking out of one shell hole into another. It was so sodden that one sank up to the knees in it: so you may guess what it was like, staggering, rather than walking, with twelve bombs in a bag, 120 rounds of ammunition, your overcoat, waterproof, haversack and rifle. Half the shell holes were half full of water: and to crown it, it came on to snow very heavily. I must have fallen down a dozen times, but finally got to our objective. One could see the effectiveness of our guns once they got on top. It was one mass of shell holes; you could not walk a foot without walking into one ... There were four of us in a shell hole, when we saw seven Germans running towards us. They did not seem to know or care where they were going so long as they got away from that awful barrage and their own lines. We trained our rifles on them, and were about to fire,

when up went their hands, and it was "No shoot, no bomb; mercy, comrade, mercy!" I have never seen men more scared. [35]

The late summer and autumn of 1917 bore witness to the Third Battle of Ypres, known colloquially as Passchendaele after the village of that name, which was the high watermark of the advance. Sir Douglas Haig was convinced that on the Somme the previous year, the Germans had avoided the issue by conceding ground of no strategic value. He believed that at Ypres the Germans must stand and fight – and their army be destroyed – or retreat and concede large tracts of the Belgian coast including their U-boat bases. After the promising start heralded by the Battle of Messines in June, the fighting around Ypres descended into a grim slogging match, as the Germans perfected 'defence in depth'. Keeping back their reserves, they held their territory with pillboxes using interlocking fields of machine-gun fire. Manxman Private Fred Curphey of the King's Liverpool Regiment was involved in the opening phase of the battle, and described Ypres as the hottest shop on the entire British front. He stated:

Well the night of the push came on July 30th. We went up at night and waited in ___ Wood, a few stumps of trees in No Man's Land which used to be a wood. Shells were dropping all about. Fritz had 'the wind up'; he must have known what was coming. He was sending torch lights up galore. About four in the morning our platoon officer came to us and said, "The biggest battle in the world is about to commence; are you ready?" And sure enough it did commence. Hundreds of big guns seemed to open up

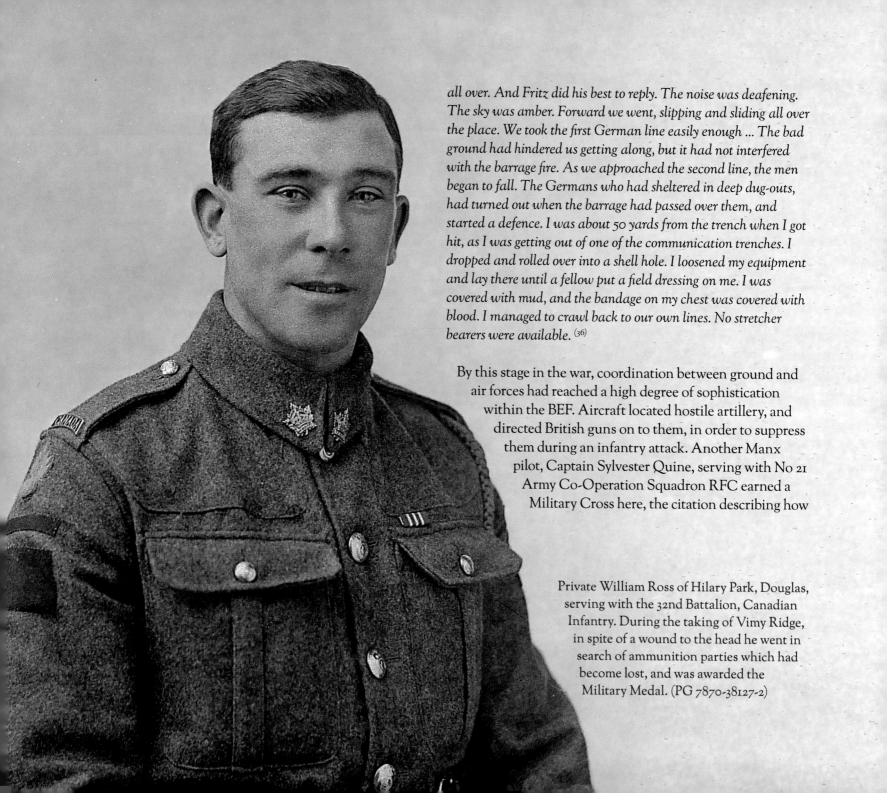

all over. And Fritz did his best to reply. The noise was deafening. The sky was amber. Forward we went, slipping and sliding all over the place. We took the first German line easily enough ... The bad ground had hindered us getting along, but it had not interfered with the barrage fire. As we approached the second line, the men began to fall. The Germans who had sheltered in deep dug-outs, had turned out when the barrage had passed over them, and started a defence. I was about 50 yards from the trench when I got hit, as I was getting out of one of the communication trenches. I dropped and rolled over into a shell hole. I loosened my equipment and lay there until a fellow put a field dressing on me. I was covered with mud, and the bandage on my chest was covered with blood. I managed to crawl back to our own lines. No stretcher bearers were available. [36]

By this stage in the war, coordination between ground and air forces had reached a high degree of sophistication within the BEF. Aircraft located hostile artillery, and directed British guns on to them, in order to suppress them during an infantry attack. Another Manx pilot, Captain Sylvester Quine, serving with No 21 Army Co-Operation Squadron RFC earned a Military Cross here, the citation describing how

Private William Ross of Hilary Park, Douglas, serving with the 32nd Battalion, Canadian Infantry. During the taking of Vimy Ridge, in spite of a wound to the head he went in search of ammunition parties which had become lost, and was awarded the Military Medal. (PG 7870-38127-2)

he went out in rough and stormy weather during an attack, and flying low over the enemy batteries reported and located those which were in action. In a letter of 17 October 1917, he describes this mission:

> I was up on another 'nasty job' today but it turned out quite well as it happened. I had another 'bus' from our flight escorting me and he stuck on splendidly. Old 'archie' [anti-aircraft fire] got very excited and fair hurled hate up at us but didn't do any damage. Then three Huns dropped down out of space and came for us. I saw them a good way off so opened up with my front gun and made some decent shooting. Then I let the observer get a shot in but his gun jammed. The Huns however didn't feel like a fight after that … [37]

His letter goes on to describe a rowdy concert in the squadron officers' mess that same evening, perhaps a way of unwinding after the tension and drama earlier in the day.

In spite of the ground gained at Vimy, and the success at Messines, 1917 had been a dreadful year on balance for the western allies. None of the major battles up to that point had been an unqualified success, and so the offensive at Cambrai in November may be seen to some degree as an attempt to even up the balance sheet. It was almost too late in the year for a successful advance, but the Tank Corps, which felt that it had been ill used in the mud at the Third Battle of Ypres, was eager for any chance to show what its machines could do in the right circumstances. At Cambrai they faced the formidable defences of the Hindenburg Line, a defensive system carefully constructed by the Germans in the wake of the Somme battle the previous year, but the terrain here was relatively unbroken by shellfire and therefore good going for tanks. Some 300 started out on the first day of the battle. Driver Herbert Mills of Main Road, Onchan, was among them and recorded his impressions of the battle, which he described as the largest he had been in, and also filled with the most saddening events. He himself was wounded in the face:

> We went over the top on the morning of the 20th [November] at 6 o'clock, with tanks and the infantry following. Everything was going on splendidly, and Fritz was either putting up his hands in thousands and coming towards our lines, or else picking up his effects and running away like rabbits. We took our first and second objectives with practically no opposition, except from snipers and machine-gunners. However we very soon put these people out of action, and allowed the infantry to come up and consolidate every position. To give you some idea of how well we did our work, the infantry operating with our section of tanks only had one casualty up to one o'clock, after seven hours in action. Our final objective was to see their gunners off with their artillery before Cambrai. Unfortunately their aeroplanes gave their gunners our range before we could spot them. The tank on our right got it first, blowing one of their tracks off, but everyone escaped uninjured. We changed our direction, to get out of the way; but instead we must have run right into the muzzle of his gun, because we got a large shell right through the front, killing our officer and the driver who was driving at the time. Only ten minutes previously I had evacuated the driver's seat for a rest. Luckily for me of course, but I am sorry for the chap who went under. As I say, it killed two; and all the rest were wounded. The tank caught fire just as

ABOVE: A British Mark IV tank goes into action. (Author's collection)

RIGHT: Herbert Mills of Onchan, in later life. As a Driver with the Tank Corps at Cambrai in 1917 he had a narrow escape when his machine was hit by a shell. (Courtesy of Sue Rimmer)

I was getting out. Once outside, we had another difficulty to get over. The same plane was hovering overhead, waiting for us. No sooner had we got out, than down it came to about 40 or 50 yards of the ground, and emptied magazine after magazine in our direction. Luckily, however, every time he swooped down at the wrong angle, and could not get good direction. The only weapon we had to retaliate with was our revolvers, which we gave him plenty of, lying on our backs. Eventually he went off, and immediately we lifted our heads to crawl along, his snipers got busy, and didn't they give us a time? For two hours we lay in the cold and rain, frozen to the marrow, in 'No Man's Land' as it was then, until I got that cramped I could have shot myself in my misery. I said to my chum, who was lying beside me more seriously wounded than I, that I was going to make a run for it. So, nipping hold of him round the waist, I practically dragged him for about 400 yards to a sunken road where we both fell down exhausted. The others followed our lead, and all arrived without further casualties. I am more than pleased that I am alive to tell the tale. However it was a glorious day, and a big victory – I believe one which I shall never forget if I live to be 100. [38]

Away from the fighting, behind the lines, there was recreation to be had whilst in rest billets and entertainment was considered a vital part of maintaining the morale of the BEF. Writing home, W.A.W. Crellin (by now a Lieutenant Colonel), revealed that:

[I] saw quite a decent show in a town close by two or three nights ago. All the artists except one were Tommies in the A.S.C. The other was a 2/Lt and he made a top

hole girl. One of the fellows I was with bet 100 francs it wasn't a man, but he found his mistake at the end & had to pay up. [39]

However, maintaining cohesion and discipline within the BEF was a combination of both stick and carrot. The executions by firing squad of those convicted of desertion or showing cowardice have remained controversial for over ninety years. Although these men were officially pardoned in 2006 after a long campaign, the fact remains that the death penalty was an accepted part of civilian life in that era, and many soldiers at the time tacitly believed that those who abandoned their comrades deserved little sympathy. Many historians have argued that in a conflict of this horrendous nature, recourse by the military authorities to the ultimate sanction was a necessary evil. One Manx soldier, Private John McCauley, was a witness to one military execution in France, his battalion drawn up on parade as the convicted man was brought before them:

I watched as if in a trance, and saw his escort guide him to the stake. He was in a stupor now – paralysed with fright. They pinioned his arms and legs, then bound his poor trembling body to the stake. A blue and white bandage which had been carried by one of the escort was placed over his eyes and firmly fastened at the back of his head ... the order rang out sharp and crisp through the early morning air: "Present arms" ... "Fire." A momentary pause, then the crack of the rifles rang out. It was not a clear volley. The shots were spasmodic; some of the firing party had hesitated longer than others .... It was a mournful body of men that tramped silently back to billets [afterwards]. Even the birds seem to be stilled that morning. We were all unnerved and disconsolate. The firing party filed back into the barn where we were quartered, and several flung themselves down and cried openly and bitterly. We could thoroughly understand their feelings. Very little food was eaten in our billet that day. It was not easy to shake off the thoughts of that early morning death parade. [40]

As the war dragged on, men fought for their comrades as much as for King and Country. A fierce comradeship grew up between the men of a platoon and their officer, and between each other. It was this which sustained the BEF in its momentous struggle on the Western Front. Private Frank Clucas, writing home about the death of a soldier who was not just his comrade, but also his cousin, was clearly bereft:

> *I expect you will be rather anxious not having heard from me for some time but really I have not been in a condition to write. I have felt I should write but have been so upset that I could not settle down to write even if I had been provided with paper and envelopes .... The last few days has been a nightmare to me but I am glad to say I am now feeling much better though fits of depression still come upon me and make me feel miserable. I expect you have heard the sad news at Home and I can only give you a brief outline of what happened ... if Tom really is gone than I have lost the best and truest chum I ever had. I can't write any more.* [41]

As well as loyalty to those they fought alongside, Manx soldiers were also defined by a sharp hostility to those in

Lieutenant Colonel W.A.W.Crellin, of Ballachurry, Andreas. In action since the earliest days of the war, Crellin was to lose his life in 1918. (MS 09412)

the Isle of Man whom they felt were not pulling their weight in the conflict. Private C.W.Lowey, of the King's Liverpool Regiment, wrote:

> I am in the trenches at present, and writing this under shellfire ... I have several Manx chums out here now ... But still there are slackers knocking about Peel and the little village of Dalby who should take a little interest in their fellow countrymen and come out and lend a helping hand. [42]

Whilst an unnamed Manx soldier wrote:

> There are lots of single men in Douglas ... it is time they were wearing the uniform of which England is so proud, because England is in the greatest struggle of history ... the enemy cannot be beaten without more help. It is through the shirkers that the war has lasted as long as it has. Always remember the motto, 'Your King and country needs you' [sic] and show that you are Manxmen and not shirkers. [43]

Private William McLean of the Border Regiment was equally vociferous in his condemnation of a civilian who had objected to the billeting of soldiers in his property:

> I wonder if Mr Cain would like to come out [to France]. Oh I do wish that nice, kind and encouraging gentleman would come; he would be able to mix with some of his countrymen. I don't want to say he is a German. Oh no; he is so kind to our comrades at home that one cannot help but think. I don't know what the troops at home are thinking about to allow such a man to be in their midst ... I hope he will take the hand of the next soldier he meets and say I am sorry for trying to stop the billeting of such men as you: I know now, lad, that we cannot do without you. [44]

The Manx, who had already paid a high price in blood for their participation in the war, were to suffer more casualties in the spring of 1918, when the BEF faced the brunt of the German spring offensives on the Somme and at Ypres. The Germans, with troops released from the Eastern Front, were going for broke before American troops arrived in France in large numbers. Their offensives were preceded by a savage bombardment, often including gas shells, and they advanced many miles using infiltration tactics. Their storm troopers bypassed strong points, leaving them to wither on the vine, whilst they pressed deep into the rear areas and knocked out artillery support. In April, further north on the Lys, a second German offensive erupted and among those captured here was Captain Ralph Stevenson, of Lorne House, a member of one of the oldest families on the Isle of Man. Also among the killed was one of the most decorated Manx soldiers of the First World War. Battery Sergeant Major R.J.Callister DCM MSM MID, of Kingswood Grove, Douglas had previously served eight years in the army, and had re-enlisted into the Royal Field Artillery again when war broke out. At the time he was working at a hotel in Liverpool. He was killed in action on 29 April 1918, whilst trying to save another soldier. Callister's parents received a letter from the other NCOs of his battery, and this provides more compelling evidence of the role that comradeship played in sustaining men under conditions of great fear and strain:

> To attempt to portray our respect for your son would be futile, as he was a man amongst us whose personality was so influencing that no words needed to be passed to realise his strength of character; and we have no hesitation in saying that his presence, when we were in some hot quarters, was sufficient to enable us to put fear aside and carry on with the particular task allotted to us. [45]

However even these shattering blows inflicted by the Germans on the battlefield were not sufficient to dent the resolve of ordinary Manx soldiers, and commitment to their cause remained strong. Private Bertie Reid of Douglas, returning to the front after a spell in England following the German spring offensives, wrote to his parents:

> By the time you get this I shall probably have started the great adventure in which every right thinking fellow should now have a hand; for after all, no exceptions are being made and we are all going out together to do our bit. I know it will be a heavy blow for you to bear, but hold up bravely and be proud rather than anxious. I know well what I have to face but I am cheerful and not afraid for, come what may, it is the right thing and therefore not to be feared. [46]

After a relatively quiet two years spent at Salonika in Greece, in spring 1918 the Manx Service Company moved to the Struma Valley front, on the border with Bulgaria, and the war in this part of the world began to move into its final phase. Through the ravages of disease – particularly malaria – rather than enemy action, the company had been depleted and made up to strength with English reinforcements. Sergeant Edward Holmes, of Douglas, was one of the luckier ones and remembered:

The lightweight cotton uniform jacket worn by Major Percy Kissack at Salonika with the 1st Manx Service Company (1972-0130)

The company never lost its Manx character or identity. Although the commanding officer Captain Gately was a Birmingham man, the other officers, including Captain Percy Kissack, along with the Company Sergeant Major Louis Meyer, were all Manx. Meyer was for many years a successful printer in Douglas. Kissack was a striking figure, some six feet four tall, and was nicknamed 'Big Sonny'. He was remembered by one veteran as armed to the teeth, and "a miniature fort".

On 15 April 1918 was fought one of the fiercest actions in which the 2nd Battalion Cheshire Regiment participated. The Manx Company took over the preliminary work, and occupied Kumli, a village well in front of the line. Two other companies passed through to other villages still further away, where they encountered the enemy in vastly superior force. After sustaining and repelling fierce bayonet and bomb attacks, both companies retired to Kumli. The casualties sustained by the battalion overall were about fifty per cent. After three days of heavy shellfire, the 2nd Cheshires were relieved. In June 1918, two members of the Manx company, Privates Joseph William Buckley, of Oxford Street, Douglas and

Sergeant Edward Holmes of the 1st Manx Service Company. At Salonika, mosquitoes and malaria were bigger threats than Bulgarian bullets. (PG 13745 Courtesy of Barry Quilliam)

Harold Dod of Onchan were captured by a Bulgarian raiding party. The incident is well documented in a report contained within Buckley's service papers, filed by his section commander Sergeant W.Easton after the event:

On the morning of the 4th June 1918 about 0415 hours I was in charge of a covering party of 6 men whose duty it was to make good the ground between [post] CW1 & the OP ... I advanced to within 500 yards when I saw a man walking about ... I took him to be a deserter, as they were accustomed to wait there ... to give themselves up. I then sent two men (Ptes Buckley & Dod) to reconnoitre the sunken road 200 yds to the left of the OP & another 2 men to reconnoitre the sunken road on the right. I myself with the remaining two men advanced direct on the OP and on arrival there found that the man who had been observed had vanished. I then saw the two men whom I had sent on the left flank looking down the sunken road. After what appeared to be about one minute's careful examination of the road & its vicinity, the two men stepped down into the sunken road. They were then immediately rushed, from about twenty yards, by a party of about 12 Bulgars. I heard two shots fired by my men as they were being rushed, but no other shots were heard from that direction. At the same time as my two men were rushed in the sunken road a party of the enemy about 80 strong opened fire on the remainder of my covering party. I immediately took cover & opened fire on the enemy who could be seen about 200 yards further along the road to where my men had been rushed. After about one minute the enemy ceased firing & withdrew towards KUMLI in small parties. I fired at them until they were out of sight. I then took two men with me to examine the ground where the enemy had been lying in ambush but could discover no trace of the two men whom I had sent to the left flank. [48]

Both men were apparently well treated by their Bulgarian captors, and were released unharmed at the close of hostilities. In the autumn of 1918, the Manx Company participated in the decisive break through on the Salonika front which brought an end to the war in that theatre. The 2nd Cheshires were engaged near Lake Doiran, co-operating with the Greek Army. Johnny Kaneen of Ramsey who had served as a 16-year-old with the Manx Service Company, recalled the time that the fighting in Salonika drew to a close:

My memory takes me back to this date, 30th September 1918 ... as a Battalion Scout of the 2nd Cheshire Regiment on my roadside post I saw the car, flying white flags, of the Bulgarian Commander-in-Chief go by to sign the Armistice. So the Bulgar, Austrian and German forces were beaten in that sector – the Middle East; formidable positions they held too as they gazed down on us for years from the mountainous terrain. The regiment I was in attacked to the right of Lake Doiran, near a village called Peroy. I was situated on the right flank of our regiment, and the Greek Venezlos Army was on my right: a Greek army sergeant scout keeping touch with me. We attacked the foothills of that formidable barrier, the Bolasico Range mountains. The Greeks did good work here. However at a later period in the scrap our regiment moved from that position and went up over Petit Couronne and Pip Ridge. The enemy trenches and barbed wire were absolutely blown flat by our artillery on these positions. These trenches were dug in rock mind you. The enemy also had

Captain John Bell Nelson, of Ramsey, 125th Napier's Rifles. He was to be killed in action in Palestine in 1918. (MS 09412)

fine dug-outs built in these rocky mountains, reinforced and propped with timber in the raw lumber state. [49]

Among the last Manx casualties of the war was Captain John Bell Nelson, of the 125th Napier's Rifles, an Indian Army regiment. He was killed in action in Palestine in September 1918, in one of the final actions of the war against Turkey. Just one month later she also would sue for an armistice. Nelson, from Ramsey, had been a promising young law student before enlisting at first as a private soldier into the 9th Lancers. Great things were expected of him, and he was just the sort of able young man that the Isle of Man could ill afford to lose.

Trouble however continued to flare up around the world in the wake of the First World War. Much of Ireland was in open revolt, and Britain became embroiled in the Russian Civil War even before hostilities in the west had officially ended. Lieutenant Cyril Corlett, who had already seen much action, volunteered to serve at Archangel in 1919 but was soon bitterly disappointed with the situation, writing to his brother:

> *About this Russian stunt. If you are sent well & good but if you volunteer you will be an absolute B.F. [Bloody Fool] There is no show of any kind here and paper twaddle about relieving hard pressed garrisons is, to say the least possible about it, All Balls. The only reason I can give for it is that volunteers for this stunt being few and far between they are trying to buck up recruiting.* [50]

Cyril Corlett was subsequently placed with other British officers in charge of a Russian battalion recruited from Bolshevik prisoners, who later mutinied, murdered their

Russian officers and took the British officers prisoner. Corlett was held captive in a filthy cell in Moscow and his family had no word of whether he was alive or dead for several months. Eventually in March 1920 he was released as part of a prisoner exchange, a Manx newspaper stating:

Thus the last Manxman to be reported 'missing' has been accounted for, and he is safe and let us hope, sound. [51]

Statistics have been quoted and re-quoted in relation the military effort of the Isle of Man in the First World War. However one chooses to quantify it, either as a percentage of total population or of available manpower, the Isle of Man's contribution was significant. Its men folk fought on every continent and in every campaign; Manxmen were present when the first angry shots were fired in 1914, and were still in harm's way after the general close of hostilities in 1918; their casualties were appallingly high, and the Island's contribution to the military effort of the British Empire was even more remarkable when one considers that it was predominantly a maritime nation, and had also committed many of its sons to the war at sea.

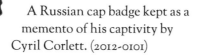

A Russian cap badge kept as a memento of his captivity by Cyril Corlett. (2012-0101)

Lieutenant Cyril Corlett in Russia in 1919. Corlett was captured by Bolshevik forces during the Allied Intervention in the Russian Civil War, and was not released until 1920. (MS 10987)

A U-boat on the surface. During the early part of the war Allied ships were often sunk by fire from the deck mounted gun, in order to conserve torpedoes. Later in the war this would become too risky. (Author's collection)

Chapter Two
Be British, Boys

In a world war, control of the seas and shipping lanes could have a dramatic impact upon the overall course of the conflict. As the navies of Great Britain and Imperial Germany battled for control of these seaways, vessels large and small, civilian and military became involved in the conflict. Although tactics such as blockades had been used in previous centuries, this was a conflict also increasingly influenced by new weapons such as submarines and ship-launched aircraft. As a maritime nation, the economy of which depended to a large extent upon fishing, and as an Island heavily reliant upon its trading links for supplies, the war at sea impacted upon the daily life of the Isle of Man and its people to a greater degree than perhaps upon many parts of the United Kingdom. This chapter examines the experiences of Manx seafarers in the First World War, the role played by the Isle of Man Steam Packet Company (IOMSPCo), and the way in which the Manx fishing fleet operating in the Irish Sea also became embroiled in the front line of the maritime conflict.

Manxmen (and indeed some Manx women) served afloat in the Great War under the flags of a variety of merchant fleets, including the IOMSPCo and a host of other companies; some of these men were engaged in maritime actions and dramas far from the shores of the Isle of Man. One such mariner, and one of the first to see action, was Frederick Teare. Born in Peel in 1877, he was

described as a man typical of the British officers bred by our tramp steamers.[52]

In 1914 on the outbreak of the Great War, Teare was a river pilot in Burma. He was aboard the *Hindu*, a small, fast coasting steamer, undertaking the work of guiding ships up the Rangoon River to their berths. On 26 July 1914, as war appeared imminent, the Rangoon Port Authorities learned that the Hamburg-Amerika line steamer *Alesia* had passed through the Suez canal and was bound for Rangoon. At first it was believed that she would probably find a neutral port and turn herself in, but out of a squall a few days later off Rangoon appeared a large liner, flying the German flag – the *Alesia*. By now Germany and Great Britain were at war, and the intentions of the German crew were unclear. Were they armed? Had they come to attack the port facilities at Rangoon?

A sharp eyed observer noticed that the radio mast on the *Alesia* was down, and so Frederick Teare volunteered to go aboard, in order to pilot the big ship into harbour. His gamble paid off, as once aboard the *Alesia* the German crew told him that their radio was broken, and quizzed him about developments with the war. With a poker face, Teare assured them that hostilities had been averted by diplomatic means. Pilot Teare then guided the mighty ship up river. There was still a chance that the Germans were also bluffing and might have had concealed armament, ready to bombard the port installations, but Teare kept his

A sailor's cap tally from HMS *Mona's Isle*. The ship was taken over from the IOMSPCo by the Royal Navy in 1915, and served as an anti-submarine net-laying vessel. (2008-0319)

nerve and remained on board all that night, guiding the ship further up river where she could do no harm. At dawn, two platoons of British soldiers stormed on board to take control. The furious German captain asked the pilot what the meaning of this was, to which Teare replied,

I am sorry to say, Captain, that our countries are at war with each other, and I have captured your ship. (53)

The *Alesia* was later offered for sale in the *London Gazette* as a prize, along with other German merchantmen seized in British or Empire ports, and was subsequently purchased by the Government of India. There was a sad sequel to the story however, for Teare returned to the Isle of Man the following year, joined the army and died leading his platoon of Seaforth Highlanders during the Battle of Arras. The story of his remarkable coolness in seizing the ship single-handed came to light through letters home to his parents in Peel.

Another Peel man, Henry Crellin of Mona Street, had had some hair raising experiences before the war; he was aboard the Peel fishing boat *Fear Not*, which was wrecked in Port Erin Bay in August 1910 with two lives being lost. He was also a member of the crew of a vessel which was sunk in the Mersey about nine months prior to the outbreak of war. Again one life was lost. In August 1914 he was one of the hands aboard a merchant vessel, the SS *Bordeland*, which found itself impounded at Hamburg, upon the outbreak of war. He and his fellow crewmen were made prisoners on their own ship for over two months, before being transferred to the German civilian internment camp at Ruhleben, a former racecourse outside Berlin.

Here the men were accommodated in stalls, which in former times had housed the racehorses. With six men to a stall, conditions were cramped. The surroundings were far from luxurious, with only straw mattresses to sleep on and at first no means of heating the stalls. Gradually conditions improved, though the harshness of the rationing system in Germany was evident, with fats of all kinds, especially butter and margarine, practically unobtainable there as early as 1915. Crellin recounted:

We had three meals a day. In the morning we had dry bread and a cup of black coffee, which was very seldom flavoured with milk. It was black bread; not the real black bread, which was better than that which we were given ... At first we were allowed a loaf of this bread every other day. Then it was reduced to a loaf every three days, and at last we were given one fifth of a loaf every day. For dinner there was sometimes soup made of sausage and vegetables, and sometimes fish. [54]

He went on:

There was not nearly enough food, and I can say with a clear conscience that only for the parcels of food from home, half of the prisoners in the camp would have died. On average there were 24,000 parcels a month received from England ... There were a great many things however, which those with money could buy; and from the spring we each received 5 marks a week from the English government ... This money was paid through the American Embassy. In addition to that, the men who were taken off the boat I was on received 2 ½ marks a week from the shipping company. [55]

One day an official list of those who were to be exchanged was posted up. Crellin continues:

The crowd was so great that I could not get near it until a policeman came and shifted some of the men. I found that I was amongst those on the list, and had only half an hour to pack my clothes and present myself in the square. When I got to the hut I found an official paper telling me what to do. There were 85 of us who were chosen to go home. We were all seamen, but no man who held a 'ticket' as a mate or skipper was allowed to go. The men were all either over 55 years of age or under 17. [56]

Whilst many Manx sailors were plying their trade in waters far away from the Isle of Man, those seas closer to home were in the grip of an ever-present danger. The Irish Sea became known in the First World War as 'U-boat Alley.' The approaches to Liverpool, Britain's largest port, were the ideal place for prowling U-boats to loiter in the hope of picking off trans-Atlantic shipping on the final leg of its journey. It is no exaggeration to say that this small stretch of water became one of the deadliest battlegrounds in the world for seafarers.

Unlike the situation during the Second World War, there was no equivalent of RAF coastal command, which took such a heavy toll of U-boats during the 1939-45 Battle of the Atlantic. Thus in the early part of the Great War at least, U-boats could operate fairly freely, without fear of being molested by British aircraft. If they were not directly engaged in torpedoing British shipping, then the U-boats often left mines in the shipping lanes, which were equally hazardous. During this four year naval war, ocean liners and merchant steamers were frequent targets, but the Isle of Man's fishing fleet was often also on the front line, with its crews either going to the assistance of stricken vessels, or even confronting the U-boats face to face.

On 30 January 1915 the crew of the first vessel sunk in Manx waters by an enemy submarine was landed at Douglas. On the following day news arrived of the sinking of five more vessels, and, not long after the reception of this news, the Extinction of Lights Order was put into operation. Under this order, all lights visible seawards, whether inside houses or in the Island's streets, were required to be kept obscured. In February 1915 the steamer *Downshire* of Dundrum was sunk by U-12, nine miles north-west of the Calf of Man. Prior to the destruction of the vessel by means of a bomb, the U-boat commander allowed the crew to board two small boats, along with water and provisions, which sustained them until they were rescued. In later instances, the U-boat crews would not be so chivalrous.

On 11 March 1915 HMS *Bayano* was torpedoed by U-27 off Carswell Point, Stranraer. She sank in under three minutes, and most of her crew were asleep below decks. Just four officers and twenty two men were saved, whilst fourteen officers and a hundred and eighty one men were lost. Some of her dead crew members were brought into Ramsey, whilst others washed up on the Manx coast over the following days. The *Bayano* was an armed merchant cruiser, a banana boat formerly belonging to the Elders and Fyffes line. She was requisitioned by the Royal Navy at the start of the war but, like many similar armed merchant cruisers she was extremely vulnerable, having limited armament, high sides offering a good target, and few watertight doors or compartments to limit flooding if she were hit.

Two days later on 13 March 1915 came the sinking of the Langland liner *Princess Victoria*, carrying cargo from Aberdeen to Liverpool. This attack struck even closer to home as eight of the twenty four crew were Manx,

including the master, Captain John Cubbon. He stated that they had kept a good look out for U-boats and would have been willing to ram one if they had seen it, but twenty miles off the Mersey Bar they saw a torpedo racing through the water, which struck the forequarter. There was a large explosion. Lifeboats were swung out in readiness for such an attack, and all twenty four crew got away in one.

On 7 May 1915 occurred the most famous attack by a U-boat on a merchant ship in history. The Cunard liner *Lusitania* was attacked by a submarine fifteen miles south of the Old Head of Kinsale, southern Ireland, whilst heading for Queenstown (now Cobh). She was torpedoed without warning, with the result that 1,198 lives were lost. Winston Churchill famously called her '45,000 tons of livebait', because he believed that the ongoing U-boat campaign, and the American lives which were being lost as a result, would eventually draw the United States into the war. One aspect of this most famous of incidents concerns the crew of the Peel fishing boat PL 11, the *Wanderer*, which at that time like many other Manx boats often fished off Kinsale. In consequence she was the first rescue vessel on the scene of the disaster, the skipper William Ball telling his helmsman, 'Go for her, be British', and as a result her crew picked up more than 100 passengers and took two of her lifeboats in tow. Ball wrote later to the owner of the *Wanderer*, Mr Morrison of Peel:

We were the only boat there for two hours, then the patrol boats came out from Queenstown. We had a busy time making tea for them – and all our milk and tea is gone and a lot of clothes as well, and the bottle of whisky we had leaving home. The people were in a sorry plight, most

of them having been in the water. We took them to within two miles of the Old Head, when it fell calm .... The tug boat Flying Fish from Queenstown then came up and took them from us. [57]

The crew of the *Wanderer* receiving medals at Tynwald Day 1915. (Courtesy of Alexander McKinnon)

Stanley Ball, one of the crew and son of William Ball the skipper, wrote to his mother:

...we saw the Lusitania going east. We knew it was one of the big liners by her four funnels, so we put the watch on. When we were lying in bed the man on watch shouted *that the four-funnelled boat was sinking. I got up out of bed and on deck. I saw her going down. She went down bow first. We were going off south and we kept her away to the south-south-west, and then went out to where it took place. We went out to within a quarter of a mile of where she went down, and we picked four yawls up. We took 110 persons out of the two first yawls, and about 50*

A medal awarded to Thomas Woods, one of the crew of the *Wanderer*, by the Manchester Manx Society (1959-0184)

or 60 out of the two next, and we took two yawls in tow. We were at her a good while before any other boat. The first person we took aboard was a child of two months. We had four or five children aboard and a lot of women. Some of them were naked. I gave a pair of trousers, a waistcoat and an oil coat away. Some of us have lost a lot but we expect to get it made up to us. One of the women had her leg broken, another her arm, and many were very exhausted. [58]

In recognition of their bravery, the Manchester Manx Society had medals struck, which were presented by the Lieutenant Governor to the crew on Tynwald Day 1915.

Later that year the steamer *Princess Caroline*, which carried nine Manx crew including the Master, William Corlett, was lost after striking a mine en route from Liverpool to Aberdeen. One of the crew, Thomas Hudson of Castletown, remarked light-heartedly after the event that he was getting used to the experience, as he had already survived the sinking of the steamer *Princess Olga* earlier the same year, though it must have been a terrifying situation. The *Princess Caroline* was prepared for the worst, having her lifeboats swung out in readiness. Even so, some of the crew were lost, including Manxman Harry Crebbin who went below decks probably to retrieve personal possessions.

Hugh Corlett, of Ramsey, began his working life as a sixteen year old cadet aboard the Harrison line ship *Gladiator*. His first voyage to Brazil was uneventful, as was the second to East Africa. It was to be third time unlucky for him however; he recalled:

We left Cardiff on August 14th, 1915 and when about 75 miles south-east of Waterford we were chased by a U-boat. When close to us it flew the German ensign and at the same time ordered us by International Flag Signal to abandon ship. The U-boat fired on the ship even while we were embarking in the lifeboats. The ship was soon sunk by the U-boat shells. We landed at Milford Haven the following day, assisted by a trawler. From Milford Haven we travelled to Liverpool by train and on arrival at Lime Street found the newspaper boys were carrying placards reading 'Harrison Line Gladiator sunk in Irish

Sea'. Security was not so tight in World War 1.

I remember the 'Daily Mail' offered a reward of £1000 to the first person producing a photograph of a U-boat. Our third officer had photographed our attacker while he was in the lifeboat. But he discovered when he reached Liverpool that in the excitement he had failed to turn the film! [59]

Corlett remained at sea, having two further clashes with U-boats. After one attack, upon returning home he was given the grim task by his employers of calling on the widows of the crew who had been lost, to offer their condolences. He recalled:

What a mission for a young man to carry out – but I did it. [60]

It is not generally appreciated that many women also served in the Merchant service as stewards, both before and during the First World War. Annie Storah, who was born in Douglas in 1864, served for most of her life on vessels of the Isle of Man Steam Packet Company. She sailed in the *Fenella* and the *Ramsey* prior to the First World War, and during the war she served in the *Tynwald*, crossing and re-crossing the war zone of the Irish Sea many times. In September 1915, Mary Ann Green of Douglas lost her life in the sinking of the SS *Hesperian*, by a U-boat, off the coast of Ireland. Employed by the Allan Line as a Matron on board the vessel, the thirty-five year old had previously spent five years at sea in the employ of the IOMSPCo. Her death was particularly tragic, as having survived the initial attack, she accidentally fell from a lifeboat. A Manxman who

was a passenger aboard the *Hesperian*, Charles Kennaugh, has left a graphic account of this horrific incident which occurred as she sank:

At about 8.30 there was a little lull in the conversation, and all of a sudden we heard something like the heavy banging of a door. I had a premonition all the time that something was in store for us. We looked at one another, and I said, "My God, there we have got it." We ran out of the cabin into the passage, and then I remembered I had left my lifebelt in my cabin, and I went back for it, and then went on deck. I saw practically nobody at that time. The water was pouring down from the top decks; the explosion had sent a rush of water fifty feet into the air ... and the first thing that happened when I got on deck was that I got a soaking from this water-spout coming from the top deck. The boat that was alongside the deck at that point was being gradually lowered, and there were a lot of ladies and children in it. While they were lowering, the ropes on the stern got fast in the falls, and somebody shouted, "Cut away the ropes." There was an axe on each boat in case of emergency, in case you could not get the blocking-tackle to clear. All of a sudden, the ropes of the boat gave way, and I saw the boat stand perpendicular, and all the people fall into the water, screaming. I turned my head away, and walked about for a moment, and then thought my best move would be to make for another lifeboat. I got into one, and as we were lowering down, the same thing happened to us as with the first boat; one of the ropes got fast, and it looked as if we were going to turn perpendicular too. However, we got half way down the ship's side. The ship stopped dead almost as soon as she was struck ... while we were being lowered, the ship gave a

kind of lurch, and the lurch caught us on the side of the boat, and nearly threw us out, but the boat righted herself and the ship righted herself. We got down, and I was thankful when we rested on the water. [61]

For many Manxmen, the living that they had made from the sea before the war was so sparse that enrolment in the Royal Naval Reserve was an attractive option for extra money. As a result, the Manx were present in numbers at several notable naval actions. The magazine *Ellan Vannin* recounted the declaration of war, adding:

> *...the Royal Naval Reservists ... had received urgent instructions to report to their depots immediately, and Sunday, the 2nd August, 1914, witnessed the departure of 85 men, mostly taken at a moment's notice from their employment on our steamers, fishing vessels, and pleasure yachts.* [62]

Some numbers of these Manx naval reservists found themselves serving together aboard the veteran battleship HMS *Goliath* in the Dardanelles. *Goliath* was laid down at Chatham Dockyard in 1897 and was commissioned three years later. She and her five sister ships were designed for service in the Far East, where the new rising power Japan was beginning to build a fleet to rival the Royal Navy. To facilitate passage through the Suez Canal, they were designed to be narrower (and lighter) than their predecessors, the *Majestic*-class battleships. In order to save weight, *Goliath* carried less armour, and this deficiency was to make her almost a second-class battleship.

Goliath was part of the Allied fleet covering the landing at 'X' and 'Y' Beaches during the landing at Gallipoli on

Mary Ann Green, a stewardess aboard SS *Hesperian*, who lost her life when the vessel was sunk off the Irish coast in September 1915. (M 00227)

Above: William Moore, of Douglas. In later life he was the Douglas Harbour Master, but in 1915 he survived the sinking of HMS *Goliath*. (PG 13761/1)

Left: HMS *Goliath*. The obsolete battleship numbered many Manxmen among her crew. (PG 13761/2)

British battleships in the Dardanelles, during the Gallipoli campaign, 1915. (Author's collection)

25 April 1915, sustaining some damage from the gunfire of Turkish forts and shore batteries, and supporting Allied troops ashore during the First Battle of Krithia that day. On the night of 12-13 May, *Goliath* was anchored in Morto Bay off Cape Helles, along with HMS *Cornwallis* and a screen of five destroyers, in foggy conditions. Around 1 am on 13 May, the Turkish torpedo boat *Muavenet-i Milliye* eluded the destroyers and fired two torpedoes which struck *Goliath* almost simultaneously abreast her fore turret and abeam the fore funnel, causing a massive explosion. *Goliath* began to capsize almost immediately, and was lying on her beam ends when a third torpedo struck near her after turret. She then rolled over completely and began to sink by the bows, taking 570 of the 700-strong crew to the bottom, including her commanding officer.

Among the Manx crew was forty-one year old William Moore of Douglas. Moore had served his apprenticeship in tall ships and during a career which had taken him all over the world had joined the Royal Naval Reserve. He was called up upon the outbreak of war, and posted to *Goliath*. On the night the torpedoes struck her, he was below decks with several other Manxmen. When the alarm was raised they struggled up the iron ladders to the top deck, but *Goliath* was already listing and the waves were lapping over her decks on one side. Moore dived into the sea but as the mighty vessel disappeared under the waves the suction dragged him under with her. He was battered against the hull and received severe injuries. A strong swimmer, he grasped first an oar and then a log to keep himself afloat. An eyewitness who was with him later reported that:

> *His head was opened like an oyster and blood was pouring from it, but for over an hour he held on to that log to prevent it from turning over and throwing us back into the water. Eventually we were picked up by a French picket boat.* (63)

Another Manxman who survived the sinking was Seaman W.H.Clark, the only one of six Ramsey men aboard the *Goliath* who was not drowned. He wrote afterwards:

> *No doubt you will have heard all about our ship by now. I can tell you I don't want to go through such an experience again. We were in the water about an hour, and it was an awful sight to see so many men struggling for life. I was almost done when I got rescued, but we proved ourselves British anyway. As the ship was sinking one chap shouted, "Are we downhearted?" and all hands replied with a shout, "No!" and "Be British boys!" As we were struggling in the water we could hear the*

> *rest on board singing "Tipperary." I have often heard about men singing facing death, but I have now seen it in reality. I don't know how any of the Ramsey chaps got on, as I was the only one on board the ship I was rescued by. We lost everything, but thank God I was spared my life … We are all suffering shock as a result of the terrible sensation, and I am not feeling up to the mark at the time of writing.* (64)

The Dardanelles campaign took a heavy toll on British warships – on 27 May 1915 HMS *Majestic* became the third British battleship to be lost in those waters when she was torpedoed by a U-boat. Seaman John Edward Kelly, of College Street, Ramsey, was among the crew; after she was struck and began to list at forty-five degrees, he managed to reach the forecastle and lowered himself down the ship's side. As she turned on her beam ends he crawled forward to get clear of the booms and nets in which many of the crew became entangled. When she had turned completely over he sat on the hull until a steam trawler arrived on the scene, and thus became the last man to leave the vessel.

In time of war it is common for the Royal Navy to supplement its strength by drawing upon ships from the merchant service. The IOMSPCo, having one of the most modern fleets in British home waters, made an important contribution to the war at sea. Of the fifteen steamers owned by the company in 1914, eleven were either chartered or requisitioned by the British government for war service. Only four of these vessels would return to their peacetime occupation at the end of the war. Of the remainder, four would be lost and three retained by the government. *Ben my Chree* and *Viking* both served as seaplane carriers. *Viking* was renamed HMS *Vindex* for the duration of the war, as there was already an HMS *Viking* in the Royal Navy. *Ben my Chree* was chartered by the government on 1 January 1915. She was one the fastest vessels in the British coastal services, and it was perhaps for this reason that she was converted to be a seaplane carrier. This was done by Cammell Laird at Birkenhead, and considerable changes were made to her superstructure, with a large hangar for the housing of seaplanes being added to her afterdeck along with cranes for lifting seaplanes on and off the vessel. There were a few of the pre-war Manx crew still on board as naval reservists, but many of the complement were wartime enlistments. Her Medical Officer, Surgeon Lieutenant L.S.Goss RN, joined the vessel upon commissioning and remained with her for two years. A detailed report about the ship which he prepared survives, and in it he writes:

HMS *Ben my Chree* equipped as a seaplane carrier. Seaplanes were carried in the hangar at the rear of the vessel. (PG 4385/13)

The Ship's Company were recruited in Liverpool from merchantile [sic] ratings and were the sweepings of the place after all the shipping companies had taken their pick. Physically they were a very poor lot but we had to take what we could get. They were signed on T124 [a naval form placing crews under naval discipline but with merchant service rates of pay, usually higher than RN equivalents]. They were a dreadful lot to start with but by judicious weeding out and a slight stiffening of RNR and RFR they are now after 9 months drilling a very good crowd ... They have had practically no leave since commissioning, except 48 hours before we left England and the stokers were [not] even allowed that. This deprivation of leave has a bad effect upon them mentally and morally they get very 'bloody minded' and *are liable to refuse duty while the lack of change of environment, diet and exercise of a different kind from their work also tells upon them ... On the other hand the only time they did get leave at home most of them got drunk and misbehaved themselves. I represented to the captain that this was probably due to the fact that leave was not given frequently enough. They have occasionally been ashore for route marches, swimming and football matches.* [65]

In May 1915 HMS *Ben My Chree* was dispatched to the Dardanelles, in order to participate in the Gallipoli campaign. Her aircraft were engaged in spotting targets for the guns of the big battleships which formed the eastern Mediterranean fleet. She saw considerable action during this period of her service, she was more than once the subject of a torpedo attack, but being of shallow draught, the torpedoes passed underneath her. The Official History of the campaign considered the *Ben My Chree* particularly valuable as a mobile self-contained air unit, and on 12 August 1915 she became part of aviation history, when she was the platform for the first ship-launched airborne torpedo attack on an enemy vessel. One of her aircraft sank a Turkish transport vessel in the Sea of Marmara, after it had flown right over the Gallipoli peninsula in order to reach it. The pilot, Flight Commander C.H.K.Edmonds, reported that, as he looked backwards:

> *I observed the track of the torpedo, which struck the ship abreast the mainmast, the starboard side. The explosion sent a column of water and large fragments of the ship almost as high as the masthead ... she appeared to have settled down a little by the stern when I ceased watching her.* [66]

Another Steam Packet ship, the *Ramsey*, was taken over by the government, and fitted out as an Armed Boarding Vessel. Her armament consisted of two twelve pounder guns, placed port and starboard, underneath the Captain's bridge. Her crew numbered ninety-eight all told. She sailed for Scapa Flow in November 1914, and now as HMS *Ramsey* was subsequently ordered to accompany HMS *Sapphire* and HMS *Sapplire* on patrol duty. They went out at dusk each day, steaming about

two miles apart in line with each other, returning the next day.

The usual procedure, when dusk set in, was for one of the Marines on board to see that all lights were screened. The *Ramsey* then steamed without navigation lights, and the gun crews were at their guns all the time. The speed of the ship was altered from time to time, from eight to twelve knots per hour, and if a light were seen, then full speed ahead was made in order to investigate it. Everyone was on the alert, even those off watch would be often leaning over the rails, trying to make out in the darkness what a light might mean, friend or foe. When a vessel was sighted, the *Ramsey* would steam up abeam of her, keeping about fifty yards off, then flash her searchlight upon her. The voice of the Commander would then be heard, calling through his megaphone for the stranger to identify herself. If all was found in order, the skipper of the vessel would be told to proceed, the *Ramsey* would sheer off, and all would become normal again.

The dangerous work in which the *Ramsey* was engaged was evident from the large amount of wreckage frequently seen floating past, showing that some vessel had met with disaster. During the last three months of her patrol work she searched a large number of vessels, and had to put prize crews on some of them in order to take them into port. The last patrol, in August 1915, is described by one of the survivors. The account is unattributed, but as it contains details which only he can have known, the author must be Engineer Lieutenant T.Fayle RNR of Douglas:

> *The Ramsey left Scapa Flow about 5 p.m. on Saturday, August 7th 1915, for the North Sea. About midnight, a*

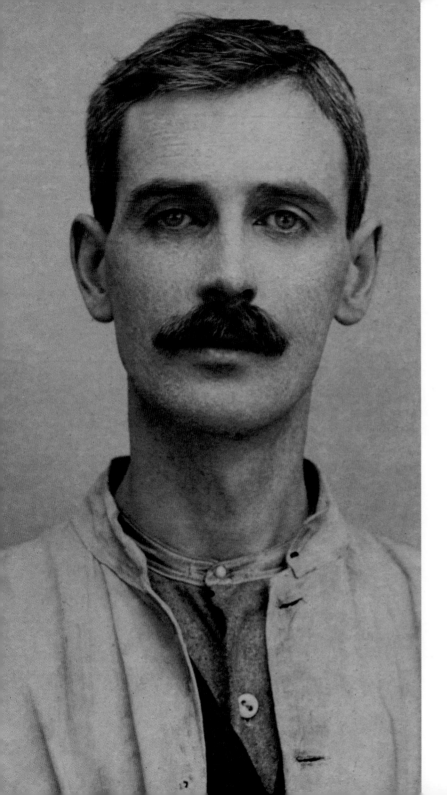

wireless message came through to the Lieutenant-Commander to keep a sharp lookout to the Eastward. All went well until about 5 a.m., Sunday morning, when the smoke of a vessel was seen on the horizon.

The Ramsey at once gave chase, and in half-an-hour came up to what, from all outward appearances, seemed to be a large tramp steamer. We blew for her to stop, as we wanted to board her. Both men and ship were well disguised, She stopped, and, when we had got to within a short distance of her, the captain hauled down his flag, which was Russian, and immediately hoisted the German flag. At the same time, the raider opened fire with machine-guns, and two 4.6 guns, which were on disappearing mounts, forward and aft. With these, she gave us the benefit of a broadside, sweeping our decks with bullets and shells, killing the Commander, Lieut. Raby RNR, and the officers who were with him on the bridge. At the same time she released a torpedo, which struck the Ramsey aft, just where the crew's quarters were situated. [67]

Another crewman, Marshall Cleator, wrote to his mother to say:

We had a terrible time of it in the North Sea. Those saved were taken to a German ship. We were taken prisoners. They treated us fairly, giving us dry clothes; but they did not give us a dog's chance to get out of the boat before they

Engineer Lieutenant T.Fayle, of Douglas. A member of the Royal Naval Reserve, he was part of the crew of HMS *Ramsey* when she was attacked by the *Meteor*. (Courtesy of Southampton City Archives)

struck us. As soon as she was hit by the torpedo we had to jump into the water. She sank in five minutes. I don't know anything about Will, George Perry, or Tommy Crosbie, or any of the other Manx chaps. It was every man for himself ... men were getting killed on the deck from the quick firing of the Maxim guns. They had all their guns covered up until we were close to them ... when the Germans came in their boats to pick us up out of the water we thought they had come to shoot us in the water with their revolvers. [68]

The survivors, numbering forty six out of a crew of ninety eight, were picked up from the few of the *Ramsey's* boats which the crew had managed to lower, and from the water. Among the latter group was Fayle, whose foot was crushed in escaping the sinking vessel. They were taken on board the German ship, which turned out to be the raider *Meteor*.

As soon as we were put on board the German ship, the Commander, who, by the way, was wearing an Iron Cross, mustered us on the deck, and then sent us below to get some dry clothes and medical comforts. He afterwards addressed us, saying that he was sorry to see us in such a plight, and sorry we had lost so many brave men, but that it was the fortune of war. He also said, that as British officers had been so kind to many of their men (Germans), who had, up to that time, come into their hands, it behoved him to do all in his power for us, and anything we wanted in reason we were to ask, and he would grant it. At the same time, he asked if we would like to have a Church service in memory of our lost comrades. We replied that we would gladly accept his offer. He then had the necessary arrangements made on deck, including a lectern, covered with a Union Jack. The German Commander with his officers who were off duty, attended the service.

We were treated very well indeed, whether it was that the code of honour was higher amongst the original officers of the German Navy than it was toward the end of the war, or whether we had struck an exception, I don't know, but they certainly were very good to us, and amongst other things gave us plenty of cigars and cigarettes. Extra privileges were also granted to all officers, but they were confined in rooms on deck. Our men were put down one of the ship's holds, and each one was given a mattress and a blanket. Here we remained until about 3 o'clock in the afternoon. We were then brought up on deck and given an hour's exercise, after which we were sent below, had tea, and lay down for the night. [69]

The *Meteor* was subsequently pursued and challenged by British cruisers. The Germans decided to abandon ship, and transferred their Manx and other captives on to a commandeered Danish lugger. Fayle continues:

The first cruiser to come on the scene was the HMS Cleopatra. After circling round us several times, one of our officers gave orders to a signalman, who was also one of the survivors of the Ramsey to let them know on the Cleopatra that we were on board. This he did, and the order came back to take charge of the lugger and steer a course that they gave.

The German Commander, however, would not allow our men to interfere with the navigation of the vessel, pointing out that we were under a neutral flag. We again signalled the Cleopatra telling her what had transpired, and she made off to Commodore Tyrwhitt on the Arethusa, who was cruising round a long way off.

We began to get a little disconsolate, not knowing what was going to happen, and thinking that they had left us to our fate. The German officers in the meantime put their heads together, and had a consultation, the result being, that we were told to go aboard another lugger, which was a Norwegian. By means of a couple of small dinghies they transferred us to the other boat, whilst they made off in the Danish one.

We were on board this Norwegian lugger about half-an-hour, when again one of our cruisers appeared. This time it was the HMS Arethusa under Commodore Tyrwhitt, himself. When they found out where we were, they lowered one of their large boats, and sent it off for us. Thus we had the unique experience of sailing under four flags in a very short space of time, being transferred from the German to the Danish, from the Danish to the Norwegian, and then on to the British.

Needless to say we were all overcome with joy when we got on board the Arethusa, knowing that if we happened to meet another raider, we would be able to hit smartly back. We now had something under us very different from the poor old Ramsey with her two small twelve pounders. [70]

The *Peel Castle*, originally built as the *Duke of York* for the Lancashire and Yorkshire Railway Company, had been purchased by the IOMSPCo before the war. She was requisitioned and commissioned into the Royal Navy as HMS *Peel Castle* on 14 November 1914. In common with many other vessels taken up from trade, her executive and navigating officers were regular members of the Royal Navy. The engine room staff however were mostly pre-war employees of the company. HMS *Peel Castle* undertook duties as a patrol vessel in the English Channel, also helping to enforce the blockade of Germany. The channel had largely been closed off by minefields and anti-submarine nets, with only a few routes open. Merchant men using these routes were subject to searches by Royal Navy vessels, looking for contraband entering German ports. This was one of the busiest sea lanes in the world, with an average of 115 vessels per day passing through it. The vessel became known as the *Terror of the Downs* during her tenure off the south coast.

The first job which she had was typical of many others. A steamer which turned out to be of Greek nationality was endeavouring to slip away in the dark. She was chased and brought back. A few days later, a large steamer flying the red ensign passed through the Downs, and, continuing to proceed after being ordered to stop, the *Peel Castle* fired at her and gave chase. When off the South Foreland, however, the unknown steamer returned the fire, by a shot from a much larger gun than any aboard the *Peel Castle*. She was left to other larger Royal Navy craft to deal with.

Whilst searching vessels, she made some valuable captures of prisoners. It was known that some Germans were returning home by stowing themselves away in the bunkers of neutral ships, so orders were received that an engineer officer and a party of stokers were to search the engine-rooms and bunkers of neutral vessels, especially those of ships hailing from United States ports. On 1 May 1915, an engineer (a Douglas man) and a party of stokers were searching a Dutch ship, whose engine-room staff were all mustered together in the engine-room whilst the search was in progress. One of the stokers, in going through a coal bunker, was surprised to see a pair of eyes staring at him from behind a heap of coal. He quickly got out and returned with the engineer. They then discovered a stowaway, who was made prisoner. On examination by the interpreter aboard the *Peel Castle*, he was proved to be a prominent New York businessman. He was sent ashore and interned, and was believed to be the first man to be found hidden in a coal bunker.

On 11 June 1915 an engineer and search-party from the *Peel Castle* examined the Dutch steamer *Rotterdam*. On board they captured the second engineer of the German auxiliary cruiser *Prinz Eitel Frederick*, disguised as a greaser. His ship was at the time interned in a United States port. On another occasion, while searching a Holland-America Line ship from New York, they captured two German prisoners, who were kept on board the *Peel Castle*, and examined by the senior Naval officer of the base. Posing as civilian businessmen, they turned out to be German agents. A diary account of some of the activities of HMS *Peel Castle* at this time reads as follows:

December 24th 1915 Picked up the crew of a Greek steamer, which had been torpedoed.

December 29th 1915 Information received that the Dutch steamer Delphland had sailed from New York with one boiler empty, so an engineer and party of stokers were sent to search it. Found the boiler to be entirely empty.

December 31st 1915 Went to the assistance of the Dutch ship Ecuador, which was mined, and sinking. Boarding tugs were giving assistance, but the ship sank on the Goodwin Sands.

January 6th, 1916 A Dutch tug brought the crew of a Norwegian steamer, which was mined off the North Galloper light-vessel. As the crew had very little clothing, the firemen being in their stokehold dungarees, we fitted them out with what clothes we could spare.

January 18th A steam trawler came alongside at night for assistance. One of the men had gone mad, and had attacked another member of the crew with a shackle. An officer and a party were sent on board, brought the man back under arrest, and, also, the wounded man, who was badly battered about the head. The wounded man was put into hospital, and the other one sent to the Naval base for treatment.

January 28th 1916 The crew of a Jersey smack, which had been sunk by a German submarine, was placed on board our ship. The men had been adrift for three days, and were in a very bad condition. [71]

Like the *Peel Castle*, the *King Orry* was fitted out by the navy as an armed boarding-vessel and left Liverpool in November 1914, bound for Scapa Flow. She was soon busy intercepting vessels in a similar fashion to the *Peel Castle*, albeit in more northerly waters. The crew were sometimes called to action stations three or four times during the night, amid driving sleet, in inky darkness, for there were times when it might have been fatal to disclose their position by showing a light. As well as danger from the enemy, she faced the hazards of terrible winter gales, because her work could not be held up by the weather. HMS *King Orry* searched innumerable vessels, and sometimes had the satisfaction of getting a significant prize. On one occasion while operating in the Pentland Firth, they boarded a big steamer, and escorted her into Kirkwall with a cargo of 10,000 tons of wheat, which her papers showed was intended for Germany, but which was shortly afterwards unloaded at a Scottish port instead. A report by one of those on board illustrates the work of the *King Orry*:

Today, June 3rd, 1915, we are anchored in the 'Flow' and are ready to weigh anchor. We had thought, at first, that we were to proceed to Liverpool; instead, we are to make a raid, along with eight other vessels, through the North Sea in search of contraband carriers. By the nomenclature of the Navy, our method of procedure is known as a sweep,

The nose of a German shell, fired at a British ship during the Battle of Jutland in 1916. It was handed in at Castle Rushen in the 1920s. (1954-0990)

that is, by steaming with the other ships on our beam, and ten miles apart, we make a sweep of thirty miles.

Saturday, June 5th, 9 p.m. We have been steaming along the German minefield, and are now about ninety miles off Heligoland. We have boarded two fishing vessels, presumably Dutch, but there was nothing we could take, other than a little fish. Our three destroyers have joined company, and have disappeared over the horizon to the South.

With the coming of night we fall in line astern of our parent ship. The destroyers, when in company, fall in behind us. There is a faint blue light to guide us, fitted close to the usual position of the stern light. The nights, so far, have been graciously fine; they have been anxious nights, and we have been ever vigilant.

This morning, the TBDs [Torpedo Boat Destroyers] have returned. They have secured a fishing vessel flying the Dutch flag. The same vessel having considerably more petrol than is required for her own use, obviously explanation is superfluous, and she is to have a long tow. We are now proceeding towards the Skager Rack [sic]. Since daybreak, we have stopped and boarded six vessels. We have put a prize crew on one big oil-tanker. She is bound for the East Coast. The waters we have travelled through are infested with submarines, but, so far, we have not got foul of one. Maybe, they are after big prey; in any case we offer them no temptation, for we are moving cautiously and quickly. Tonight we are making the Islands of Orkney; the weather has been beautiful and calm, now there is a change, the visibility is failing. We are approaching the Pentland Firth, and we have received orders to make our own way into Scapa. [72]

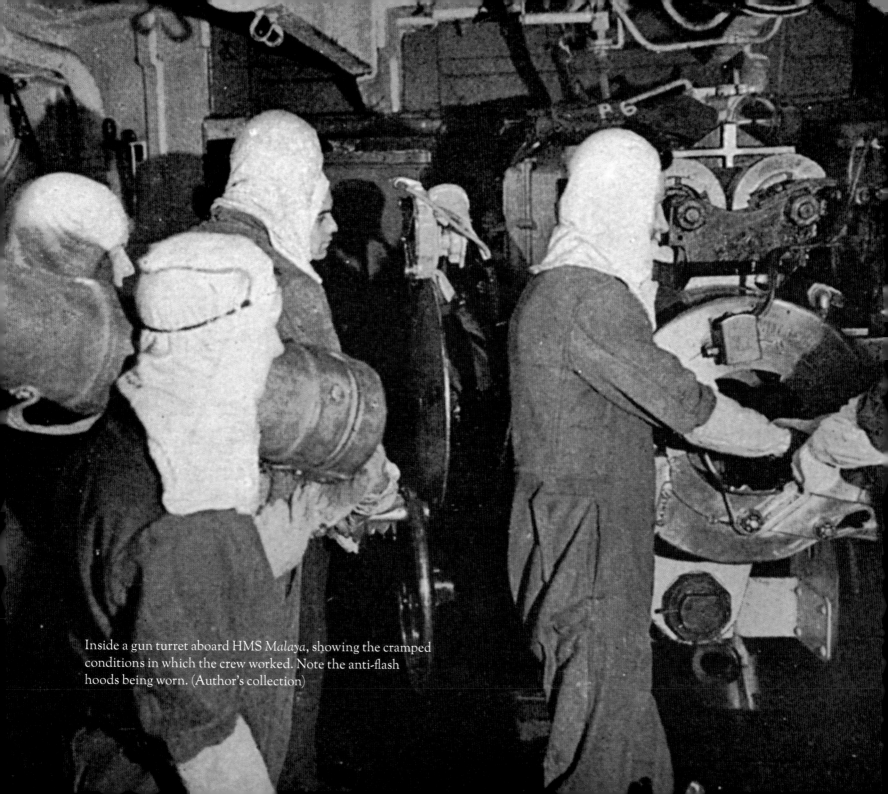

Inside a gun turret aboard HMS *Malaya*, showing the cramped conditions in which the crew worked. Note the anti-flash hoods being worn. (Author's collection)

In May 1916 in the North Sea came the Battle of Jutland, still the largest naval battle in history. The numerically inferior German High Seas Fleet left its bases and put to sea, in an attempt to lure the fast British battlecruisers away from their heavier dreadnought sisters, and into a trap. The German plan to defeat the Royal Navy piecemeal almost worked, though the result of the battle was inconclusive, and both sides claimed victory. A number of other Manx sailors were with the Grand Fleet and participated in this action. George Kewley of Castletown was aboard HMS *Warspite* and was part of a gun crew of nine. Whilst in the act of firing, a shell landed close by his turret, killing or injuring all of the other men, only Kewley being unscathed. Isaac Kelly of Baldrine was aboard HMS *Mandate*, and wrote to his father afterwards:

> *We had it a bit lively last week; it was hell let loose for a while. But we came out on top all right. Wait until you get the full result of it, and then you will see what we have done. Of course we lost a bit heavy. But when you are in the thick of it you can see for yourself what is going on.* [73]

Able Seaman James Bridson of Malew Street, Castletown, was part of a gun crew aboard HMS *Malaya*, a super-dreadnought battleship. *Malaya* was in the thick of the battle and Bridson afterwards commented that

> *The German fleet suffered a severe defeat, and ... the British Navy is quite prepared for the enemy whenever his ships venture out again – if they ever do.* [74]

Able Seaman James Bridson, who served aboard HMS *Malaya* at Jutland, and later became a Master with the IOMSPCo. (PG 13769/11)

In fact the outcome of the Jutland battle has remained controversial ever since. In part the absence of a decisive victory was blamed upon poor gunnery, and in late 1916 it was decided that battle practice was to be carried out by the Grand Fleet with a view to increasing the efficiency of its gun fire. The tugs employed for towing the huge targets were considered too slow for the purpose, however the *King Orry* was ideal for this task, and was fitted with towing gear. She was then able to tow the largest targets at about twelve to thirteen knots per hour. When it is remembered that the range at which the battleships had to practice would be somewhere about ten miles, it is not surprising that sometimes the *King Orry* herself came under fire, and numerous shells dropped about her. On one occasion a shell actually struck her, passing through the vessel just above the water-line, at the after end in the men's quarters, and, although a number of the crew were at mess at the time, not one of them was hurt. Her captain, Harry Tylden Mosse remembered:

...all of a sudden I felt something had hit me, and the First Lieutenant went down and chased out about it, and we discovered that a 6 inch 'proj' had come in about a foot off the water and gone straight across and through and out the other side ... I signalled to the Admiral that I had been hit and thought it better for me to go back into harbour because we hadn't got watertight doors or anything of that sort and I was put into the dockyard for 5 days... [75]

The working party on the *King Orry* had an anxious time during these operations. A former Royal Navy rating, Mr W.H.Banham, recalled these exercises many years later:

On various occasions [I was] on board the King Orry. It required four seamen with an officer in charge to record the splash of the shells so that the range and corrections could be reported and from it find out where the firing ship went wrong. Volunteers were called for from the fleet and I found it was a welcome change from being stuck below in a turret magazine on board HMS Monarch, a Super Dreadnought.

The King Orry was not a perfect lady. At times it was difficult to stand – she would roll, pitch and yaw. On she'd go for a few yards then come to a jerky halt as the target pulled her back. The tow hawser flew from side to side of the 'horse'. It would slacken and then – wham – up it would spring bar taught. [76]

In the autumn of that year, the *King Orry* was taken off these duties and ordered to the Norwegian coast to intercept contraband carriers, who apparently were operating between Norwegian, Danish, and German ports. For this purpose, the ship was disguised as a peaceful trader. The breaks in her side were closed up with canvas; these and the hull were painted black. Derricks were fitted to the masts, fore and aft. The guns were covered by a temporary superstructure; the funnel painted yellow, with a black top. The embossed name on the bows was easily transformed by the addition of the letters V and I, into *Viking Orry*, *Viking* being a common name for a ship in those waters.

Thus disguised, she cruised out of sight of land during the day, and, when night came on, would close the land, cruising along territorial waters. Not a light was visible on board, and in this way they were able to approach another vessel to within a stone's throw, form their own opinion of her, and if all was in order steam away again. In this way they sailed in territorial waters round about the islands on the Norwegian coast, sometimes chased by Norwegian destroyers, but never caught. An account survives of one incident here:

> We were cruising along at about nine knots per hour, with a visibility of about a couple of miles, having previously had a submarine scare, when out of the mists came a large cargo steamer. Immediately she was seen to alter her course, her object obviously being to get into neutral waters, before we could overtake her. In order that she might 'heave to' immediately, we dropped a couple of 4-inch shells across her bow. Then we closed down on her and lowered a boat. Upon our officer going on board, the Captain informed him that, directly he sighted us, he knew the game was up. The profile of our vessel, much disguised as she was, left something 'rakish and warlike' about her, to use his own words, and that was his reason for endeavouring to make for neutral waters. He appeared to blame the fog for his capture, having been drawn from the shelter of the islands to the safer navigation of the open sea. [77]

It is said that one of the enemy crew, who had previously been employed on the Birkenhead ferries, recognised the *King Orry*, and made her true identity known to his captain, who, to his regret, ignored the advice of the sailor. As this ship turned out to be carrying a valuable cargo of magnetic ore destined for Germany, a prize crew was put on board and she was taken to Kirkwall.

HMS *Ben My Chree*, whom we met last in the Eastern Mediterranean, was to meet her fate in the early spring of 1917. She was the last warship to withdraw from the Dardanelles, when the Gallipoli adventure was finally abandoned in January 1916, and had spent the time since providing mobile air support to Allied operations in the Middle East. Life for those on board was not entirely unpleasant during the two years she was on war service. She had a piano, and an orchestra which gave concerts for the crew and also for visitors when in port. The hangar, when the seaplanes were removed, made for a fine concert hall, capable of accommodating about 400 people. The crew also had their own football, hockey and cricket teams and often played against local sides when in port. Captain William Wedgwood Benn joined the vessel in 1916 and remembered:

> She was a new fast tripper recently built to do the journey from Liverpool to the Isle of Man. As that passage was a short one, the bunker accommodation in the ship was of a scanty kind by no means fitting her to cruise about for days, especially as her consumption of coal was commensurate with her fine turn of speed. To adapt her to her new work, a certain number of the cabins had been converted into coal bunkers, and in addition when long trips were made, as, for example, down the Red Sea, the decks as well had to be piled with fuel. Add to this the fact that the forced draught blew the dust through the lids of the coal holes in the deck and it will be seen that except in port, when she was a shining model of beautiful cleanliness, our ship was apt to be somewhat grimy. Aft of the funnels there had been a large deck or hall, once used, I believe, as a tea pavilion, and it was this which was converted into the hangar in which five or six machines — folded, of course, and in case of the single seaters, with

the tails taken off — could be stored. We carried Shorts (two-seaters) and Sopwiths. Aft of the hangar was the launching deck with bollards, derricks, and steam winch.

The ship's company was split up between the airmen and the seamen. It is surprising, although we were a naval unit, how distinct, even divisive, was the class-consciousness of these two groups; though nothing in the least disturbed the magnificent esprit de corps which made the old Ben-my-Chree an imperishable memory for those who ever had the privilege of sailing in her. [78]

Her skipper at this time was the famous Commander Charles Rumney Samson (who was remembered as the first British pilot to take off from a ship, on 10 January 1912). Having returned to the Mediterranean, the *Ben my Chree* was lost in February 1917, whilst on patrol off the coast of Asia Minor, searching for Turkish gun batteries. She was in harbour at Castellorizo, an Island held by the French at the time, when a salvo was fired from a Turkish battery on the enemy-held mainland. The *Ben* was hit immediately, the explosions puncturing her petrol supplies. Burning petrol ran down on to her lower decks and she was quickly ablaze. Valiant efforts were made to extinguish the fire, but with her steering gear crippled as well, after half an hour the order was given to abandon ship. Wedgwood Benn remembered:

I was resting in my cabin on the upper deck at half-past two when I heard a tremendous explosion and saw a column of water rise not fifteen yards from the ship. I was not surprised, for I imagined it was just the first of the usual two or three shots from an ordinary Taube [German aircraft], to which during the last few months we had been

getting quite accustomed. The first explosion, however, was followed quickly by two real smashers, neither of which, so far as I remember, hit the ship. I went to find Samson; it was clear that something more than a mere aeroplane attack was in progress, and our minds turned to the battery, the presence of which the French had suspected some months before. I found the CO on the main deck quietly giving orders; he was in no doubt about the source of the attack. Just as I reached him, a shell, which must have been the third or fourth, set fire to the hangar. Nothing now could prevent the ship from burning, and as further hits occurred, huge scarlet flames and masses of black smoke poured from the vessel. A few moments later the petrol store was hit and with it the fate of the ship was sealed. We were, of course, an actual 'sitter' for the Turks.

Direction and range offered no difficulty to their gunners; they could see us and our position relative to the town and could measure us off to a millimetre, and shoot simply from the map. Some minutes after the first attack a shot hit the whaler and swept it clean away; the bow was left dangling from one davit like a leg of mutton. In the meantime 'fire stations' had been sounded and the whole ship's company, except the crew of the twelve-pounder, was engaged in trying to quell the outbreak.

The gun was manned in the perfectly vain hope that it might make some reply to the 6-inch Howitzers, which had us in hand. The rest of us meanwhile were very busy dragging hoses into the hangar with the intention of putting out the fire; but flaming petrol is not extinguished with squirting water and it was soon clear that we were finished. We had steam, of course, and could have left the harbour, but what was the use of going to sea in a furnace with half a gale blowing, amid the certainty, at the best, of having to beach the ship on the Turkish coast and lose all the crew? Bitter as the decision was it was clearly the right one when the commanding officer ordered the quartermaster to pipe 'Abandon ship.'

In the meantime I was sent to the engine-room to see that there was no one left below; others went forward to the 'sick' bay, where some wounded were being attended to. One man, I remember, had the curious idea that the 'sick bay' was a sort of sanctuary where, according to the rules of The Hague Convention, he was immune from enemy attack. He accordingly refused to budge.

As soon as the order was given the motor-boats were lowered and trips were started to the shore. Each man acted according to his temperament. Scores dived over the sides and swam ashore; others behaved in the most leisurely manner. I recollect a very quiet and shy individual, who was our head photographer, coming up to me just before the last boat left, asking "if I had any objection to his taking a few photographs". I need not say that he was given the necessary permission and secured some excellent views showing the ship burning. [79]

Petty Officer Alma Dougherty, who was awarded the Distinguished Service Medal and French Croix de Guerre for his services during the sinking of HMS *Ben my Chree* in 1917. (Courtesy of Southampton City Archives)

Fortunately all 250 crew were able to escape safely and there was no loss of life. Among the Manx crew members on board at the time of the sinking was the ship's Third Mate and quartermaster, Chief Petty Officer Alma Dougherty of Douglas, a member of the Royal Naval Reserve. He received the Distinguished Service Medal and French Croix de Guerre for his bravery during this episode. Also present were two Manx engine room crewmen, Stokers Bell and J.Corlett.

However, as Wedgwood Benn acknowledged in the title of his memoirs, the operations in the Mediterranean were really only a sideshow, with the real war being fought out in the waters of the Atlantic, where the coming year was to see Britain almost face disaster. Great Britain was not alone in using blockade tactics to try to force her enemy into surrender. In 1917 the Germans would declare unrestricted submarine warfare, in an all-out effort to choke off supplies to Britain, and thus starve her into submission; the toll of merchant shipping being lost as a result began to reach crisis proportions.

After Jutland, the attention of the Royal Navy turned increasingly and more directly towards hunting U-boats, as they tried to protect merchant shipping. James Bridson for one was re-deployed away from HMS *Malaya* and transferred to Q-Ships, the secretly armed merchantmen used to lure U-boats in before finishing them off. The Q-ships carried double crews, and when a U-boat surfaced nearby, one half, the so-called 'panic party' would take to the lifeboats as a normal merchant crew might. Ideally the U-boat would then move in closer to finish off its prey, whereupon the remaining crew would open fire. He was not the only Manxman engaged in this type of dangerous work. Assistant Paymaster Thomas Fleming Green, one of the six Green brothers from Douglas, was drowned on 20 May 1917 when his Q-Ship, HMS *Paxton*, came off worse against a U-boat. Disguised as the merchantman *Lady Patricia*, the vessel had earlier that day survived an encounter with a U-boat in the North Atlantic, about 100 miles west of Fastnet Rock. Then at 19.15 hours, now disguised as the Swedish *Tosca Sverige*, she was torpedoed by U-46 and two men were killed. She remained afloat, but a second torpedo fifteen minutes later sank her. The only survivors were the captain and one of his officers, who were taken prisoner.

Another Manxman who hunted U-boats during the Great War was Thomas Cain, who achieved the astonishing feat of sinking five enemy submarines during the course of the war. Tommy, as he was known, was born at Port St Mary in 1886. His father was part-owner of two schooners and when Tommy left school he began an

Sub-Lieutenant Tommy Cain DSC, the Manx fishing skipper who hunted U-boats. (Courtesy of Adrian Cain)

apprenticeship as a ship's boy aboard one of these, the *Venus*. By the time war came in 1914 he was master of the vessel, and immediately enlisted in the Royal Naval Reserve. He was soon promoted to Warrant Officer and by July 1916 was skipper of the armed trawler *Mafeking*, which was guarding the Western Approaches. It was during a subsequent posting, to the Q-ship HMS *Glen*, that he was to sink the first of his U-boats.

Cain's first taste of action came on 22 April 1917 when HMS *Glen* sighted a U-boat on the surface. Without hesitation he called for full speed, and rammed the U-boat which sank at once. For this incident Cain was promoted to sub-lieutenant. Later that year, in June he was back aboard HMS *Glen* and again she encountered a U-boat. This incident was described by Admiral of the Fleet Lord Jellicoe in his account of the conflict at sea, *The Crisis of the Naval War*:

> On July 10 1917 a decoy ship, HMS Glen, a small schooner with auxiliary power and armed with one 12 pounder and one 6 pounder gun, commanded by Sub-Lieutenant K. Morris RNR, was in a position about forty miles south-west of Weymouth when a submarine was sighted on the surface some three miles away. She closed to within two miles and opened fire on the Glen. The usual practice of abandoning ship was followed, the submarine closing during this operation to within half a mile and remaining at that distance, examining her through the periscope, finally coming to the surface about 50 yards off on the port quarter. Almost immediately she again started to submerge, and fire was at once opened. The submarine was hit three or four times before she turned over on her side and disappeared. There was every

> reason to believe that she had sunk, though no one was on deck when she disappeared. No survivors were rescued. The feature of this action was again the restraint shown by the commanding officer of the Glen and the excellent discipline of the crew. [80]

Cain was now promoted to Lieutenant and awarded the Distinguished Service Cross. Before the end of the war he was mentioned in dispatches twice for his part in damaging or sinking a further three U-boats. Another Manx U-boat hunter was Lieutenant Commander John Lindsay Quine, brother of Sylvester (mentioned in Chapter One). He was born in Douglas, and from an early age was interested in marine engineering. He studied with Knox engineering in Douglas, and later became a marine engineer with the Harrison Line. In 1914, due to the shortage of engineering officers within the Royal Navy, he was commissioned into the service and joined HMS *Achilles*. He later served in a number of destroyers, and in 1917 was engaged in hunting U-boats aboard HMS *Termagant*. Off Fair Isle she attacked with depth charges a U-boat, believed to be that which sank the *Lusitania*; Quine tells us:

> It happened just after 4.30 in the afternoon. [I] had just finished ... afternoon tea and was in the wardroom, when [I] was aware of a sudden acceleration of the propellers, and realised that not only had the speed increased, but that the ship was making a rapid turn. The ship was at its extreme NW end of its beat, but [I] did not expect the turn so soon. The signal received from the Chief at Scapa Flow, Sir David Beatty, began; 'Commander in Chief to Grand Fleet, Senior Officer of Patrol, Fair Island reports

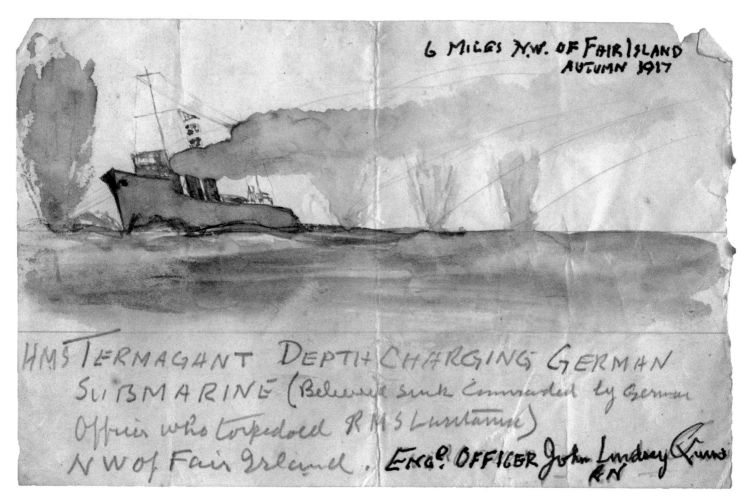

6 MILES N.W. OF FAIR ISLAND
AUTUMN 1917

HMS TERMAGANT DEPTH CHARGING GERMAN SUBMARINE (Believed sunk Commanded by German Officer who torpedoed RMS Lusitania) N W of Fair Ireland. ENG^r OFFICER John Lindsay Quine RN

Depth charging a U-boat off Fair Isle in 1917, a watercolour by Engineer-Lieutenant John Lindsay Quine of HMS *Termagant*. (MS 11835)

"*Enemy submarine on surface proceeding on N easterly course, distant, 6 miles, four of our destroyers in sight but do not appear to have seen him!* Why the hell don't you do something about it?'

On the receipt of this message things began to happen, lookouts woke up, and would you believe it, there he was, six miles or so away in the direction of Fair Island. Once sighted, all destroyers turned eight points towards the Hun, and in line abreast, the order to chase and depth charge him was given. Our leader, Commander Benson, in HMS *Medea*, now at the rear of the line, had signalled 'Chase', and the chase was on.

The submarine did not appear to have noticed the change in direction for some minutes nor that one of the destroyers was bearing down on him at high speed. [I] surveyed the "U" boat through [field] glasses. Yes, there in the conning tower hatch were the Captain and his 1ˢᵗ Lieutenant perched on the edge of the hatch, their legs inside. The Captain was in dark naval monkey jacket the other in a white sweater. Both wore dark naval caps and had their backs to us.

When Termagant was about one minute away from the intercepting point of their respective tracks, the men turned round and saw 'her'. They must have been old hands as without any trace of excitement they calmly watched the Destroyer approaching. Eventually without the slightest sign of hurry or haste, they withdrew into the conning tower and the lid swung over and closed. In a few moments the submarine submerged. In a few more, down went the depth charges from the Destroyer. No depth charge attack on a submarine could have been carried out with a better chance of success, as by means of predetermined signals, cross bearings were used to give the exact spot on which the depth charges should be dropped. As no oil ... came to the surface after the depth charging, the Admiralty could not agree that the submarine had been put down or damaged. [81]

Two IOMSPCo vessels, *Mona's Queen* and HMS *Peel Castle* mentioned previously, would also be in action against U-boats in 1917. The wartime duties of the *Mona's Queen* consisted of carrying troops across the Channel, generally between Southampton and Le Havre, after she was chartered by the British Government. The distance she had to cover each trip was about double that between Liverpool and Douglas, but she was required to do this all the year round, and in virtually all weathers. The Engineering Superintendent of the fleet, C.J. Blackburn, had occasion to inspect the ship as part of his duties:

In the early days of the war, the men returning from France on leave came aboard in all their mud and filth from the trenches, there being no opportunity of getting cleaned up before embarkation. It was a sight which called forth one's admiration, to see them arriving in the early morning, marching through Southampton before the people were astir. Very quiet and uncomplaining, and in good spirits.

When the boys from the United States began to come, later on, they seemed lonely. When speaking to some of them on one occasion, I mentioned the Isle of Man. At once they showed the greatest interest, and said "So and so in our Company came from there to the States about twelve years ago". They then insisted on going to find him,

An artist's impression of the Manx paddle steamer SS *Mona's Queen* ramming a U-boat in the English Channel. (PO 45)

so that we might have a talk.

On another occasion when a company of three men were gathered together in the shed waiting to embark, a regiment of our own boys were also going in the same ship. Plenty of good-natured fun was shown by our men as usual, when going on board ship. Their band was playing popular airs, and there were loud jests, but the Yankees maintained a gloomy silence, keeping to themselves. Then the band struck up "Way down upon the Swanee River" and the atmosphere was changed immediately, laughter and cheers were heard from all quarters, the ice being broken, and they were all companions in arms. [82]

On 6 February 1917, *Mona's Queen* left Southampton for Le Havre with over a thousand troops on board. It was a fine night and there was a full moon. At 11.15 pm, when about twelve miles from Le Havre, a large submarine was seen coming to the surface of the water about five hundred feet away on the port bow. The *Mona's Queen* went right on without reducing her speed or altering her course, and, when within about thirty feet of the submarine her Manx Captain William Cain distinctly saw a torpedo discharged, which must have passed underneath his ship, for immediately afterwards he saw the track of it away to starboard.

The situation called for a prompt decision on the part of the Captain, as to what action he should take. He decided to go straight ahead at full speed. A few seconds after firing her torpedo, the submarine was buried in the port paddle-wheel, the steel floats of which must have struck her forward of the conning-tower. The paddle-wheel was twenty-five feet in diameter. Each of its ten floats consisted

of a steel plate, twelve feet by four feet, a full inch in thickness, and weighed, with its brackets, over a ton. It caused such damage that the U-boat immediately sank. Those on the bridge of the *Mona's Queen* could see the submarine, behind the port paddle-box, disappearing below the surface of the water, bow first, her stern lifted well up, and her propellers revolving in the air.

The effect on the *Mona's Queen* was tremendous as she heeled over until her starboard paddle-box was nearly half submerged. Some idea of the force of the impact may be gained from the fact that in the engine-room the port paddle-wheel with its shaft, weighing altogether more than thirty tons, was lifted to such an extent that the cover of the outer bearing was smashed. The *Mona's Queen* was now in a semi-disabled condition, like a bird with only one wing. By working the engines slowly, however, the crew were able to creep into Le Havre and discharge their troops quite safely.

To make repairs, it was decided to tow the ship to Southampton, and using a tug boat, the return journey was commenced. It was soon realised, however, that the tug-boat was not powerful enough to tow the *Mona's Queen*, particularly as the weather was bad. A decision had to be made, as to whether to continue or not, and Captain Cain decided to try to struggle back across the Channel without aid, depending upon the crippled wheel to hold out. The tug-boat accompanied the *Mona's Queen* to render assistance in case of a breakdown, and there were also two destroyers as an escort to look out for submarines. Although going rather less than half-speed, and in bad weather, the *Mona's Queen*, was able to keep well ahead of the tug. Soon it left her out of sight, arriving at Southampton before her. The homeward journey took eighteen-and-a-half hours whereas the usual length of passage was around eight hours. C.J. Blackburn was again present:

> I awaited her arrival with some anxiety and went out in a motor-boat to meet her. On getting near enough, the "bumpaty bump" of the revolving broken wheel was distinctly heard. After going aboard, I was able to test whether the shaft, nineteen inches in diameter, was bent by the severe treatment that it had received, and was surprised to find that it was quite true.
>
> The greatest praise is due to Captain Cain and the Chief Engineer, Mr. George Kenna ... for successfully bringing the ship across under such conditions. In addition to the danger of a complete breakdown, there was the risk of attack by submarines, which were no doubt in the neighbourhood.
>
> When the ship was surveyed in the dry dock, there were clear indications, from the indented and grooved plates, that the submarine had scraped along the port side, before she was finally engulfed in the revolving wheel. [83]

After the necessary repairs the Mona's Queen resumed her war work on 17 March 1917 and continued in government service for a further two years, when she left Southampton to be re-conditioned at Birkenhead for the passenger trade.

In spite of the danger of attack by marauding German vessels in the English Channel, aboard HMS Peel Castle there was still time for recreation and relaxation, and on 14 November 1917 the crew went in for a little sport in the way of a regatta. The stokers and the RNR sailors had an eight oared race in the ship's lifeboats. There was great excitement when the stokers, under Coxswain Morrison (a Douglas man) won the race. Part of the prize was a pint of beer for each man. The officers rowed the petty officers, and the marines rowed the stewards. Altogether they had an enjoyable afternoon, and finished up with a concert party at night. The Peel Castle was able to put up quite a good concert party. One member of the crew had been a pianist in a cinema so he made an excellent accompanist, whilst the ship's electrician was conductor and managed the lighting effects. The serious business of war was never far away however, and another account highlights an incident which occurred on 24 November 1917:

> At 7am a call to action stations. Received a signal that a submarine was north of the Gull Light vessel, so proceeded there at full speed, and found a German submarine ashore on the Goodwin Sands. The mine-sweeping drifter Feasible, when sweeping the Channel off the North Foreland, fouled the sweep. Presently a submarine broke the surface of the water, on which the sweeper opened fire. The submarine returned the fire, and, as the water was too shoal to dive, attempted to escape by zig-zagging, when she ran ashore on the Goodwins. The other sweepers closed round, and shot one end off the submarine. When the Peel Castle arrived, the crew were in the conning-tower with, their hands up, so we stood by for a while, and a torpedo boat came, and took off eighteen prisoners out of a crew of forty men. About 4.30pm one of the boarding officers went to see the submarine, which was then dry on the sands, and when walking over the deck was surprised to see a man come up from below, and stagger about. The officer brought him back to the Peel Castle, where our doctor

patched him up, and sent him ashore to the hospital, but he was so badly damaged that he died three days afterwards. He was the boatswain of the submarine, and could speak English perfectly. [84]

For the last two years of the war there were no further major fleet actions, and for the crews of the bigger Royal Navy ships, the battle was one against boredom and monotony as they watched and waited. A young Manx naval officer, Kenneth Fleming Green (the younger brother of Thomas), served as a clerk aboard the cruiser HMS *Inflexible* in 1917. Described by his seniors as a steady clean living well-mannered young officer, and as most capable, hard working and zealous, he was an old boy of Douglas High School. With an eye for detail, Green has provided a remarkably complete sketch of life aboard a Royal Navy warship in this era, as seen through the eyes of a seventeen year old. It captures the aura of tradition in the Navy, as well as underlining the sense of tedium which characterised service at sea in this part of the war:

Life in the largest ships in time of war is not so thrilling as some people might imagine. The newcomer on joining his ship has probably visions of great engagements and crushing victories, in which he himself takes no small part ... but later he discovers to his disappointment that such actions seldom take place, and that instead he is destined to experience long, uninteresting periods of waiting and patrolling, which produce in him a feeling of "boredom."

... Since I am a member of the Gun-room, I trust you will excuse my mentioning that part of the ship first. The Sub. who is president of the mess has lordship over two dozen peace-loving (?) midshipmen, and is responsible for law and order in his 'realm'. One night a week is set apart as guest-night, when officers from the Ward-room, or even from other ships are invited to the Gun-room to dine. At dinner on such occasions the Sub. proposes the toast "The King". The band, which on guest nights plays just outside the Gun-room, immediately strikes up the National Anthem, but the officers remain seated, preserving the custom of the days when, owing to the limited space, it was impossible to stand up between decks.

After dinner the mess is sometimes the scene of a great 'scrap', and potatoes, plates, and furniture are found useful missiles to hurl at one's opponents. This uproar continues for a while, but order finally being restored, officers and 'snotties' [midshipmen] begin to try and extricate themselves from the mass of wreckage, and retire to rest, sore in every limb....

Early in the morning one is awakened by the blast of shrill whistles, followed by weird calls, which sound rather like the shouts of a coster, but which are, however, those of the bo'sun's mate piping the hands to work. The decks are scrubbed till they are quite white, and on Sunday morning, when the Captain inspects the ship, everything has to be spotless ... And so time rolls on, while the efficiency of the Navy is kept up by continual practising and careful training for the day when the Huns will at last come out and show fight. In the meantime, our routine varies but little, and I have tried to briefly describe in these notes the impressions I have formed of the work carried out in this ship, which is but one of hundreds patiently biding its time. [85]

1917 was to be a particularly bad year for those sailing under the red ensign, as Germany intensified her U-boat

Thomas Henry McGratten of Castletown, a merchant seaman lost in the *Belgian Prince* incident. (PG 13743)

war, and allied merchant ships were lost in alarming numbers. Ned Maddrell of Glen Chass, a fluent Manx speaker, spent the entire First World War in the merchant service, braving U-boats and other hazards. He was lucky to come through unscathed, as other Manx crewmen were lost on SS *Laurentic*, sunk off the Irish Coast on 25 January 1917, SS *Princess Alberta*, sunk in the Mediterranean on 21 February 1917, on SS *Sonnie*, (sunk by enemy submarine on 11 August 1917), and on SS *Storm* (sunk by enemy seaplanes on 9 September 1917) to name just a few.

Two other Manx merchant sailors, Thomas Henry McGratten of Castletown and Henry Taylor of Four Roads, Port St Mary, died in the worst single incident involving a U-Boat in Home waters. The two were members of the crew of the SS *Belgian Prince*. Previously known as the *Hungarian Prince*, in 1915, following the onset of war, the ship was renamed *Belgian Prince* as Hungary was now an enemy nation. The ship had one narrow escape on 24 February 1915, when she was chased by a U-Boat in the English Channel, but managed to outpace it. On 29 July 1917 the *Belgian Prince* left the port of Liverpool to cross to Newport News, USA with a cargo of blue clay. The ship was unescorted, and under the command of Captain Hassan with a crew of forty three, all British.

Just before 8pm on 31 July she had passed the Isle of Man and was heading around the northern tip of Ireland. The ship was 175 miles north-west of Tory Island, when she was hit by a torpedo. It struck the after part of the ship, exploded and broke the propeller shaft, engine and generator. The *Belgian Prince* was doomed and Captain Hassan ordered the crew to abandon ship as it heeled over to port. Three lifeboats were lowered, though one crewman was left aboard by accident and yet survived the sinking.

A U-boat surfaced nearby, and opened fire on the sinking vessel in order to destroy the telegraph equipment and thus prevent a distress message being sent. The crew had rowed the lifeboats away from the ship, but the U-boat then trained its machine-gun on them. The enemy submarine, U-44 was commanded by Kapitan Leutnant Paul Wagenfuhr; he then ordered the lifeboats to come alongside, as it was stopped in the water, and demanded that Captain Hassan identify himself. Fearing for the safety of his crew Hassan stood up and was immediately taken on board the U-boat.

Wagenfuhr ordered the lifeboat crews onto the deck of the submarine where their life-jackets and outer clothing were taken from them and thrown overboard. The

U-boat crew then smashed the lifeboats with axes. Within a short time the U-boat started its engines and motored along the surface with the forty two survivors clinging on to the deck. After about two miles the U-boat stopped, the conning tower was closed and as it blew its tanks began to submerge. Many of the survivors were washed from the deck casing, while others jumped into the sea to avoid being sucked under by the wash of the submarine. A number of the crew were at this point drowned and an account by one of the three survivors who were later picked up by a patrol boat, recounted that:

> It was almost dark when I heard a voice calling for help and I found the youngest member of the ship's crew, a 16 year old apprentice drifting nearby ... The boy had managed to find a lifejacket but was near death, having swallowed a lot of water. He died from shock and exposure about midnight. [86]

The survivor eased the boy out of the life-jacket and allowed him to slip beneath the waves. The three crewmen were picked up after eleven hours in the sea. Captain Hassan also survived, having spent the rest of the war in a prisoner of war camp in Germany. The *Belgian Prince* incident was probably the worst case of murder on the high seas in a U-boat war which was littered with atrocities. McGratten was commemorated on the roll of honour at Queen Street Mission, Castletown, where his name was justifiably annotated 'murdered by the Germans'.

With seafarers facing such awful fates, it can hardly be considered surprising that they were as conscious as were soldiers of the divisions that the war was creating in Manx society, between those that were in the danger zone, and those that were not. One man, calling himself a 'patriotic Manx sailor' who had spent most of his life at sea, wrote to the *Isle of Man Times* to protest at:

> A certain class of strong, robust, young, single or recently married [men] trying to save their skin. There is not one of these shirkers or their parents but will stick at nothing to break the laws of the country to get clear ... The Island will be up in arms about it when it is more fully known. This war is not going to be fought without a great sacrifice to all... [87]

This man added that his own son was serving in the Royal Navy, so his family had certainly faced their own share of the danger. The hazards which merchant mariners faced would have been all the more apparent to Manx people, as the list of naval and merchant shipping casualties in the Irish Sea also grew as Germany intensified the U-boat campaign. Indeed it would not be until the final year of the war that the Royal Navy would begin to bring the enemy submarines operating in these waters to heel, using the specially-designed Sea Scout series of airships to patrol coastal waters. The American liner *New York* struck a mine off Liverpool in April 1917, and her passengers were rescued by the Steam Packet vessel *Tynwald*. The liner was on a voyage from New York to Liverpool, and when she had arrived at a position three miles north by west of the Bar Lightship, a terrific explosion tore a large hole in the hull below the water-line. The *Tynwald* was about a mile from the liner when she struck the mine. Her master, Captain Cregeen, signalled to the Liverpool Pilot Boat, No. 1, which was in the vicinity, and both vessels hurried to the rescue. After the first surprise of the explosion, there was little confusion on the liner as the passengers, who had received daily lifeboat drills, took up the stations that had been assigned to them at the boats. These were quickly filled and lowered to the water. The *Tynwald* was the first vessel to arrive, and took on board the occupants of five of the liner's boats, including Admiral Sims, of the United States Navy.

Later that same year, HMS *Champagne* was torpedoed off the Isle of Man. Another armed merchant cruiser, she was built in 1895 by Harland & Wolff as the passenger steamer *Oropesa*. Owned by the Pacific Steam & Navigation Company of Liverpool, in November 1914 she was taken over by the Admiralty for war service. In 1917 she was lent to the French navy and was renamed HMS *Champagne*, but retained her British crew. On 9 October that year she was torpedoed and sunk by the German submarine U-96, when eight miles north-west of the Calf of Man. Fifty eight men were killed in this incident, and the report of her commanding officer Captain Percy Brown RN reads:

On the 9th October at 6.10 am, mean course N 21 deg E (mag) zig-zagging, Lat 54.17' N, Long 5.10' W, speed 13 kts, the ship was struck by a torpedo in the engine room the starboard side. The lookout at the starboard after gun saw a periscope and gave the order "Close up", we were struck by the torpedo almost instantaneously, and the periscope disappeared.

Ship's company automatically went to action stations - the leading torpedo man put the depth charges to safe and reported to me, the confidential books were locked up in the steel safes by the decoding officers and other confidential papers destroyed. All steam was cut off by the explosion. I believe the Engineer Officer of the watch was blown to pieces and there were several other casualties in the engine room ...

The main engines were stopped by the explosion, and we could not go astern, but the ship lost way almost at once, the wind was WNW Magnetic, squally, force 5 to 7, sea state 6.

The 1st Lieutenant asked me to give the order to abandon ship, I said "No, not yet, as the ship may float for a considerable time, and we may bag the submarine if he comes up." Almost immediately after this there was a second explosion on the port side in the forepart of the after welldeck. I at once gave the order "Abandon ship"; up to this time not a single grip had been cast off, nor any attempt made to go to the boats. The ship remained on an even keel but began to settle rapidly. The boats, with the exception of the collapsibles, were got away smartly, although difficulty was experienced owing to the rough sea.

Four men Oliver Ward, AB, RNVR, AB Ryan RNVR, LS Watkins RNR and LS W. Cox RNR volunteered to remain by foremost pair of guns. Ward saw a submarine come to the surface about 300 to 400 yards away on the port beam. The port foremost 6" gun was fired at once, projectile apparently went just over. The submarine at once dived and the gun was reloaded and a tube inserted. These men remained by their gun and I regret to say that Cox was the only one who was picked up. [88]

At 6.30 a third torpedo struck the ship, which broke her in two, whilst due to the heavy sea the boats experienced difficulty in rescuing men from the water. Two boats sailed to the Isle of Man and others were later towed there by trawlers. Brown concluded his report:

The ship went down with a portion of her guns manned

and ready to fire and traditions of the Service were upheld. At the time of the attack we were going as fast as we could keep up, lookouts were stationed all round the ship and were alert. We had no escort. [89]

Captain Brown and forty six of the crew were landed at Port Erin. At 1pm, the Peel lifeboat was launched, and all fishing vessels lying in Peel Harbour were requested to proceed to the scene of the incident. Later that day 150 of the crew were landed at Port St Mary, and at 5pm the Peel lifeboat returned to port with twenty one survivors. For these men, clothing was obtained from Knockaloe Camp, and medical aid was also provided. Harbour Master Elliot of Port Erin, the local representative of the Shipwrecked Mariners Society, provided clothing for the men landed at the southern ports, and billets were found for the survivors. On 10 October 1917 Captain Brown wrote:

> *[I] would like to take this opportunity of thanking the Authorities for the extreme kindness and hospitality which has been shown to [myself], officers and men during their stay in the Island.* [90]

Several Manxmen were amongst the crew of the *Champagne*, and at least one Manxman was in each of three of the boats of the ship which reached the Island with survivors. In one case, a man who had been married only a few days before the disaster and whose wife lived at Port Erin, arrived with a boat-load of survivors at that same port. C.H. Cowley in *Caves of Peel Hill* wrote of the famous Ooig ny daa Kione (Cave of the two ends):

> *This cave seems to be the receptacle of all the flotsam and jetsam carried on the sea from any point South to the Calf of Man, and one is never sure what they expect to find, especially when the rats are in possession. During the Great War, plunder of all descriptions was to be found. I went in after the loss of HMS Champagne, and the interior was littered with driftwood, boxes, hatches, etc., etc ... I went up to Corrin's Tower after the disaster became known in Peel that day, and could see shadowy forms of ships racing through the haze to save lives. One life-boat, No. 8, made of metal, was picked up by the Peel Lifeboat between Peel and Glenmaye. The boat was cast adrift, and floated on to Treiga Beach, and 21 men and a dog taken into Peel.* [91]

In late 1917 came another thrilling rescue, this time by the Manx collier *Sarah Blanche*. She left Garston at 4.30pm on 8 November, and the following day had passed the Skerries battling through a heavy sea. The *Sarah*

The Manx collier *Sarah Blanche*, which rescued the crew of the SS *Marquess* following an encounter with a U-boat. (PGN 13256)

A porthole recovered from the wreck of the *Romeo*, more than 90 years after she was torpedoed. (2009-0019)

The transport vessel *SS Romeo*, sunk by a U-boat off the Isle of Man in 1918 (Courtesy of Hull Museums)

Blanche had difficulties of her own with the weather and a shortage of coal in her bunkers, when at 8.30am the skipper Captain Robert Callister saw on his port beam an object projecting out of the water which, he continues:

> *...we could only see at intervals, on account of the high sea which was running. We thought all kinds of things, such as that it might be the periscope of a submarine. A minute or two later we made it out to be a boatload of men. Considering the state of the weather, and the high sea running, it seemed almost an impossibility to have got those men; but I wasn't going to stand by without a try; and in a quarter of an hour from the time of sighting them, we had them all on board ...* [92]

No sooner had the men been brought safely on deck, and the skipper had given orders to let go the lifeboat, than a heavy wave struck and capsized it. The shipwrecked men proved to be the crew of the SS *The Marquess*, which had been bound from the Welsh quarries to Ayr with a cargo of limestone, when she was sunk by gunfire from a U-boat on the surface. The crew of ten were in a pitiful state, having spent sixteen hours in the open boat in a high sea. Their boat was so small that they had to throw the water beaker overboard in order to lessen the weight. The *Sarah Blanche* turned about and landed the exhausted survivors at Holyhead.

Early the following year, the Wilson liner *Romeo* of Hull, travelling from Scapa Flow to Liverpool was torpedoed off Peel by U-102. She was on Admiralty charter for carrying meat and provisions to the Fleet, but was returning to Liverpool in ballast after having called in at Stornoway. Her only defence against enemy submarines was a twelve pounder gun. On 3 March 1918 at 2.40am she was about ten miles south of the Mull of Galloway, steaming at ten knots and zig-zagging. The weather was fine with occasional snow showers, the wind light and the sea smooth. The first officer was in charge on the bridge. There was a lookout on the forecastle head, another on the bridge and one on the gunner's platform aft. All lights on the ship were carefully screened and no navigation lights were burning. At this point a green and red light appeared off her port bow. Fearful of a collision with another ship, the order was given by the captain of the *Romeo* to show the navigation lights on her bow. This was a fatal mistake as she had been tricked by the German submarine into giving away her exact position. Within a couple of minutes a torpedo slammed into the *Romeo's* port side between the stoke hold and the engine room. The explosion was terrific and split the ship in two. At first she took a list to port, then righted herself before sinking in less than two minutes. One of the gun crew, William Camomile, stated afterwards:

> *There was ... no time to get away any of the boats and we were left struggling in the water, but managed to get hold of a swamped boat, which we clung to. The only other survivor that I saw was one of the sailors, who we hauled into the boat with us, but he died about 10 o'clock in the morning. Before I ... got into the boat I observed Morse flashing, but could not say who was making the signal or whether it was a submarine ... At daylight we managed to get up the mast and sail, when wreckage was all around us, but we did not see any other survivors ....* [93]

Camomile and his two companions were picked up by

The liner *SS Celtic* in Peel after being torpedoed off the Calf of Man. Note the dazzle camouflage intended to break up the outline of the ship. (Courtesy of Alan Kelly)

the steamship *Ardgarvel* at 11am, and later landed at Greenock. Only one other survivor from the *Romeo* was picked up by a trawler; the remaining crew of thirty four were presumed to have drowned.

On 31 March 1918, news was received on the Island that a large vessel had been torpedoed about twelve miles from the Calf of Man. The lifeboats from Castletown and Port St. Mary proceeded to the spot, but were turned back by a destroyer. The next day it transpired that the vessel in question was the White Star liner *Celtic*, which was being towed by a tug and patrol boats into shallow water at Peel, en route for repairs at Belfast. Seventeen of the engine-room staff had been killed by the explosion of the torpedo. The *Celtic* lay at Peel, surrounded by patrol

vessels, for some days, while temporary repairs were being carried out. Terrible as these attacks on large vessels were, in plying their trade between belligerent ports in time of war they might be regarded as legitimate targets. There were also however numerous attacks by U-boats on Manx fishing vessels, many of which can only be regarded as petty and spiteful, though in their defence the Germans seem to have regarded fishing crews as partisan, acting as the eyes and ears of the Royal Navy. A marvellous contemporary account survives from an Irish fisherman named Patrick Cadogan, who sometimes fished out of Peel. Written to a Manx skipper and dated 12 May 1917, it shows that but for the predations of U-boats that year might have been a bumper season:

I am sending you a few lines letting you know we are stopped of fishing [sic] since the 4ᵗʰ May we have our nets in the loft as we were afraid of the submarines that

Thursday night he sunk seven boats but for the cruser [sic] meeting him he would have the most of them sunk before morning and gave them a poor chance of their lives he took four men of one small boat aboard the submarine he sunk the Sideward and put two of them into her punt with her own crew nine men in one boat and done the same to the Fastnet about 14 miles off the stags and all came safe and they would not leave more of them take the oars and they were making great money there was never anything like it iff [sic] we were home the day we left Peel we would have a great season the Ripple made 220 pounds them two nights and the following Monday night some of the boats had a season the Thomas Joseph made 392 pounds one night we had only 10 shots and we had 13 pounds a man all the boats that was out the week we left Peel have from 25 to 30 pounds a man the ripple have about 35 pounds a man. John Cadogans boat have £56 and the Glen Dawer have £71 a man ... they would all make plenty money this year but for the submarines .... [94]

In February the following year, a Peel fishing boat *Girl Emily* was attacked by an enemy submarine. The skipper's son was ordered aboard the U-boat and was about to comply when the rope holding the fishing boat gave way and the two vessels parted. In 1919 John Hughes the skipper attempted to claim compensation for the damage to his vessel and loss of his catch, writing to the War Pensions Committee:

On Saturday 23rd February 1918, I being master of the fishing boat 'Girl Emily' of Peel put to sea with a crew of four men, about four o'clock pm. Whilst about ten miles off Peel, fishing for cod, we encountered a German submarine

John Hughes, the skipper of the *Girl Emily*, who was fired upon by a U-boat whilst fishing off Peel. (Courtesy of Jane Coomer)

which came alongside of us. They asked if I was fishing, I answered "yes". He then left us and came around on our starboard quarter, and when about one hundred yards away he fired at us, I was at the tiller and the shot struck a stanchion not a yard away from my front. I was severely wounded in the face with splinters. Some splinters entered beneath my right eye, and have seriously affected my sight.

The Germans then fired three times again the shots going through the bulwarks and the sail. They came alongside and demanded our fish which, as we were quite helpless we gave to them. There was £20 worth of fish, and they took all. I was in the Doctor's care for three weeks, and the experience has also shaken my nerve, so that as a consequence I have not been able to prosecute my calling as a fisherman as profitably as before the accident.

I am sixty eight years of age and I might add that two of my sons served with His majesties [sic] Navy during the war, and one lost his life whilst serving King and country. I would respectfully ask if you can assist me to procure some compensation for the loss I sustained through the attack made on my boat by an enemy submarine. [95]

A month after the *Girl Emily* incident a similar event occurred. The Manx fishing smack *Marguerite* was on her way from Bangor to Douglas on the evening of 9 March 1918 when she encountered a submarine, later identified as UC-75. In a sworn statement the master, Thomas Lee, stated:

... about 25 miles N ¼ E of Beaumaris, as we were going to frame a sail I heard a shot. About 20 yards astern I saw a shell hit the water, and then I observed a submarine about ¼ mile off. I put the vessel's head to wind and immediately another shot was fired. I then lowered the sail of the boat and ran her towards the submarine. My brother Richard [Dicky] Lee signalled to the submarine that we had no rifle. The submarine then came astern of us and fired a third shot. We signalled again that we had no boat, when the submarine came alongside us, and we were told to come on board. We were taken on board the submarine and at 7.30am on 10th March the commander informed us that he would put us off in a boat on meeting

Douglas fisherman Dicky Lee, who in 1918 encountered a U-boat whilst aboard the smack *Marguerite*. (PG 7531/11)

a sailing vessel. The submarine was on the surface from 7.30 to 11.00am but we were below. About 1pm on 10 March I was in the Marconi room and saw the man in charge apparently preparing a bomb. We were then told to get ready to go ashore as we were being put out in a sailing boat belonging to the *Wave*. The crew of the *Wave* were already on it and we saw the *Wave* sunk. We then came on to Whitehaven with the crew of the *Wave*, where we arrived at 6pm on 10 March. [96]

It was said that after this incident, Dicky and Thomas Lee were able to provide the authorities with valuable details concerning the submarine which they had observed during their captivity. In this incident, the U-boat commander seems to have been favourably

A Sea Scout airship lands at King William's College, 1918. This particular craft was based at RNAS Anglesey and operated on anti-submarine patrols over the Irish Sea. (PGN 01742)

The crew of a US navy destroyer, on anti-submarine patrol in the Irish Sea, mingle with local girls on a visit to Douglas in October 1918. (PG 13783)

disposed towards the fishermen, as he allowed them to take lamps and other items from the *Marguerite* before destroying her. By 1918, however, the U-boat threat in the Irish Sea had largely been contained. The presence in Irish and Welsh ports of squadrons of fast United States Navy destroyers, combined with that of Royal Navy airships, now able to cover greater ranges and stay airborne longer, had done much to reduce their effectiveness.

With the signing of the Armistice in November, one of the terms imposed upon Germany was the internment of her High Seas Fleet. HMS *King Orry* had the distinction of being the sole representative of the British Mercantile Marine at the surrender of the German fleet in the Firth of Forth, on 21 November 1918, on which occasion Admiral Beatty gave her the place of honour, in the

middle of the centre line. Her commander, Harry Tylden Mosse remembered:

As soon as the [German] ships had been brought in and our own ships came back with them, everybody went mad. We didn't go into harbour, we simply careered round, each ship individually, irrespective of the Commander in Chief or anybody else. His ship was just the same, they were all going up and down ... doing nothing else but making a noise. There were no guns or anything of that sort, but everybody was sort of cheering and when you came abreast of Admiral Beatty you gave him three cheers... [97]

In her 'dazzle' camouflage paint of diagonal yellow, dark blue and dull red blocks the King Orry made a striking sight, and it was said that in the Royal Navy she was known as the 'Devil Ship' of the North Sea. When it is considered that the *King Orry* was designed as a pleasure steamer, sailing principally in the summer season, it is remarkable that she was able to survive so well the severe buffeting she received during her four winters in the heavy seas encountered off the northern coasts of Scotland. Her chief engineer during the whole of *King Orry*'s war service was Engineer-Lieutenant John Keig, son of the late Captain Thomas Keig, commodore of the IOMSPCo fleet.

The service of the *King Orry* from the beginning of the war to its very end symbolises the commitment and resilience shown by Manx men and women at sea either under civilian or naval colours during the conflict. Whether in craft large or small, armed or civilian, Manx seafarers during the First World War upheld a fine tradition. It was a tradition which stretched back to the Napoleonic Wars and beyond, when their skills had also been highly prized. Braving the perils of the wind and waves as well as enemy action, theirs was an often unglamorous war, though it was by no means without hazard. There was certainly no kinship of the sea between them and their enemies, who often attacked without warning from under the waves. Boredom and monotony were punctuated by moments of extreme danger. Above all, theirs was a heavy responsibility, because although they could not win the war outright, either under the white or red ensigns, they could potentially lose it.

Fireman Ernest Cregeen of Four Roads, Rushen. A member of the Merchant Fleet Auxiliary, he served aboard the requisitioned HMS *King Orry*. (PG 13536)

Tents at Douglas Internment Camp, the former Cunningham's Holiday Camp on Victoria Road, which held civilian prisoners from 1914-1918. (1954-6978)

Chapter Three

The Torment of Captivity

During the Great War, both sides interned enemy civilians who were living or working in their territory upon the outbreak of hostilities. For the British part, the idea that civilians might be partisan and therefore must be controlled first gained ground during the South African War of 1899 to 1902, when members of the Boer civilian population were held in Concentration Camps. The term 'prisoner of war' is now generally only used to describe someone who is a military combatant and who is captured by the opposing armed forces. However, it is important to remember that during the First World War, the term 'prisoner of war' was used for both military prisoners captured during battle, and for interned civilians.

At the start of the First World War, in 1914, there were approximately 60,000 Germans living in Britain. On 5 August 1914, the day after war was declared, the Aliens Restriction Act was passed by the British Government. The Act allowed the Government to control the movement of 'enemy aliens', and to regulate where they could live and what they could do. Following the outbreak of war the notion that all such Germans could potentially be acting as enemy agents developed into a veritable 'spy-fever'. The initial decision to intern enemy aliens was made on 7 August 1914 and by 23 September 10,500 civilians had been arrested. The Home Office in London, through the Destitute Aliens Committee, proposed the opening of a camp on the Isle of Man and the first group of 200 internees

arrived on 22 September 1914, barely a month after the outbreak of war. Ultimately up to 29,000 Germans, Austrians, Hungarians and Turks would be interned on the Isle of Man. Many of them were merchant sailors, others had been waiters, barbers, small tradesmen or servants. A smaller number were business-men or clerks. There were also what might be termed 'quasi-military' prisoners, such as army reservists, and colonial troops captured on the high seas going to or from Africa. A certain number of those interned had been resident in England since early childhood, and when they entered internment camps some of these could not actually speak German.

The first internment camp on the Isle of Man was the Douglas Holiday Camp (also known as Cunningham's Camp), a large tented holiday complex above Douglas Promenade. However even at this early stage it was clear that Cunningham's Camp alone could not accommodate the number of prisoners which mass internment could potentially produce. The Government Secretary, Bertram Sargeaunt, remembered:

On 24th October [1914], I accompanied a deputation from Whitehall on a tour of the Island in search of a suitable site or sites. It was a pouring wet day, and before we started I said there was only one site which could accommodate a large number of prisoners, and that was Knockaloe. However certain members of the deputation turned their eyes to the Calf. I knew the proposal was impossible, as there was little water on the Island and communication was extremely dangerous. I went to an hotel at Port St Mary with one member of the deputation while others proceeded to view the Calf Island in the teeth of the gale that was blowing. They soon came back, more or less drenched, with the remark "hopeless". We then went to Knockaloe, and in a very short time after the deputation had left the Island huts were being erected on this site. [98]

The newer camp which was to be built occupied farmland known as Knockaloe Mooar near Peel, a site which had been used before the war as a camping ground for territorial troops, and one of the few locations on the Island which possessed an adequate water supply for a large number of men. However it would be some months before Knockaloe could receive its first prisoners, and at Douglas Camp a combination of poor winter weather, overcrowding (there were over 3000 internees housed in the camp by that stage instead of 2400 as suggested) and complaints about the food in which weevils had been found led to a riot on 19 November 1914. After dinner the prisoners refused to disperse and instead began hurling plates and cutlery at the guards. The atmosphere turned violent as – ignoring the pleas of their more peaceable compatriots – some internees advanced towards the kitchens brandishing broken chair legs. The women in the kitchens became hysterical, and the guards after first shooting over the heads of the rioters, fired directly into their number. Five internees died, some in the resulting stampede. One member of the Isle of Man Volunteers, William Spence, who as a fifty-one year old served as a guard at the camp, remembered afterwards:

William Spence, a member of the Isle of Man Volunteers and a guard at Douglas Camp. (PG 5406/1)

It was here that members of the [Volunteers] were first called upon to shoot in deadly earnest – the only shots fired in anger on Manx soil during the whole war. An attempted rebellion was launched by the interned men, and before it was put down the guards were compelled to open fire and several of the aliens lost their lives. [99]

Another guard, a National Reserve soldier named James Bailey, was a former Regular who had spent eight years in India. He told the subsequent inquest that the guards had stood the barrage of plates, knives and furniture for about ten minutes, receiving not just splatters of soup and jam but also cuts to their hands and faces, before opening fire:

[I] aimed for the gallery, at one man I had been watching for several minutes, firing all sorts of missiles ... He seemed

to be a ringleader ... I aimed at the main part of the body. We haven't much chance to aim at any particular part of the body. [I] then fired at the body of prisoners formed in mass before the guard. The row continued, and they were still coming forward, [I] and the others considered it necessary to fire again. [I] only fired twice [and] could not tell what effect the second shot had; four or five of [us] fired together. After that, the prisoners cleared out of the dining room. [Then] the guard got the word to double round through the kitchen to the other side of the dining room, as the prisoners had gathered there, but they found it a false alarm, as the prisoners had got back to their tents ... It was [my] firm opinion that we were justified in firing, otherwise something much more serious would have happened. [100]

The inquest found that the guards had acted lawfully, both in self-defence, and also because if the prisoners had managed to seize their rifles a breakout might have followed. As a result of the riot, the transfer of prisoners to the new purpose built camp at Knockaloe was speeded up. Douglas Camp however remained open, containing a Privilege Camp (for those internees with money) and a Jewish Camp (for those with special dietary requirements), and a camp for the residue of ordinary prisoners.

Dr Charles L. Hartmann a fifty-nine year-old author, scholar and former Honorary German consul in Japan

A sketch of the riot at Douglas Camp, drawn by an internee, and claiming six dead. (2011-0073)

arrived in the Privilege Camp in November 1915. He left a fascinating portrait of the extraordinarily luxurious lifestyle of its inmates. In his diary he wrote:

The Privilege Camp, in which I find myself, is home to about four hundred people. A part of them are housed in tents, the rest in newly built huts, for three to four men. The huts mostly have a small garden planted in front of them, and depending on how they are furnished, are more or less comfortable. There are carpenters, upholsterers, and furniture makers available to work on them. A few of the huts are even luxurious with curtains, pictures, vases, good lights and are equipped with portable paraffin heaters. The walls and roofs of the huts are covered with asbestos sheets, so they grant considerably better protection than wooden barracks against the cold ... I was allocated a bed in a hut which previously was occupied by just two internees. One, an old man, very quiet with a white moustache, does not leave the hut all day but lies down or reads a book. The other is an exceptionally stout butter trader from London, very loquacious and a great patriot. Before he goes to bed, when he has undressed down to the underpants, he kneels down before his bed, and shouts three times in a ceremonious and completely sincere tone "Gott Strafe England! Gott strafe England!" Then he quietly takes off his underpants, without a word climbs into bed, and after two minutes is snoring loud enough to make the walls tremble.

...Without doubt this is the best internment camp not only in England, but also probably – with the possible exception of Japan – of all the warring nations. However, one must not forget that it is established for just 400 people who have money and for whom the bourgeois government holding us prisoner has a certain class sympathy. Naturally this institution becomes an object of admiration for the committees from neutral governments which are supposed to inspect prison camps. It overlooks completely the fact that presently in England some 45,000 equally pitiful and innocent civilians are accommodated and treated quite differently. [101]

Hartmann, having been transferred to Douglas via Knockaloe, was acutely aware of the contrast between the two. Indeed, it seems that at Douglas the threat of transfer to Knockaloe was used as quite an effective means of control:

.... The Privilege Camp is the only one in Great Britain in which the prisoners are permitted wine and beer. Of the former a daily small bottle of Niersteiner or Medoc, of quite good quality, is priced around a shilling, and we may have a further three bottles of beer. We have some who drink ten to twelve bottles of wine in an evening; sometimes they are caught, as yesterday was a Hungarian count, and immediately are sent as a punishment to Knockaloe. The latter is our equivalent of Siberia, as a threat of punishment it is highly effective. For holidays we may also order better wines, however there is no champagne, which I find completely justified given the seriousness of the times. The catering for these 400 privileged prisoners is cared for by a restaurateur who is under the control of the kitchens committee. Three tables have their own waiter, all qualified fellows and with a quite excellent Head Waiter in charge, who had worked for years in Paris and London. Many, who were quite unnoticed outside of the camp, here play swanks, and order extra luncheons for four or five invited

guests, or extra food for themselves, so that they take up three quarters of the time of our waiters by themselves. Because they have no interests other than food, drinking, blethering and boasting, the torment of captivity barely enters their consciousness.... [102]

Ultimately, Hartmann's nationality was recognised as French (he was from the territories of Alsace-Lorraine seized by Germany in 1871) and he was released. Also in Douglas Camp around the same time was Frederic Dunbar-Kalckreuth, a German of Scottish and American descent. The son of a high ranking German naval officer, he had been in London learning English when war broke out. He also wrote of his experiences at Douglas where, being from an upper class background, he too was accommodated in the Privilege Camp. In December 1915 a month after his arrival he noted:

Our hut looks quite comfortable now. Herr von Beyerheim had a carpet, two padded wicker chairs, a paraffin lamp, a wire bed and a folding screen sent to him from his house in Chichester. He also had cutlery sent. But instead of a coffee-machine, only a coffee-mill was packed. A Viennese carpenter has panelled the thin asbestos walls with a layer of wood, painted green, and a skirting board. At my instigation an imitation fireplace with a mirror on top and an opening for the paraffin stove underneath has been fitted into one wall. By the window there is a folding table, with two seats, where we work.

Frederic Dunbar-Kalckreuth. The aristocratic son of a German naval officer, he had been in England to improve his language skills when war broke out. (M 24060)

Herr von Beyerheim copies pictures, while I study books on artists from the camp library. On the wall hangs a picture that Herr von Ramenz painted of me as well as an original by Lenbach... [103]

However the arrival of Christmas, as well as stirring the emotions of those prisoners who had families (and particularly children) still in Germany, was a particular source of irritation to Dunbar-Kalckreuth:

I went into our hut, where a few Chinese lanterns were giving an illusion of 'merry Christmas'. Hot wine bubbled away on the paraffin stove. It gave off a nice scent of cloves and cinnamon. Everyone was given over to his own thoughts ... Here, where every day is a day off work, and where the same daily routine dominates, I find the official days of celebration particularly oppressive. I'm not surprised that people take to drink and that Mr Slyshanks' wine canteen makes a roaring trade as a result. [104]

'Slyshanks' was the nickname (a play on his surname) given by the prisoners to Joseph Cunningham, the owner of the camp; who they viewed as profiting from their misfortune both through the rent he received for his holiday camp from the British Government, and also through the sale of provisions to the prisoners. Religious celebrations however were not confined to the Christian element of the camp. The Jewish portion was also highly organised in this respect. Maurice Jeger, an Austrian Jew who had worked in Cardiff as a printer, remembered that the Passover story of the enslaved Jews in Egypt had added resonance in the circumstances of captivity on the Isle of Man:

Again the Passover holidays had arrived, for the second time in our captivity, and even though many expected to be freed, nevertheless, we put all our energy into preparations for this holiday. The Jewish committee, which had been formed from representatives of the Jewish barracks, uniformly took the decision to celebrate the Passover in the traditional way, and immediately began its preparations ... they had access to 'Kosher' meat here, and a separate kitchen for which they had to pay the small amount of 1 shilling weekly. The spiritual head of the Jews was an interned Rabbi named Silberman, a Hungarian who had also spent some years in Vienna, and the Viennese Jewish community is well-respected. The commandant now promised to provide everything which the religion requires, and also agreed to provide financial help....

650 Jews assembled, all looking their smartest in their best clothes, from all areas of Austria, Germany and Turkey, in the decorated barrack hall, to mark the Exodus from Egypt and to celebrate freedom from slavery. The Jewish tragedy, a tragedy so sad as rarely befell any people, made itself obvious here in all its naked reality; is this not the night in which all Jews in the whole world celebrate the foundation of their nation? Are the Jews a nation, and if so, why does their blood flow so richly on all fronts, why do we find her sons in all the armies, of the friends and of the enemies ...?

But Mr Rabbi Silberman, wearing his white cap decorated with golden embroidery, stands on the platform, which is surrounded so beautifully with vases of flowers, begins to speak, while he lifts up a bowl: "This is the bread of the sufferings which our forefathers have eaten in the land of Mizrajim; who is hungry, come and

A Jewish religious service at Douglas Camp, around 1915 (PG 5290-16)

In contrast with Douglas, Knockaloe Camp was originally built to accommodate 5,000 internees, but finally it was extended to 23,000 prisoners, making it the second largest settlement on the Isle of Man. Among the earliest occupants was Karl Berthold Robert Schonwalder, a thirty-two year old German who had been resident in Birmingham since 1900 and who had married an English wife. Schonwalder kept a meticulous diary of day to day events in Knockaloe, and his notes reveal the severe hardship experienced in the depths of a Manx winter. On 10 November 1915 he wrote:

> It is very cold and wet & [we] are walking about in the house [hut] with an overcoat on. This afternoon we have 2 stoves put in, to warm 2 huts or 6 rooms & me being in the middle hut which has no stove the fire makes no difference... [106]

Later that month he added:

eat with us; who is destitute, come and join our celebrations with us, this year here, in future years in the land of Israel, this year slaves, in future years as free people!"

...The week soon was over and we returned to the reality of life, to the life of a "prisoner of war". Would we really be free men next year, I thought - my friends were accustomed to look upon me always as an 'unbeliever' - and I am heartily sorry that we could not celebrate the next Passover together, even if not in Israel then at least at liberty, but most however, are still in captivity behind the barbed wire. [105]

> ... here at Knockaloe up to date a great many sleep on a mattress or rather a straw sack which lies on the floor the damp penetrating not one has a Govt. Bolster & only 3 blankets are allowed & no more fires have been put in our huts. As regards clothing I myself have been waiting and am on the list ever since I have been here for a pair of pants, vest & clogs (boots we don't get) but have not seen any, nor anyone else, only one shirt & one pair of sock & a pr of slippers which can be bought anywhere at 1/11 ½. There are doz[ens] in our Comp[ound] who cannot go outside theyr [sic] huts when raining no boots & trousers all patched together with all sorts of rags overcoats we have not seen yet but a few suits have been given to the very worst cases. The

material of these suit [sic] is about the worst I have ever come across you only have to touch it & it tears. [107]

Knockaloe had a reputation as an unpleasant location not only at Douglas Camp, but also among Germans and Austrians interned in England. Even two years later, conditions were still harsh. Major Paul Stoffa, an officer in the Austro-Hungarian army, was transferred there from Alexandra Palace Camp. He published his memoirs after the war as *Round the World to Freedom*. In the book he wrote:

> *After the usual formalities we were distributed to the various camps: my new home was Camp III. As it was mercifully dark, camps and compounds conveyed little to us: I was taken to one of the many army-huts, each divided into three sections with a double row of bunks ranged alongside the wall. My first thought was that I was back in the fo'c'sle, only on dry land. The sea of mud round the camps provided a substitute for the missing element .... Waking up on the 1st of January, 1917, I soon discovered why the camp at Knockaloe inspired such dread amongst the inhabitants of the Alexandra Palace. Here internment was reduced to its simplest elements: barbed wire, huts and mud. There were no 'frills', no panorama of London stretching for miles, which in itself was an element of qualified freedom, no permanent buildings and no visitors, it was the home of make-shift,*

Major Paul Stoffa. An Austrian army officer, he was captured by the Russians on the Eastern Font. After escaping from captivity he was disguised as a sailor aboard a merchant ship, which was intercepted by the British. Unable to prove his true identity he was regarded as a civilian, rather than military prisoner. (M 07821)

Prisoners rush for dinner at Knockaloe in this scene painted by internee George Kenner. (2006-0063)

grim, cold and monotonous. The incessant drizzle outside supplied the key-note of our existence ... it gave one the ... feeling of utter isolation, a complete severance from the outside world. No wonder that so many men degenerated here by degrees into something near a state of savagery: the decent majority struggled hard to keep afloat in a sea of hopeless despondency – many went under, insanity claiming not a few. [108]

In 1932 Paul Cohen-Portheim published his memoir of Knockaloe, *Time Stood Still*. His view of the camp was more benign, but he acknowledged that much of this was down to his personal outlook. He wrote of his arrival there in the dead of night:

The chains of light came nearer and nearer ... Barbed wire appeared, long, endlessly long stretches of barbed wire, five or six yards high. And faces and faces behind the wire, thousands of caged animals. They called out to us, and as in a nightmare they repeated the cries of the East End crowd: "Huns! Baby-killers! Have they caught you at last!" This was not meant unkindly, but the form of humour peculiar to prisoners was as yet unknown to me, also I was very, very weary. At last a gate opened in the barbed wire wall, we entered, one's feet sank deep into slippery clay. In front of us lay on the left free space, on the right tightly-clustered wooden huts, the whole surrounded by tall barbed wire and arc-lamps. This was called a compound; it held one thousand human animals. Five compounds formed a camp, and this was Camp II. There were five camps altogether, I believe. The gate closed behind us. This, then, was 'the second camp,' there was nothing more to be done but wait for liberation – which already seemed much, much farther than twenty-four hours ago in Stratford – or else for the end of the Great War.

First impressions are by no means always right but they are frequently decisive. My first impression of Stratford had been sickening; my first impression on seeing Knockaloe Camp in daylight was one of delighted surprise, brought about, no doubt, by the contrast with the scene that had met my eyes the previous morning. Stepping out of the hut I found radiant sunshine, marvellously pure and bracing air, and a panorama of turf clad hills. That is how, in spite of all that was to follow, Knockaloe has remained in my mind, for I am what the French call a type visuel, which means that the look of a thing, place, or person matters most to me. When choosing a house or flat I have always been apt to consider the view from the window more important than more practical matters, and if I had to choose an internment camp – which I hope to God I shall never have to again – I should be guided by similar considerations. This is apt to annoy other people a good deal. Knockaloe was considered the most distasteful of all camps, the one where hardships were worst and conditions most unpleasant, that is why I feel apologetic to my fellow-

prisoners when I state that I rather liked being there. It is only fair, however, to add that my stay there was short and that we had marvellous summer weather. The case of the men who were there for years ... is, of course, a very different one. [109]

His induction consisted of a speech from the commandant, translated afterwards into German:

And that ended the ceremony. And now, what next? Now there was nothing to do, nothing at all, nothing whatsoever, nothing-for how long? There was a sort of shanty called a canteen, standing just outside the wire, with its counter open to the camp, where one might try to buy something. No matter what, one had nothing one needed, so everything would be welcome. Hundreds were waiting already; I waited for about two hours and everything had been sold out when my turn came. [110]

Herein lay the problem. Although some internees were hired out to farmers for labouring purposes during the war, many refused, perceiving this as co-operation with the enemy. With so little to do, time hung heavy on men's hands, and much of the illness suffered by the internees was psychological rather than physical. Boredom was a serious problem, and many prisoners developed a listlessness as the weeks of internment turned to months then years. Schonwalder noted in his diary for January 1916:

Everybody seems to get tired of this awful monotony a great many are getting sallow looking and thin altered in their features ill tempered & nervous getting exited [sic] at

J.T.Baily, of the Society of Friends (Quakers). The Society sought to alleviate the hardships of war wherever they were found, but Baily (second right) found himself mistrusted by both sides in Knockaloe. (PG 38039)

nothing or fly in a temper all caused through this monotony. [111]

One laconic guard officer, talking to a journalist, neatly summed up the whole situation in one line when he commented:

You must either give 'em something to do, or let them go 'dotty'. [112]

In order to combat this problem, the Society of Friends (Quakers) established workshops for the internees, in which to produce goods for sale outside of the camp. In 1915 work also began on improving living conditions by making equipment for games, libraries, gardening and by building camp theatres. J.T.Baily of the Society of Friends was invited to become involved in the setting up of workshops and occupational activities in a number of internment camps. In October 1915 he came to Knockaloe. He observed:

Probably the worst disease to be combated in a civilian internment camp came to be known as 'barbed-wirelitis'[sic]. It could soon develop into incipient insanity; prisoners of war who were readily subject to it were those who felt most acutely the injustice of their incarceration, particularly when they had adopted Britain as their home by having been resident over many years; such had usually married a woman of British nationality and had British born children – it was remarkable that such men had failed to take out naturalisation papers – their feelings were accentuated by the sudden unexpected separation, the loss of the means of a livelihood and the consequent anxiety concerning the family's welfare. Another contributory factor to those of a more cultured life was the promiscuous herding together of all types and the lack of privacy; then again to have no idea of the duration of their internment was a case of 'hope deferred maketh the heart sick', and further to all this was the absence of occupations.

It will be obvious how different was the condition of combatant prisoners of war to that of civilian internees, for the former internment was one of the expected fortunes of war often welcomed as a deliverance from the risks of the battlefield and to such, idleness was not their lot as employment could be imposed upon them, choice they had none, but the civilian could refuse to work because of the terms of the Hague Convention, only need he do that which was necessary for his own wellbeing. The symptoms of the disease were moroseness, avoidance of others, and an aimless promenading up and down the barbed wired boundary of the compound... if this could not be stopped insanity would follow and probably suicide ... the surest way to prevent and cure the disease – while the war continued – was occupation and it was to the provision of this in every possible form that the Friends Relief Service ... gave every attention and to the promotion of which I was called to organise. That such provisions were effectual was proved by the fact that where the disease developed it was among those who stubbornly refused to engage in any activity. [113]

In spite of his efforts, Baily was viewed with suspicion by both sides; the camp authorities questioned the motives behind his sympathy for enemy prisoners, whilst many of the prisoners, at first at least, believed that he was some sort of spy. To his credit he persevered, and by 1916 the American Embassy in London was able to report that:

Nearly 72 per cent of the interned men in the camp are at work. Many of the men were employed as bootmakers, tailors, joiners, cap workers, plumbers, woodworkers, gardeners, latrine men, police, coal and railway workers, quarry workers, post-office workers, and parcel-post workers, etc. [114]

Much of the recognition for this must go to the Friends' Emergency Committee, a Quaker organisation, which helped to provide books, tools and equipment for the internees to work with and to start workshops in the camp. Never the less, an appeal from Baily appeared in *The Friend* of 16 November 1917 in which he stated:

The Industrial Committees of all four camps, together with myself, are viewing with much anxiety the prospect of another winter for the interned spent under trying conditions of camp life and Manx weather. To many men it means a fourth winter of internment ... there are now large numbers seeking occupation who have hitherto held indifferently aloof, and even those who opposed all such efforts from a mistaken idea of being patriotic to Germany are now co-operating in these efforts. [115]

The physical hardship of daily life in a camp comprised of wooden huts, in a climate as harsh as that of the Isle of Man in winter, can be imagined. One internee who found it particularly difficult was Otto Schimming, a missionary from Togoland who was more used to the heat of East Africa:

The life in the hut compartments with at most 30 inhabitants has a more comfortable character than in the large halls of the Alexandra Palace[,] if it were not for the adverse climate and the mud. Our hut floor was always damp. The sun warmed only the 'B' huts, they have the windows facing the south. 'A' huts have the windows to the north, and the sun's rays never fall through them. In December and January the sun only comes out from behind the mountains after 9 o'clock in the morning and at 3 o'clock is already disappearing again. I felt certain that I could not for long bear it in this damp hut, in mud and slush and storms of snow and rain. In the last week of January I was struck down with a fever. First I believed it was an attack of malaria, but quinine did not help. I became more and more wretched, but hoped for improvement and refused to call the doctor. After five days other prisoners brought the doctor, as I could no longer get up ... My temperature was 106 degrees ... he had me taken to the hospital. I had pneumonia with an almost intolerable headache. [116]

A Turkish prisoner in Knockaloe. For these people in particular, the Manx winter spent in draughty wooden huts would be harsh. (PG 7870-38267)

It is also an often overlooked fact that the camps contained numbers of subjects of the Ottoman Empire, Germany's ally with which Britain was at war in the Middle East. The voices of Turkish internees are seldom heard when internment is discussed, but we are fortunate in that we have at least one source upon which to draw. Mustapha Shefket, who gave his address as Camp 3, Compound 2, Hut 5a at Knockaloe wrote in September 1917 to a Swedish diplomat about the various hardships which he was experiencing:

I am a Turkish subject and 17 months ago was arrested by the British at the Isle of Chios where I had lived since a very long time, and, together with German and Austrian Consul I was brought to this country. Being 56 years of age and having passed all my life in a hot country, I find it very difficult to stand the hardships of an internment in a northern country. I am especially afraid of the coming autumn and winter and, once again, beg you to endeavour to get me exchanged, liberated or, at least, sent to a place more suited to my condition of health.

Besides this I beg to draw your attention to another matter. Since about 4 months I have not received any money from Chios. Formerly I regularly got remittances from the Chios Dock Company where I was employed, but now the Greek Government has prevented my company from sending me money. I am absolutely destitute and beg you to get permission for my company to send me money. (117)

The special dietary requirements of Muslim prisoners in Knockaloe must have presented some challenges to the camp authorities, but it should not be forgotten that a number of the Ottoman subjects who were interned on the Isle of Man were actually Jews, hailing from present day Israel, and would have been accommodated in the Jewish compound at Douglas.

Maurice Jeger's description of the Passover in Douglas Camp raises interesting questions about which side the internees identified with, and exactly how they perceived themselves. It could be argued that Jeger saw himself as a Jew first and foremost, and an Austrian second. It was a question which would take on a more sinister significance in the years which followed, but during the First World War the Right Reverend Herbert Bury was given responsibility for religious matters throughout the prisoner of war camps of the British Isles. He visited the Isle of Man in 1916, and reported not just upon the Jews but also the inhabitants of Knockaloe, who he perceived as being largely pro-British:

One's sympathy could be given to those — far and away the greater number of them — who have loved England, and all things English, and never wished to leave, nor thought of leaving, it again. Some have sons fighting for us in France and some of their sons have died for us. But still I said to them frankly — I was very frank throughout — that though it was an embittering thing to feel that because some were suspected, and rightly, of being spies, and some were evil and treacherous, so many of the innocent had to suffer, yet they must bear the burden their nationality had laid upon them, and suffer with their country-men. They were quite sensible about it, and said afterwards: "We don't know ourselves, though here with them, who the spies and undesirables are, and it must be still more difficult for the authorities to track them out."

On the Sunday morning I attended an Old Catholic celebration in one of the compounds, taken by Pastor Bollman, formerly of St. Mary's, Charing Cross Road, at which I preached, helped to administer, and gave the blessing. There was some Roumanian music and we administered to Roumanians and other members of the Orthodox Church, some Old Catholics and a few Anglicans — about twenty altogether — but the large hall was packed from end to end with German Protestants who sang their own chorales, listened to the sermon, and followed the service with the keenest and most reverent interest. The friends of the pastor had worked for a whole day at preparing the altar and getting flowers, and for the time being it was really an impressive and beautiful sanctuary, quite astonishing to those who were only familiar with it in its ordinary and everyday appearance.

The same afternoon I addressed some three thousand men in a great hall, with a gallery, in the camp at Douglas, and had a magnificent orchestra to help us with the service. Amongst them were about seven hundred Jews whose representatives and spokesman, presented to me on arrival, told me how glad he and they were to be at the service. The keen interest and gradually awakening sympathy — at first it seemed to be prejudice, hostility, and curiosity only — nearly swept me off my feet by its reality, and when I offered a little prayer at the end for their homes and wives and children to be kept happily and dutifully together until they could return to them again, praying that it might be soon, I could see that those about me were in tears. And indeed I was very near to it myself as I gave the blessing. [118]

A Ciborium used by Father Thomas Crookall, the Catholic priest from St Mary's in Douglas, at Knockaloe during the First World War. He was held in such high esteem by the prisoners that many wrote to him after the war. (2013-0010)

There were nonetheless many within both camps who vigorously and vociferously identified with the German cause. Pastor Rudolf Hartmann in a sermon given in Knockaloe in November 1915 stressed the part being played by the internees in a greater German struggle, and urged them to remember the sacrifices being made on the battlefields of Europe:

Our dead – in this hour, we remember in particular those, both young and old, who have been taken from our midst

litho
by AG0.

G St
23.7.17

Rudolf Hartmann, Pastor.
Knockaloe Camp. Joll.

and will never see the homeland again, because they have
been brought over to the greater homeland. Our dead –
for whom we should see it today as our solemn duty to
provide a worthy place of burial. Yet those who have died
in Knockaloe are but a few among the thousands who
will return to the homeland, who will once more be able
to serve life. Our dead – those are the others over there
who will not be able to return, whom we will never see
again, never be able to embrace again, our friends, our
brothers, our sons, our fathers, and we are helpless, far
away, cut off, alone, imprisoned! But today is Totenfest,
today we are able to commemorate them, and we want to
allow our thoughts of them to stand before us in all their
warmth and strength, in all their youthful vigour, in all
their seriousness, and in all their love. We want to pledge
ourselves to them once more with the best that we have,
and that bound us to them. Friends, brothers, fathers, we
have lost you, but in the depths of our hearts you live on,
and in the peace of our souls you celebrate resurrection
from day to day. [119]

The same month Schonwalder, in his diary
describes the sullen and truculent anti-British
mood in the camp. He noted that:

It is getting a bit weary here they don't seem the
same sort of chaps as at Wakefield if you speak
English to anyone they don't answer you or tell
you that this is a German camp. [120]

A charcoal sketch of Pastor Rudolf
Hartmann, a Lutheran minister in Knockaloe.
(Courtesy of Frances Coakley)

Later he seemed to take positive delight in the difficulties which Britain was experiencing, commenting:

> I don't think [the war] will last much longer the English have this time what they have been asking for[.] this is no Boer War ... they are on the road to Bankruptcie. [sic] [121]

In June 1916 Schonwalder gleefully recorded the names of the British ships lost at the Battle of Jutland, the news of which was clearly common knowledge in the camp, adding:

> This will take the swank off John Bull. [122]

He also records numerous escape attempts by his comrades including trying to cut the wire, construction of a tunnel, and a party of sailors who managed to get as far as Peel with the intention of securing a boat for return to Germany; Schonwalder, who had lived in England for many years and thus might be expected to be pro-British, added that he wished the participants the best of luck in these attempts. Overall, these were hardly the actions of prisoners who loved England and all things English. Protest and patriotic expression took whatever form it could. Schonwalder records on 1 May 1916:

> In Comp[ound] I they have been upholding May day making a procession headed by theyr [sic] band with the red flag & a green one for Ireland the Sub. Com. came in with a few soldiers and told them to stop which they did but boot [booed] him out of it loud enough for us to hear & then they shouted 3 cheers for Little Willy [Crown Prince Wilhelm]. [123]

Not surprisingly growing frustration and resentment in Knockaloe led to violence, as it had at Douglas. In October 1916, Schonwalder wrote:

> When the sub com[mander] came in [compound] IV this eve he ask [sic] one officer what was the matter & he told him they want their liberty, he gave them a speech & after he had gone they broke the canteen open, 2nd time this week & practically cleared it. Its only 5 yards from our wire & the chaps in [compound] V watched them carry the stuff away. I heard tonight that they want the soldiers from the other camp drafted up here & then they start in other camps they been talking about setting the hall on fire. I trust they will do nothing of the kind, but you cannot blame them giving trouble after 26 months behind wire. [124]

This incident was followed the next day by a proclamation informing prisoners that combining together to cause trouble amounted to mutiny, for which they were liable to be court martialled and shot.

As well as the anti-British sentiments expressed within the camps, there was also a considerable amount of hostility directed *towards* enemy aliens, much of it from the English press. Based it seems on the Isle of Man's pre-war reputation as a place for fun and frolics, the idea grew up in some quarters that the internees were somehow on holiday. Under the heading 'The Huns Paradise' in May 1915 the populist weekly *John Bull* took an ill-informed swipe at both the internees and the Manx authorities:

> Some of the newly-interned aliens are said to be destined for the Isle of Man, and they are probably congratulating

themselves on securing such pleasant quarters. The place has been made very comfortable for them – almost, in fact "a home from home" .... Certainly for some weeks past the Isle of Man has been a pleasant sojourn for Germhuns [sic], who have been permitted, encouraged and assisted to have a good time. [125]

The *John Bull* article alleged that the *Isle of Man Times* had carried a report to the effect that a party of Germans allowed out on a picnic had cheered a placard carrying news of the *Lusitania* sinking, adding:

A state of things is here revealed that calls for instant and drastic alteration. There must be no more ... picnics for Germhun [sic] skunks who celebrate an unnecessary outing by cheering the crowning crime of the murdering nation to which they belong. [126]

The *Isle of Man Examiner*, no friend to the *Times*, investigated this last report and found it to be wholly without foundation. However there were many others within the Isle of Man who held similar anti-German views. Mary Faragher, a Douglas woman who had gone to Vickers in Barrow to undertake war work, wrote to her mother in April 1918 about a German aristocrat who due to his rank was allowed special privileges whilst interned:

I ...read in the paper about Baron von Bissing being over on the Island I must say we have the elite of German society there now it is disgusting such vermin as Von Bissing are allowed to pollute the earth he ought to be transported to Germany along with his brother the dirty pup who shot (not caused to be shot) Nurse Cavell[,] interned is too good for

the likes of him, he is able to live in peace & quietness while real Manx people have to go into the danger zone to earn a living for in England one never knows when we are to have a visit from the Germans (airships I mean). [127]

The same year, Douglas Councillor Knox objected to the use of internees outside on the roads, stating:

As long as he was a member of the Council he would never agree to a halfpenny of the ratepayers' money being spent in employing Huns. He had come to the conclusion that alien labour was only justified when it was employed within barbed wire, and certainly it should not be utilised by the Council. [128]

There were also wider objections to outside work based not on hatred of the men themselves, but on the fact that their employment on farms at low rates of pay was both enriching landowners who were already wealthy, and at the same time undercutting and thereby undermining the wages of the Manx agricultural workforce. Section 5 of the Regulations governing internee labour also stated:

A farmer employing an Alien will be required to give an undertaking ... that he will not permit him to have any communication with any person other than himself or his authorised agent. [129]

Yet in spite of the attempts by the authorities to prevent as far as possible contact between the internees and the local civilian population, it was inevitable that such contact would occur, particularly as the war went on and internees were increasingly used for labour outside of the camps. This of course coincided with the disappearance of a large portion of the local population of young males. In November 1918, Alice Kerruish, a forty- year-old married woman from Kirk Michael was charged with communicating with an Alien prisoner, contrary to camp regulations. In her statement she said:

> *Two aliens named Willy and Harry from Knockaloe Camp were working for my husband John R.H.Kerruish ... in the harvest, putting in corn, when I got on friendly terms with them. I wrote on two occasions and I sent a shilling's worth of sweets on two occasions to Willy and the last time I sent a shillings worth of sweets to Harry. Willy, when working in the stackyard, got in conversation with ___, and he asked me if I would see her and ask her to write to him ...* [130]

The High Bailiff clearly believed that in Mrs Kerruish's case matters had gone beyond 'friendly' to 'extremely intimate relations', and furthermore she was attempting to induce other women to behave similarly. We cannot know the full extent of her relationship with Harry, but in the circumstances it is not wholly surprising that such liaisons occurred, and Mrs Kerruish was by no means the only Manx woman charged with communicating or 'trafficking' with aliens. Tom Lilley of Castletown was perhaps better qualified than most to understand the impact of the war on personal beliefs, having one son in the army and another in prison as a conscientious objector. Writing in 1917 he said:

> *There has just passed the house under escort between 30 & 40 aliens from Douglas who are working at Scarlett breaking stones for the Highway Board they are singing and marching in tune as if they were happy as the customary trippers that pass through here in normal times. They are mostly young fellows ... they appear to be inoffensive, good looking and by their actions, good natured lot of young fellows; they are followed night & morning by a crowd of children boys & girls who march behind them during their holidays. Until recently they have been in the habit of regaling the children at the Railway station on their return to chocolate and sweets, bought at the automatic machines, out of their scanty earnings, and even bringing sweets from Douglas to them .... But latterly the Police have prevented the children from gaining access to the Railway station and consequently the little kiddies are despondent. I suppose the authorities were afraid if this sort of thing continued the children would begin to love the aliens, instead of hating them as they are taught to do.* [131]

A forgery of a ten shilling note, produced in Knockaloe (note the miss-spelling of 'amount'.) Such notes are known to have been passed in Michael Street, Peel. (2008-0135)

Within the camps of Douglas and Knockaloe there were also printing presses, upon which the prisoners could produce their own German-language camp magazines. Numerous issues of the various titles which were published by civilian prisoners during their internment have survived. Some examples are *Camp Echo, Das Schleierlicht, Die Lager Laterne, Unter Uns, Lager-Echo, Knockaloe-Lager-Zeitung, Lager Ulk, Werden* and *Quousque Tandem*. Every magazine had its own editorial staff, its own character and its own target audience, which they met with varying degrees of success. While *Lager-Echo* and *Knockaloe-Lager-Zeitung* were published regularly for almost two years, other camp magazines like *Quousque Tandem* ceased after only two issues, and there is only one issue known of the magazine *Werden*.

Whilst the short term objectives of the camp authorities, in allowing the internees to produce such magazines, were focused upon the maintenance of morale and of their mental well-being, the longer term value to historians is incalculable in reflecting both everyday activities, and the hopes and concerns of those interned. They also include political opinions, and attitudes towards the war, insofar as the normal restrictions of censorship would allow this. In contrast to the documents of military authorities or relief organizations, which represent the 'view from above', they convey the 'view from below', the perspective of the ordinary men. Two of the longest-running magazines, *Knockaloe-Lager-Zeitung* and *Lager-Echo* offer sufficient material to be able to draw conclusions about the different aspects of camp life.

The former newspaper had its roots in a publication which was founded by internees at Stobs camp in Scotland in September 1915. In June the following year publication ceased, when several of the editors were transferred from Stobs to Knockaloe. In Knockaloe these amateur journalists re-united to found, in October 1916, *Knockaloe-Lager-Zeitung: Zeitschrift des Zivil-Gefangenen-Lagers Knockaloe, Isle of Man*. They had received the permission of the camp commander to continue their previous activity. Every issue of *Knockaloe-Lager-Zeitung* covered four pages and cost one penny. The editorial staff worked as volunteers, the proceeds from the magazine were given to charity organisations in the camp like the Hospital Fund and the Burial Expenses Board. Apart from some odd issues the magazine was published monthly. Circulation ranged from 1600 to 4000 copies. Some issues like the Christmas issue of 1917 were soon out of print. The internees were able to send magazines to Germany without limitation, apart from the fact that they only were allowed to send twenty copies to any one address.

The first issue of *Knockaloe-Lager-Zeitung* did not refer at all to hope or to the future, as had those in Stobs; instead there was a sense of despair, bitter irony and the fear of being interned for an indefinite period:

We are still interned: Our acute wailing over the loss of freedom has changed into chronic resignation. We appreciate our transfer as a lovely inspiration for our literary subject needs. There was nothing more to tell about Stobs that could have interested refined German readers. One year ago when we started our career in journalism, a joker suggested that we should not forget the words 'volume one' under the title of the magazine. We did what he wanted, though we would never have thought it possible that there would be a 'volume two'. However we were wrong and today we wonder if there will be a third volume? (132)

Despite this uncertainty the editors continued their work. It was their aim:

> to provide a connection to the almost forgotten home, to give our relatives and friends an idea of our situation and our feelings. (...) We also wanted to ease the burden of life in the camp....with the little money that was left over from our work. (...) We also wanted to write a chronicle which will tell about the labours and joys of German prisoners of war and civilian prisoners in England in the future and we wanted to produce a small contribution to the history of the war. (133)

Simultaneously with the *Knockaloe-Lager-Zeitung* of Camp IV, a group of prisoners in Camp III began publishing a similar magazine, *Lager-Echo*, and in June 1917 H.Behrens who had belonged to the editorial staff of *Knockaloe-Lager-Zeitung* moved to Camp III and began work for the rival title, so there was some degree of editorial crossover between the two. The editors' aims were clearly reminiscent of those of the *Knockaloe-Lager-Zeitung*:

> There are different points of view which seem to make the publishing of a camp magazine necessary, but first of all it is to tie the same bonds around those of us who have been forced in to this quite unusual life. (...) But we also want to create a picture of the bustle we've kept for those who stand in the middle of the camp life with all its differences, its worries, its wantings and its not-able-to-be, and also for

those who are on their own way and separated from the others. (...) Last but not least we wanted to spin the thread again which connected us with the homeland and which now seems to be cut off. (134)

Like all the other camp magazines the *Knockaloe-Lager-Zeitung* and the *Lager-Echo* also had to pass through the camp censorship office; in some cases the editors had to leave blank spaces in the magazine with the note:

> Because some of the articles in today's magazine were objected to by the censors, we beg our readers pardon for the white gaps. We guarantee to write more in the next issue. (135)

Whilst the editors of the *Lager-Echo* described in their first issue the conditions of publication:

> All articles which should be printed have to pass the censor and we want to emphasize that in order to avoid needless entries. (136)

In the final issue of the magazine censorship is referred to explicitly:

> The publishing of this issue of Knockaloe-Lager-Zeitung was unfortunately delayed, because two articles (about compensation and exchange) were objected to by the censor's office. We therefore had to submit new ones for approval. (137)

The censorship of personal letters meanwhile was the subject of a satirical commentary in *Knockaloe-Lager-*

Zeitung in July 1917:

> *Three weeks ago I was called to go to the censor. I went there. The stern man showed me a letter and asked me in English if I was the author. After I agreed he wanted to know why I had rubbed something out. Immediately I remembered that ages ago I had made an inkblot on a sheet of paper which I wanted to remove with soft rubbing. I took the letter and examined it with great interest. Only with every effort did I find the scene of the crime.* (138)

The magazine mocks the efforts of the camp censors, but control of information passing in and out of the camp was taken very seriously. Archibald Knox, the Isle of Man's greatest artist, worked as a parcel censor at the camp, one of many civilian staff in Knockaloe and Douglas. After the war he wrote to a friend:

> *I had the same post from the day I started work Nov 9 1914 until I left Oct 25 1919: 1,207,000 parcels passed through my department and up to about the end of 1915 it was a hard worked post: the office was understaffed and you would have laughed I think if you had seen me at some of the jobs I had to do: but after that time the staff was enlarged and I had an easier time of it: but the staff was too small and I had more work to do than could be rightly and completely done ... our business was to intercept communications: there was always some new trick – an epidemic of the same trick; but for the last 13 months we had comparative peace: they must have admitted defeat for we seldom found anything. At one time for several months there were tins of preserved meat – according to the label assurance also it was made in a neutral country: for*

Archibald Knox, the Isle of Man's greatest artist, worked as a parcel censor at Knockaloe during the First World War. (1954-6003)

> *'meat' would have been comforting if they had got it for it was a fortnight's newspapers rolled and folded and packed and sealed to deceive even a censor. Those were specially prepared for PsOW [sic] parcels but the same game was tried in all sorts of amateur ways, baked in loaves, in tins of fat, sewn up in a chest protector, sewn in pieces of cabbage leaf and buried in a tin of sauerkraut, cuttings fitted in medical [globules] packed in an [odour] bottle and so on. The last parcel that arrived in October 1915 was a long*

canister of 'tobacco substitute' but ¾ of its contents were German newspapers: papers with the story of Kitchener's death, the battle of Jutland reached the office within 10 days of the event: the wonder was why they persisted so long in the effort to get their newspapers into the camp: their loaves cakes sausages were relentlessly opened everything that might contain a message: for their own comfort one would have thought they would have told their friends to stop: but the yearning for authentic news seemed strong to the last. I was interested very much at first: the advertisements, the get up of the paper containers and wrappers were always decorated in interesting patterns and bright colours: but they disappeared and the foods came more or less without wrappering [sic]. [139]

It is perhaps tempting to think of the internees as a homogenous mass, but it is important to remember that German society was as divided by class as was that of Great Britain; perhaps more so. This was naturally reflected within the camp populations, where ethnic and other social divisions were also to be found. George Kenner, an educated and intelligent German artist resident in London before the war, found the arbitrary mix of classes and types in Knockaloe to be one of the most difficult aspects of internment. The first hut occupied by Kenner contained mostly ethnic Poles, from the eastern German territories which would later form part of Poland. They spoke no German, and had nothing in common with Kenner. Later on, he was granted a transfer to be with his brother, but this brought its own difficulties:

George Kenner (wearing shorts) and his brother, interned at Knockaloe. (PG 8327-1)

I loaded boxes and mattresses on a two wheeled barrow and, under guard, pushed it over [to the other compound] where my brother welcomed me at the gate.

Unfortunately I learned here were many gamblers. They gathered up to 20 and 30 round the table in our hut, and sat together by candle and petroleum light (smoke hung in blue clouds). Long ago the electric light had been turned out for the nights rest, yet, under such circumstances one could not think of sleep. Several times the enclosure sergeant had rebuked them by taking away all the money, but now they put out spies to betray his approach. All this, through years, made a bad influence upon the mind of my young brother. It required great perseverance to lift him upon a higher plane. (140)

Sometime later, Kenner was offered the opportunity to move again:

I did not consider very long, since I was not liked much for not gambling with them, to the contrary, I had rather a sharp argument about it. I looked at the place and gladly moved. That white-washed corner I liked more than my last place. A cupboard for dishes, folding table and folding stool, trunk seat, a flower picture over the bed, and little evergreen trees on the window shelf increased my comfort. By fixing a curtain I could retire undisturbed. Besides the mates around me were more agreeable. (141)

Opportunities for work have already been discussed, but theatre, film, music, art, sport and lectures on different subjects also offered the possibility of occupying oneself with something outside of working hours. In the printing office of Camp IV were produced not only the *Knockaloe-Lager-Zeitung*, but also Almanacs, Christmas and Easter cards for the camp, as well as various theatre programmes, and it is these which reflect the importance of cultural life within it. Every issue of *Knockaloe-Lager-Zeitung* and *Lager-Echo* reported on theatre productions and concerts in the different compounds and also about lectures and seminars on different topics. A common pastime was acting in plays at the theatre. Camp IV at Knockaloe had a theatre in each of its seven compounds. In six months the theatres put on 113 comedies, forty-two plays, fifteen dramas, twenty-one variety shows and a pageant. The men also had to play female roles which sometimes caused difficulty:

The association had to struggle a little with the lack of suitable ladies' players. (142)

But this challenge also seemed to encourage some actors:

We wanted to highlight the extraordinary portrayal of the character of Gertrud Gronau whose actor (Mr. Ehlers) not only distinguished himself because of his pleasant voice and female appearance but also because of his sensitive appreciation of this role. (143)

Indeed, some of the actors even specialised in female roles:

Mr Buerkle is one of our best ladies' actors but he is more suited to playing the intriguing woman in her mid thirties. (144)

The extent to which some prisoners seem to have immersed themselves in an adopted female persona – a persona which seems to have extended in some cases far beyond the boundaries of the theatre – has led to speculation as to whether or not they had fully adopted the role of women in a closed all-male society. Cohen-Portheim tells us:

> The first and obvious conclusion anyone considering the matter dispassionately would arrive at is this: when you lock up thousands of men between eighteen and fifty years for a very prolonged period and prevent any intercourse with the opposite sex, you inevitably drive them, indeed almost force them into homosexual intercourse. As this conclusion would have been considered painful and not good for the ears of the public, the matter was never discussed or even alluded to in the papers, and the whole problem was ignored, but it can and should not be ignored by any writer on the subject of prison life .... Such acts were, I should say, extremely infrequent, and personally I know of none at all. This may seem improbable, and would be more than improbable if there was not one most important point to be considered: The camp offered no possibility of isolation ... there was no possible privacy for anybody, and such intercourse would have had to be conducted within hearing (if not seeing) of others, and therefore to the general knowledge .... As to their committing sexual acts of any kind whilst under observation – as they always were – that was almost unthinkable. [145]

The case of Alice Kerruish discussed earlier also demonstrates that if prisoners were determined enough, contact with females was not entirely beyond their reach. Undoubtedly a well-executed play made it possible to forget about camp life for a short time as the *Knockaloe-Lager-Zeitung* commented in July 1917:

> There is an amazing tension in the air. The tension of a premiere. The lights in the audience hall are going out, the last acts of the overture are gone. The bell is ringing for the last time, the curtain is raising - and we are looking forward to forgetting for a few hours that we have been prisoners of war for three years. [146]

Besides the theatre concerts, music provided a diversion. In Camp IV at Knockaloe there were four string orchestras, three choirs and a military brass band who put on eighteen general concerts, twenty-two classical concerts, five open-air concerts and eight zither concerts in six months. Many prisoners also tried to occupy themselves with reading, which caused some trouble as the *Lager-Echo* reported in July 1917:

> Reading and always reading is one of the best possibilities for diversion. In the first days of our arrest we were always occupied with finding a book, it didn't matter if it was a detective novel or a little girl's novel, and then we absorbed it line by line as a narcotic against all senseless brooding over events which have taken place. Unfortunately, our private stocks were not very large in the beginning, when the connection to the homeland was still present, so we had to go all around the houses to get any book. Really good books could only be received from best friends and only after passionate persuasion. [147]

In December 1916 in order to try to end the shortage of good books (which was a problem in every compound), the *Knockaloe-Lager-Zeitung* published a call for the donation of books to the library of Camp IV, which already possessed some 8,000 titles. It is perhaps surprising that the internees were missing scientific books, rather than fiction, but the magazine explained:

> *After two years of internment some of us do not feel like being shown the pleasures of freedom in novels and novellas. We prefer practical lectures which could be necessary for the future.* [148]

One year later the magazine again emphasised the importance of reading in order to gain the stimulus which, under ordinary circumstances, would be provided by the natural world:

> *The internee is virtually cut off from the whole wide world of nature, the plants, animals and free living and unrestricted men, the beautiful, colourful world is somewhere outside behind the wire, and nearly every impulse we need in order not to become intellectually stunted we have to obtain from books. The book is of great importance to us, and the ones who don't want or aren't able to read in the camp are poor ones, very poor.* [149]

Those who wanted to widen their horizons could join numerous classes and lectures about different topics. In a single camp at Knockaloe, there were eleven different schools in operation in June 1917. Seven general schools provided lessons ranging from popular arithmetic and three types of shorthand, through to ten different languages, electro-mechanics and hotel book-keeping. Three advanced schools specialised in preparation for matriculation exams and a preparatory class for army service and nautical school. *Lager-Echo* claimed that the German internees were predisposed towards organisation along educational lines in the camps because of their nationality:

> *Everywhere the German school system is described as exemplary. In particular those Germans who are living abroad, who have gained positions across the world because of their knowledge and their skills, and who have claimed those positions as pioneers for German work and creativity in spite of real competition, know this for certain. It is also common knowledge that a German is always interested in learning new things even if he has left school some time since.* [150]

The seminar programme of the literary-scientific association of Camp IV offered a wide variety of topics including the work of medieval poet Walther von der Vogelweide, the production of gunpowder, the mining of gold in the Transvaal, and wireless telegraphy to name just a few. As the annual report stated, the association intended to:

> *...bring some diversion amid the monotony of camp life and to show that we will not lose our confidence, even under difficult conditions, and that we aspire to the cultivation of the mind. In our hearts we hope that the voice of peace will soon drown the sound of the weapons in the world and open the gates. Until that time we must follow our own path.* [151]

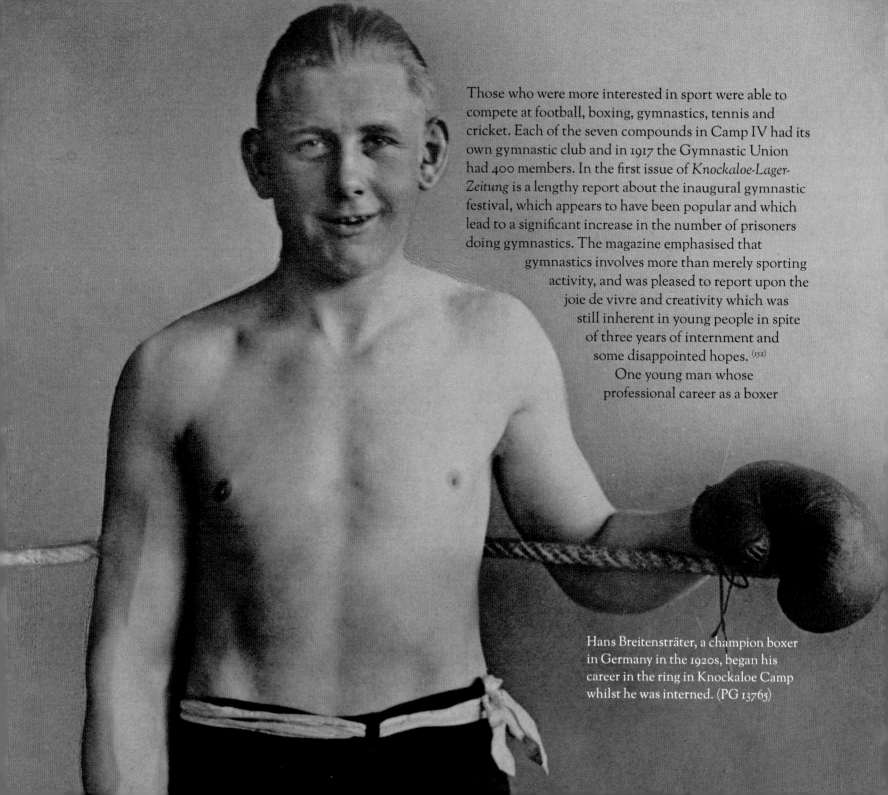

Those who were more interested in sport were able to compete at football, boxing, gymnastics, tennis and cricket. Each of the seven compounds in Camp IV had its own gymnastic club and in 1917 the Gymnastic Union had 400 members. In the first issue of *Knockaloe-Lager-Zeitung* is a lengthy report about the inaugural gymnastic festival, which appears to have been popular and which lead to a significant increase in the number of prisoners doing gymnastics. The magazine emphasised that gymnastics involves more than merely sporting activity, and was pleased to report upon the joie de vivre and creativity which was still inherent in young people in spite of three years of internment and some disappointed hopes. [152] One young man whose professional career as a boxer

Hans Breitensträter, a champion boxer in Germany in the 1920s, began his career in the ring in Knockaloe Camp whilst he was interned. (PG 13765)

A view of Knockaloe camp, painted by George Kenner. The flower garden cultivated by the prisoners is visible in the foreground. (2006-0067)

began in Knockaloe was Hans Breitensträter, who remembered:

No one can understand what it means as a young man to spend so many years behind barbed wire, if they have not experienced this themselves. In the camp, sport became our only salvation ... [our sports were] football, baseball and tennis, but primarily boxing.

The best boxer in the camp was "Nigger Charley", who was not a true black man, but was so-called on account of his Negroid looks. His real name was Charley Browning, he came from Bremen, but had spent many years on American ships. I had barely been in the camp two weeks when I began to dislike him. He however weighed 170 pounds and I only 140, I therefore had no desire to fight him, as defeat would surely be the result; nothing would have become of this if Nigger Charley had not irritated me so.

He made all kinds of disdainful allusions to me, and I did not want to allow him to accuse me of cowardice. Courage, however, was not my companion when in the end I had to climb the ropes into the ring. The referee was the lightweight champion of the British Army, Fitzpatrick. The spectators were our fellow internees, almost all the English officers and many soldiers. Everyone believed that the fight would be over very quickly, and indeed it did not last long. The match was to be over 20 rounds, but no one had foreseen what would happen.

In the first round, I noticed that my opponent was not completely made of timber. He tried to overwhelm me. He pressed me against the ropes and in the close fight landed some low blows. Fitzpatrick warned him, and I immediately hit him with my left, which probably showed him that I was not intimidated by him.

Already by the second round it appeared that I was considerably quicker than him, and with a right hook I brought him to the ground for the first time. Loud applause proved to me that I had the sympathies of the spectators on my side and this raised my confidence quite enormously. The desire to win became uncontrollable, I could hardly bring myself to rest between rounds. A right jab brought Nigger Charley to the ground for a second time. And then the fourth round brought the decision. With a right hook I hit my opponent so hard that his nose was broken. He was a tough one, and he was not yet out, but as I feinted to the left, with a straight right hander I knocked him down hard, and he was counted out.

The cheering of my companions was indescribable. They carried me on their shoulders to my barrack, and I was the champion and the darling of the whole camp.[153]

As well as the applause of his peers, Breitensträter received a significant purse of prize money, which he recalled was useful in purchasing additional food supplies. Away from the boxing ring, many internees occupied themselves with gardening and a horticultural competition was held on 24 August 1916. The judges were the owner of the Knockaloe farm and the head gardener of Kershaw Nursery at Douglas. The internees were very creative, especially in the category of gardening tools. One of the winners was awarded a prize for his watering can made from corned beef cans. The results of the competition were applauded in the Knockaloe-Lager-Zeitung:

More than 55,000 cabbage plants have been planted, which will provide a full harvest, as well as the usual

useful plants like peas, beans, carrots, different sorts of salads etc., which will provide a pleasant diversion in the internees' diet. The camp itself contains many garden plots of a decorative nature which we like to see. When we have portions of vegetables at lunch in the vegetable season we will remember our gardeners thankfully and in our imagination we will shake their hands.[154]

But even this plethora of activities ultimately could not make the internees entirely forget their internment. In September 1917, when many had been imprisoned for three years, the *Lager-Echo* comments:

How many men are able to occupy themselves still! Not everybody is educated or young enough to work intellectually, to learn languages, to study mechanical engineering, to read a chemical book or something similar (...). The average one is only suited for manual crafts: fretsawing, wood and bone carving, painting, knotting and things like that. The ones who really felt like working have tried all possible crafts. But after three years of internment and all the attendant circumstances even the most eager person is fed up with carving vases from bones or making wooden frames en gros. [155]

The editors of the magazines, in spite of their efforts to draw the attention of their readers outside of the camp through reports about flora and fauna, or philosophical debates, inevitably held up a mirror to the captive

A pastel drawing of Thomas Cowley, the water engineer at Knockaloe. The civilian camp staff wore blue uniform, and were known as 'blue staff'. (1994-0007)

population. If one takes their articles as a barometer of the mood of more than 20,000 men in Knockaloe, one finds quite differing emotional reactions. Resignation, defiance, irony, hope, pride, sadness, rage and ridicule are all to be found in the magazines, which incorporate in their variety the different personalities of their authors. Numerous articles however reflect despair and hopelessness. In a November 1916 piece, there was an admission that theatres or orchestras provided merely a temporary distraction from reality:

We can see on the left fellow prisoners going to and from the wire, driven by their inner restlessness.... Whatever you do is characterised by nervousness. Nothing seems to succeed, nothing can satisfy us... Those who can practise their professions, even in a very moderate way, are luckier than others... The shrill laughing which is heard sometimes coming from our lips now, has nothing in common with the hearty laughter of freedom. It is a discharge of the permanent tension we are living with. One can't strike the right note in the confusion of the wire. Our ambitious theatre associations and brave musicians try sometimes to cheer us up and sometimes they really succeed in relaxing our strained faces. But when the game is over and the music has faded we are even more imprisoned by the feeling of loneliness. The desire for freedom, the yearning for the homeland is increasing. [156]

In spite of its efforts to put a brave face on things, *Lager-Echo* could not avoid the hopelessness of everyday life in the camp:

We have always been famous for our patience. Patience

in general is the most striking quality which characterises our life. We are just waiting because there is time enough. Our life is permanent waiting. Sometimes we are waiting for the autumn, for which we have high hopes, sometimes we are waiting for the spring, sometimes for the summer. Only the winter we are never waiting for... What we don't need, there is plenty of, for example, our fellow prisoners, but what we really need we don't have, especially at the moment when we most want it. We never have what we need most, whether it's a piece of string, a nail or money, or to be truthful, a little Gretchen we could talk to. [157]

The "little Gretchen" represents the wife or the fiancée at home from whom some of the internees had been separated for more than two years by this point. There can be little doubt that internment caused serious mental health problems, on a scale perhaps not previously understood. Ballamona Mental Hospital records show that for the period from November 1917 to May 1919 some sixty six internees were admitted with a variety of mental health conditions. A typical example is perhaps that of Ludwig Albach, admitted to Ballamona in July 1918 with Melancholia. In his admission notes, Dr George Kelman stated:

This p/w was a very good athlete in the camp, being the best high jumper in it, he was also a very successful theatrical manager, but within the last year, he has gradually gone down, become morose & keeping away from people, getting into dark corners, hiding away from the light with sudden attacks of crying & wringing his hands, of late he has not slept well & has been secreting pieces of rope, necessitating constant watch being kept on

A medal made by internees for themselves from the melted liners of tea chests. (1974-0291)

him, also breaking out at night to catch the train home. [158]

As an indication of how serious this situation was, by contrast in the same period some forty five civilians and three guards were admitted to the hospital. Given that the internee population was perhaps half the size of the civilian population of the Isle of Man, then an internee was almost three times more likely than his civilian counterpart outside of the wire to develop mental health problems. Of course, there were as many different reactions to internment as there were internees.

R.F.Koch, writing of his time in Knockaloe stated:

I consider myself lucky to have been there, it was not so bad, after all, we had our school and our football grounds and that was the most important thing at that time ... at that time I spoke English and my best friends were the 'sentries' marching along the barbed wire, I often talked with them, they were all rather elderly men and they brought me in some chocolate, woollen socks, fresh collars for shirts and many other little things that really were not allowed to come in, but they were kind to me. [159]

Koch was aged twenty, and as has already been stated, it was those older men longer established in England who perhaps found internment hardest to cope with. Another ex-internee with fond memories of Knockaloe was Ricardo Fadum, who was born in Germany of Danish parents. He stated:

I enjoyed many privileges which enabled me to ramble through the most picturesque parts of [the] Island, and thus become fairly well acquainted with its land, sea and sky scape, and with many Manx people as well. [160]

As the war drew to a close, concern grew among them over what the future held for those who had been interned in the Isle of Man for the duration of hostilities. How would they be perceived in a post-war Germany? Would they be shunned for not having played their part in the carnage on the battlefields? This concern is clearly evident in a paragraph in the *Knockaloe-Lager-Zeitung* in the final months of the war:

We are not deserters, and he who dares to deny our right of public work after the war, because fate has banished us to this island, is out of his senses. We would give him the correct answer: (...) Every conscientious and honest man has his civil rights, and on the Isle of Man we didn't gain those rights spectacularly, but instead with patient study. [161]

For many in the post war years, internment was a chapter of history that they wished to forget. It was certainly a chapter which relatively few who were interned wished to talk about – the number of published memoirs or monographs which describe life in Douglas or Knockaloe camps can almost be counted on the fingers of one hand. There was no glory to be won in an internment camp, and no medals to be awarded except those which the internees made themselves. When such souvenirs of internment do survive, and are passed down through families, often they pose more questions than answers, for "grandfather never spoke about it." Little wonder then, that for so long internment has been one of the untold stories of the First World War.

Ramsey Harbour Guard in 1915, comprised of National Reserve soldiers. Note the Boy Scouts who were possibly messengers. (PG 7493-3)

Chapter Four

Our Greatest Agony

Perhaps even more than internment, the First World War as endured by the domestic population remains one of the least researched aspects of the Manx war experience; and yet it could be argued that the impact of the war on society in the Isle of Man was more dramatic than in any other part of the British Isles. The effects of the conflict upon domestic life in Britain as a whole are well documented: the introduction of rationing and British Summer Time, mechanisation of agriculture, the attempts to control the licensed trade, and the massive increase in the role of women in the work place to name just a few. Political tensions were also exacerbated by the pressure of war; in the case of Ireland, this led to the complete fracture of relations with the Imperial government and political dislocation.

Whilst the Isle of Man undoubtedly shared much in common with its neighbours on either side of the Irish Sea, some aspects of its war experience were highly unusual and were brought about by its unique position within the British constitutional framework. Having stated that the impact of the war on the Isle of Man, politically and constitutionally, was greater and more sweeping certainly than that in England, one might even go further and argue that the Isle of Man as a modern state was created during the First World War. The conflict threw into sharper focus than ever before the ongoing constitutional problems which had troubled the Isle of Man since the institution of Lord Raglan as Lieutenant Governor in 1902. Prior to the war, the deeply conservative Raglan had used his position consistently to block legislation which would have led to legitimate and popular reforms. These proposed reforms closely paralleled measures being introduced at the same time by the Liberal Government in London. The war forced the issue in respect of reform and modernisation of Manx society – so much so that the Island almost tore itself apart – and Raglan was ultimately compelled to back down. Things however started quietly enough. With the war just a week old, Catherine Craine in rural Ballaugh commented in a diary entry of 13 August:

> Today the Captain of the Parish and John Kirjairg have been round collecting for the mother of our station porter and the wife of a man at Ballawhayne, both of whom will be very badly off with their bread winners away. No one has refused to give to them.
>
> Of late years .... the putting down of herring for winter stock has fallen very much out of fashion. Farm labourers and the poor people who once dined on potatoes and salt herring, four days out of seven, have outgrown such food, but this year people are buying in larger stocks again. "Aw, maybe thou'll be glad of a salt herring yet gal," I heard one man say. Maybe we will. It's a good thing that the harvest of the sea promises to be a plentiful one this year. [162]

She also recounts that the older people in the village were comparing notes on how the Crimean and Franco-Prussian wars (and even the American War of Independence) had affected the Island, in an effort to gauge what lay in store. One early effect of the war was the darkening of streets, perhaps not noticeable in the rural areas which would have been without public lighting anyway, but certainly more so in the towns. This blackout was not introduced as a precaution against air raids, because air power was in its infancy and no German aircraft yet had the range or speed to bomb the Isle of Man (though Zeppelins and Gotha bombers would attack London and other cities later in the war). This measure was introduced in the main to economise on coal, which produced town gas used for lighting the streets. As a result travellers late at night and early in the morning had to grope their way through an inky darkness.

There was a general shortage of coal across the British Isles in the First World War mainly due to the large numbers of miners who had enlisted in the army. However the situation was worse in the Isle of Man due to the fact that this fuel does not occur naturally, and there was reluctance on the part of ship owners to carry coal to the Island. In the early part of 1915 U-boats had accounted for several colliers lost whilst sailing out of Liverpool, and coal as a result was both scarcer and dearer. Newspapers implored readers to accept this as cheerfully as possible, and suggested going back to turf as an alternative fuel, though they acknowledged that this would have to be open to all and not just the Lord's tenants as had historically been the case. Coal on the Isle of Man was more closely controlled than in England during the First World War. All coal supplies, upon arrival in the Island, were immediately taken over by the Manx government. They were then distributed through coal merchants. Each Manx household was issued with coupons by the local authority, and one of these was surrendered to the coal merchant for each hundredweight of coal drawn.

It was not long before anti-German feelings began to swirl around the Manx 'chattering' classes. As was often the case in the British Isles at the time, these sentiments were misdirected, in this case towards a Douglas pork butcher named Peter Luft, who was alleged to have raised a German flag over his premises. Luft for his part protested vigorously that he was a 'Britisher' born on the Isle of Man. One of the instigators of the rumours against Luft, the well known artist John Holland, was eventually compelled to print an apology in several Manx newspapers:

> I ... have lately made certain statements that Peter Luft, of this town, butcher, is of German nationality, and that his sympathies are with the German cause, I wish to declare that I am now satisfied that such statements were false and to express my regret that I should have been the means of spreading such false reports. [163]

The *Isle of Man Examiner* noted that in the prevailing climate it was by no means a joke to call a Briton a German.

In the early days of the war, many men expressed a wish to form a corps for service in the Island, to be composed of those who, for one reason or another, were unable to join the active forces of the Crown, and who would practise drill and shooting. The formation of this body would not only set free younger men for more active duties, but it would itself be in a position to render valuable service in the Island in case of need. On 12 August 1914 the Lieutenant-Governor Lord Raglan authorised the formation of a National Reserve, to be termed The Loyal Manx Association, for the enrolment of such men. Guards were posted nightly over the Government Offices where the wireless station was located, and over the General Post Office at Douglas. The Loyal Manx Association undertook these duties, together with escorting prisoners of war between the harbour and the camp at Douglas. Those men who volunteered for this work were sworn in as special constables and were supplied with arms. In January 1915, the strength of the Loyal Manx Association stood at around 690 members across the Island. From then onwards the Loyal Manx Association provided a nightly guard for the prisoner of war camp at Douglas, which was additional to the regular camp guard. For a short time also, when enemy submarines in the Irish Sea first appeared, the Association provided guards for some of the harbours of the Island.

The loyalty and devotion to duty displayed by the members of the Loyal Manx Association were noted. From all parts of the Island, week after week, these volunteers, many of them quite old men, came to Douglas Camp to take their turn at guard duty. No matter the state of the weather or the time of the year, they arrived and performed their task. They received no pay, and, after a cold night

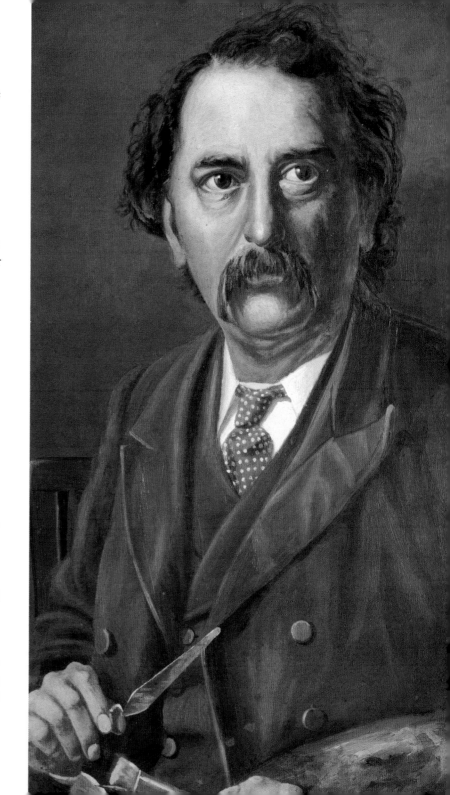

The artist John Holland, who subsequently apologised publicly for spreading anti-German rumours about Douglas pork butcher Peter Luft. (L21819)

This Terrible Ordeal

guarding prisoners of war, would pursue their daily occupations. The Association comprised all classes and there were included in it lawyers, farmers, managers, clerks, and others all working shoulder to shoulder for the war effort. It was a monotonous duty and without glory, but it was loyally performed.

In May 1915, the Loyal Manx Association was formed into the Loyal Manx Volunteer Corps, and affiliated to the Central Association of Volunteer Training Corps. As the Corps undertook to continue to perform guard duty at Douglas prisoner of war camp, 300 of its members were clothed in the standard uniform for Volunteer Corps, at Government expense. Members of the corps were required to give an undertaking that they would continue during the period of the war to perform guard duties over prisoners of war (unless relieved from their obligation by the Commandant) and such other duties as might be required of them, provided such duties did not interfere with their livelihood.

From late 1914 appeals began in Manx newspapers for funds to support destitute Belgians, Leigh Goldie-Taubman asking the Island's people to:

> ...give a penny a week towards the Belgians ... even the poorest hardly feeling this small sum ... [164]

From January 1915 onwards Belgian refugees, who had fled their homes in advance of the German invasion of their country, began to actually arrive in the Isle of Man. Collections were taken in parish churches, and whist

Fundraising for Belgian refugees at the White House, Kirk Michael. (PG 10524)

drives and other charitable events took place to raise funds for their upkeep. The refugee families were distributed throughout the Island with some at Jurby and Bride. A home for Belgians was set up in Ramsey, and the proceeds from a performance in the town by the Peel Players (organised by Sophia Morrison and the Manx Language Society) were donated to their cause. There was deep gratitude from the refugees themselves for all that the Manx had done for them, one Lieutenant Messagie of the Belgian artillery writing to the Ballaugh Belgian Refugee Committee:

> It is with heart overflowing with gratitude I write these few words to thank you for the warm welcome and cordiality with which you received me during my stay in your country, and the way in which you have shown hospitality to my wife and her family, for I wish to say that it is through your kindness that they do not suffer much during their exile. [165]

However radical journalist 'Walter C' in the *Examiner* questioned the prevailing wisdom, writing:

> Long lists of presidents, vice presidents, secretaries, treasurers, committees, subscribers and patrons [are] all interested in giving a good time to a handful of Belgian refugees, while tons of misery and anxieties beset daily our own people. But then Belgian refugees are fashionable – our own poor are ever with us. Refugees are so interesting you know; not so tiresome as our own destitute. [166]

The effect of the war was immediately felt in the economy of the Island, in particular in the visiting industry upon which the requisitioning of the Isle of Man Steam Packet Company fleet had a devastating effect. A letter to the *Examiner* in February 1915 was hopeful that the season that year would not be as bad as predicted. The author stated that the IOMSPCo would surely hire other steamers, and continued:

> *Let us remember that all the continental resorts are closed and this being so, we should have a fairly good season* [167]

By the end of 1915 however it was openly acknowledged that the industry was in crisis, the same newspaper describing visitors to the Island as akin to shells for the army – in both cases vital, but in short supply that year. The same article observed that the rival resorts of Blackpool and Lytham St Annes were booming, so there were still people taking holidays in spite of the war.

In the summer of 1913, three boats had left Liverpool for Douglas daily and a relief boat often had also to be sent. On Saturdays in August there had been six sailings per day to the Isle of Man and each was packed. It was not uncommon for 4000 visitors to sail each day and for 7500 to arrive on Saturdays. By contrast, in wartime there was only one boat a day from Liverpool and services from Fleetwood, Whitehaven and Glasgow had been suspended altogether. On average only 400 visitors per day were arriving during the summer of 1915. In addition to the reduction in steamer capacity, two other problems beset the Isle of Man. One was the submarine peril – the fear of U-boats operating in the Irish Sea was understandably deterring visitors from making a sea journey even if shipping was available. The second

problem was the withdrawal of cheap railway bookings (presumably because so many of the UK railways were engaged on government work) which made access to the ports from the industrial towns expensive.

The *Examiner* estimated that 90% of householders on the Isle of Man depended upon what they could make out of summer visitors to keep them alive in winter; many, saddled with debts taken on in order to acquire or improve their premises in times of prosperity, simply could not survive. Predictably, requests for help made to Lord Raglan fell upon deaf ears. This economic pressure caused by the war quickly began to make itself felt upon the Island's constitutional framework. Even as early as 6 August 1914 Catherine Craine reported on one malcontent, a sadly unnamed Ballaugh hedge trimmer, who she states was:

> *Of the opinion that "The sooner the Germans win, the better," and he "Hopes they will win, as wages are better and food is cheaper in Germany than here and our government doesn't look after the people at all."* [168]

By 1915 suggestions were being made in some quarters that the Island should seek annexation, and link up with Lancashire. It was noted that the Isle of Man had no direct taxation, only indirect taxation on foodstuffs and tobacco, the burden of which fell disproportionately upon the poor rather than the rich. It was also noted that the Manx were debarred from English benefits such as old age pensions, National Insurance and so on. The question had already arisen in local newspapers as to what would be the position and status of Manx soldiers after the war. Would they still be treated as English citizens, or transferred back to their home government, and in the case of old age pensions, be told that the revenue was too poor to be able to afford it?

It was the collapse of the tourist industry, upon which so many Manx people depended for their livelihood, which led to a vociferous renewal of the pre-war castigation directed against Tynwald and Raglan. In September 1915 there was severe criticism of the Lieutenant Governor from Douglas Corporation. The local boards had asked Tynwald for relief, because they could not meet their own financial obligations if their rate payers were unable to pay them. They argued that certain sections of their population were in distress through no fault of their own, but the towns had been rebuffed by Raglan, who told them to raise the rates instead! Douglas in particular was incensed at being told to cut its coat according to its cloth. Douglas Corporation had fixed charges which it had to meet, and when the crash came, Douglas had stepped in to provide relief for its boarding house keepers, because the government would not do it. Alderman Cowin spoke for many when he said that,

Douglas has always been regarded as the milch cow of the country, but they had stopped all the cow's fodder with the result that the milk was no longer flowing into the pails and the farmer – the Governor – now sees £27,000 of it short. He (the Governor) now thought that the cow should give milk

George Henry Fitzroy Somerset, Lord Raglan. As Lieutenant Governor of the Isle of Man he was deeply unpopular, yet there was no democratic method by which the Manx people could remove him. (PG 0625)

without getting fodder, and said that the cow which could not give milk without fodder was a poor kind of cow. [169]

There was no doubting the patriotism of the vast majority of Manx people. They were overwhelmingly in support of Britain's cause. Every night at the Grand Theatre Picturedrome on Victoria Street a film called the *Douglas Roll of Honour* was shown. It comprised photographs of Manx soldiers who had been killed and others who were still serving at the front, and it drew warm rounds of applause from every corner of the house. In Castletown, Queen Street could reasonably lay claim to being the most patriotic community in the British Isles, because at the height of the war no less than forty-four men from this little row of cottages had joined up. Sophia Morrison, writing in March 1915, commented:

> *At the present time Manx hearts are especially drawn together in the thought of the gallantry of all the fine Manxmen who are fighting for us by land & sea. May all of [them] come safely through this terrible ordeal, & may Peace soon bless us.* [170]

But the evident unfairness of the prevailing situation was threatening to cause social divisions and political tensions to worsen further. In September 1915 at a public meeting in Douglas there was open anger not just towards the Manx government but also towards the British government. It had cut off the Island's livelihood and was now refusing to do anything to assist it, whilst at the same time piling up debts upon the Island. Speaker after speaker stressed the patriotism of the Isle of Man – it had after all sent thousands of its sons to defend the empire - but what was

happening at home was clearly unreasonable.

In September 1915 the rate collector reported to the Onchan Commissioners that month that rates were down on the previous year. This in part was due to the attractions on Onchan Head being closed for the duration of the war, but worryingly he also reported that there had been much agitation and disturbance in the lower part of Onchan from many people who could actually afford to pay the rates, but had outright refused. In December 1915, Samuel Norris, a journalist and printer formed the War Rights Union to represent those boarding-house keepers and others dependent for livelihood upon holiday-makers, and who were now in financial distress. That month, during the north Douglas by-election, there was much criticism of the Lieutenant Governor, in particular his use of non-Manxmen in key jobs – probably a jibe at Bertram Sargeaunt, the Government Secretary, who was an English civil servant. It was also said that the House of Keys was weak because too many of its members were in the pocket of the Lieutenant Governor. That same month, £25,000 was voted by Tynwald for the relief of distress caused by the war, but it was immediately condemned as not enough.

The answer was some form of direct taxation, but Raglan was adamant that income tax could not be levied until April 1916 at the earliest, so in the meantime, to try to plug the shortfall in the public finances, duty on sugar and tobacco were raised, hitting the poor harder than the rich. The constitutional crisis deepened, with the elected members of the House of Keys, men like Ambrose Qualtrough, T.H.Quine, J.Qualtrough, T.H.Cormode and W.F.Cowell directly opposed to the increase in indirect taxation, and at loggerheads with the un-elected

Samuel Norris, the journalist who defied the Lieutenant Governor. "In the Isle of Man," he said, "Raglan was Caesar." (M 08164)

Licutenant Governor. Christopher Shimmin of Peel, a stonemason by trade, but also a radical socialist playwright, wrote in 1916:

> ... the Lieutenant Governor has succeeded to all the power and prerogative of the ancient kings and lords. He has power of veto on all expenditure. He summons and dismisses Keys, Council and Tynwald at his own sweet will. His approval is necessary on all laws and taxation ... He has infinitely more power in the Isle of Man than King George has in England. The House of Keys, the so-called representatives of the Manx people, have little power ... This is Manx Home Rule. Unfortunately the majority of the members of the House of Keys represent land and property rather than the physical and moral welfare of the men, women and children of Man.
>
> The workers, the labouring men and women, are penalised for being Manx. For them only, of all the rest of the British Islands, there is no attempt at modern social legislation. In Manxland there is no state insurance, no workmen's compensation, no factory laws, and for the aged worker, when poor and feebly tottering to the grave, no old age pension. Rightly has the Isle of Man been called "A paradise for the rich but a purgatory for the poor."
>
> The Manx working men are losing faith in the present one-sided legislation, and are asking for annexation, so as to share in the juster British laws. In opposition there is strong national sentiment, anxious to preserve what still remains of our nationality.
>
> If this patriotic sentiment is true and real it will develop along modern progressive political lines. Sentimentality alone will not prevent annexation, it must interest itself in the affairs of the people, and become constructive and economic, or the present generation may see the extinction of the "Little Manx Nation." [171]

The annexation debate rumbled on, in spite of Raglan's attempts to pour cold water on the idea. One correspondent in the *Isle of Man Examiner* wrote:

Lord Raglan some time ago wakened up sufficiently to utter a feeble protest against the desire for annexation. "No sane ratepayer," he said in effect, "would want annexation if he but knew the heavy addition to his rates which annexation involves" [but] it was an absolute distortion of the truth to say that annexation would bring higher rates ... There is no reason for any such fear. Annexation does not mean the surrender of our autonomy in local government, but the surrender of our very doubtful autonomy in national government. [172]

There is no doubt from the tone of letters such as this and others like it that Raglan was growing more unpopular by the day. The infamous Tynwald Day of 1916 saw public resentment against him boil over. Samuel Norris, in *Manx Memories and Movements*, described the scene:

Tynwald Day in 1916 dawned in all the glory of a mid-summer holiday. Only once during the previous 25 years had rain fallen during the annual ceremony of promulgation; this day was no exception to the rule, but in most other respects July 5th 1916, the 'Manx Day of Independence' was memorable for scenes and incidents which have probably had no parallel in the Island's history and are, perhaps, never to be seen again... When the Peel fishermen, in 1880, made their protest against the Governor's policy of taxing their fishing boats without providing harbour accommodation, they received Governor Loch as he arrived at St. John's between their silent lines, and cheered him as he entered and left their ranks. The leaders of the demonstration in 1916 did not follow that or any other precedent. The main contingent

in three horse-drawn 'roundabouts', holding about ten each, left Douglas at an early hour and took up positions in the field adjoining the path from the church to the Hill - using the vehicles as platforms, one near the church, one about mid-way, and one near the Hill.

From each of the three platforms large cards were displayed... bearing the following words in large type and red ink:

WE WANT A NEW GOVERNOR
TAXATION OF WEALTH
NO FOOD TAXES
REVENUE FROM THE CAMPS FOR WAR
DISTRESS
REDRESS, RETRENCHMENT AND REFORM! [173]

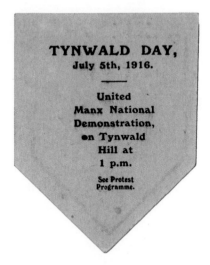

A badge worn at the anti-Raglan protest at Tynwald, 1916. R.M.G. stood for Raglan Must Go. (M 07136)

As well as shouted demands for reform there was also a considerable amount of booing and hooting. The chorus of disapproval grew in intensity as the procession made its way along the path to Tynwald Hill. Any cheers were completely drowned by groans. Lord Raglan was apparently unswayed by the hostile crowds; but more than verbal abuse was hurled. A few moments later he was 'sodded' by a clump of grass thrown from the crowd – an extraordinary incident but a measure of his deep unpopularity amongst ordinary people. The demonstrations on Tynwald Day 1916 were followed by the presentation of more peaceful resolutions in 1917, perhaps due to the hard line stance taken by the courts in dealing with Samuel Norris. Norris was sent to gaol for contempt of court, in hindering and obstructing the sale of the goods of those who had defaulted on their rate arrears. He almost immediately petitioned the Home Secretary Herbert Samuel for release. Samuel however, declined to interfere with what he saw as the prerogative of the Lieutenant-Governor, and Norris, after undergoing twenty-eight days' imprisonment, was forced to apologise for his contempt. In the Isle of Man, Norris declared, Raglan was Caesar.

The ongoing debate over annexation was now splitting the Manx people along class lines. By 1916 many of the working class were in favour of abandoning the Island's independence and joining with England. To them, home rule offered none of the benefits of direct rule, along with a host of disadvantages. It was argued that only the landed interest and professional classes were in favour of the status quo, but this was not wholly true, as the debate also split the Manx along nationalist lines; Sophia Morrison in August 1916 wrote:

...the Island is seething with excitement over the questions of Annexation and Reform. I feel strongly that [we] should have something to say on the subject. We are a national society and we should speak out against annexation. We of the Manx Society who for the last 20 years have worked for Manx Nationalism – music, language, folk life ... sentiment - whilst agreeing that the Insular Government needs reforming, do not see that that is a sufficient reason for the adoption of a course that would end in the destruction of the Manx national existence – the absorption of the Island into an English county. These rabid people certainly do not speak on behalf of the Manx people in total. [174]

None the less, at a public meeting in Peel, it was wryly observed that when the Imperial Government was handing something out, for example old age pensions, state insurance or workmens' compensation, the Isle of Man was not included. When the Imperial Government wanted something, then it was!

Perhaps the greatest threat to the cohesion of the political system – and indeed of society as a whole – in the Isle of Man was presented by the controversy over conscription. The Military Service Act was passed by the Westminster parliament in January 1916 making all fit males of military age in England, Scotland and Wales liable for call up into the armed forces. Questions were immediately raised as to what the position of the Isle of Man was in relation to the Act. Some members of the House of Keys argued that the Island was not represented in the Imperial Parliament, therefore the Act did not apply. Others argued that as the Manx are the subjects of the Crown, the Crown may call upon them at a time of crisis, and in effect the Isle of Man already had a form of conscription through its ancient militia acts. The net result was a fierce debate on the constitutional position of the Island; many stated that the position of the Isle of Man was no different from that of Australia and Canada, which had autonomy from the Westminster government, but it was hard to argue with those who questioned what Manx home rule was worth, if Ireland was excluded from conscription but the Isle of Man was not. In the event, the extension of the Military Service Act to the Isle of Man was not imposed, but voted for by the House of Keys, leading to a strong reaction from workers' leaders that, as old men it was not their own liberty that they were voting away but that of others.

There were continuing references to Ireland during the months which followed; it was hard to avoid the irony of the situation in that Ireland was supposedly subject to direct rule from Westminster and thus in an inferior position to the Isle of Man, yet it had received thousands of pounds in subsidies from the British Government, which the Isle of Man had not, and had been exempted from conscription because that government did not believe that it could force the Irish to fight. In March 1918, Joseph Qualtrough in Tynwald stated:

> We in the Isle of Man are drained almost to the last man. But what have the [British] Government done with Ireland? [175]

This sense of indignation and injustice united both the radical union leader William Clucas, and the conservative journalist 'Junius Junior', the latter comparing the temperament of the Isle of Man unfavourably with that of Ireland:

> There is no compulsion on Irishmen to join the army ... the Irish would not have it and the British government dare not force it on them. I do not say it was forced on the Isle of Man; but it would have been forced on us if we had not accepted it because we have no teeth and claws as Ireland has... [176]

Clucas for his part declared that he was:

> In favour of some drastic measures. Ireland is a country worth imitating in several respects. [177]

One effect of conscription was to force into public view those who for political, religious or other reasons could not support British involvement in the war. The Military Service Act allowed the right of appeal for exemption on grounds of conscientious objection as well as on grounds of ill health or economic hardship, or indeed if one's occupation was of vital importance to the war effort. When a man failed to substantiate his claim at a Local Appeal Tribunal (where the objector had to overcome the weight of both public opinion and the influence of the military representative) if he continued in his objection he was arrested and handed over to the military authorities. The stance of conscientious objectors (COs) in the Great War was against the overwhelming flow of public opinion at the time. There was much bitterness over their perceived lack of 'patriotism' and they experienced open hostility from some sections of society. Nevertheless, it sometimes requires considerable courage to stand up for ones beliefs in such circumstances. The stance of the British government in the Great War was less than sympathetic towards these men, particularly the so called 'absolutists' who would brook no compromise with the military authorities. These men held out for absolute exemption, and would work neither in hospitals nor on farms. Most COs who failed in their appeal were drafted into the Non-Combatant Corps (NCC). Once in the army, refusal to obey orders would result in a court martial. In 1916 a party from the NCC were shipped to France where their refusal to obey orders led to their being sentenced to death, a sentence later commuted to ten years' imprisonment.

Across Britain as a whole some 16,000 men claimed some form of conscientious objection, of whom over 6,000 men resisted the Military Service Acts and 843 men spent two years in prison as a result of their convictions. In acknowledging the courage of such men in facing such consequences, we must also be aware that public opinion was overwhelmingly out of sympathy with them. A number of such men of conscience were to be found on the Isle of Man in the Great War. One of them was Elijah Oliver, clerk and rate collector to the Education Authority of Lonan, and agent of the Liverpool, London and Globe Insurance Company. A member of a staunch Primitive Methodist family from Agneash, Oliver was called up for military service in May 1916, and claimed conscientious objection on religious grounds. He appeared before a tribunal and made an eloquent statement of his position, stating that war was organised murder, and he was ready to endure any penalty, privation or suffering – even to death itself – than to take part in causing human suffering directly or indirectly. The love of his heart bade him to assist rather than destroy even the so-called enemy.

In a subsequent letter to the *Isle of Man Examiner* he claimed that the frequent interruptions to which he was subjected made it impossible for him to put a reasoned case forward. He said that he was opposed to ambulance work because:

> *The presence on the battlefield of extensive services for the relief of suffering helped to smooth over the horrors of the scene in the eyes of the public, which in its turn, had an appreciable effect upon recruiting, as, viewed in that light, war did not appear to be altogether bad. But if there was no attempt to relieve suffering, possible voluntary recruits would have considered the fact, and some would not have gone at all. The same consideration would have made conscription much less welcome. So, even in that sense, Red Cross work helps to promote and to develop the war in no small measure.*
>
> *Secondly, as the soldier goes forth to battle, the very knowledge that behind the firing line there are hundreds of doctors and thousands of nurses, encourages him to take the risk of getting wounded, thus nerving him to bring about far greater execution.*
>
> *Thirdly, all ministrations to the lightly wounded, only enables them more quickly to get back to the firing line, to kill more people. So ambulance work on the battlefield is a most valuable agent in helping to carry on the war … My attitude, as now defined, does not mean that I am opposed to the relief of suffering , for I would do anything within my power, night or day, to stop or alleviate it –*

that is, in my private capacity and not as a unit of a war organisation. [178]

Nevertheless he was arrested and incarcerated in Victoria Road prison, Douglas. Two days later, he was transferred to Liverpool, but refusing to co-operate with the military authorities in any way had to be carried to the steamer strapped to a stretcher. As he was loaded aboard he was jeered and booed by the local population. The *Ramsey Courier* reported that:

About five minutes to nine this morning the crowd who were down at the Victoria Pier, Douglas seeing the boat off were amazed by the spectacle of a small posse of soldiers wheeling a handcart, on which lay a man strapped on a stretcher. It was Elijah Oliver, late clerk to the Lonan School Board, who has added to his role of 'Conscientious Objector' that of 'passive resister'. Oliver was charged before the High Bailiff of Douglas yesterday with being a deserter from military service, and was fined 40s and remanded to gaol for a military escort to take him to his regimental headquarters. He refused to go with the escort unless he was physically 'fetched' ... When the escort halted the cart at the top of the steps leading to the gangway, and were about to unstrap him, he refused to go down the steps, and the escort had to leave him on the stretcher and carry him aboard the ship. There however he consented to stand upon his feet and the next minute he was seen smiling at the crowd and endeavouring to engage his guards in conversation. As the boat moved off, he waved his handkerchief to the crowd and then resumed conversation with an acquaintance aboard the boat. There was very little

demonstration, the crowd displaying contemptuous amusement rather than hostility. One knot of women who were seeing soldier sons and sailor husbands off were not so tolerant. They shouted derisively "Thou shalt not kill!" and "Coward!" and expressed their indignation freely amongst each other, "Yes", said one, "my husband has seen 27 years service and has to go on for the sake of that creature," "We are to give up everything," responded another, "to the last child in the house, but that coward is to get off." [179]

Oliver was sent to Kinmel Camp in North Wales, the depot of the Non-Combatant Corps, where he was tried by court martial for refusing to obey military orders. Whilst maintaining his stance as an objector to military service on religious grounds, he argued that technically the army had no right to issue orders to him at all, stating:

Gentlemen, I contend that my call to join the forces was irregular and illegal. If you have a copy of my notice to report for service, you will see that the notice calls me up under the Military Service Act, 1916. Being a citizen of the Isle of Man, I was not amenable to that Act, but to the Military Service (Isle of Man) Act 1916, which is the English Act altered and adapted as to apply to the Isle of Man ... not having been called up under the proper act, no person had any right to give me any military orders until I was called up in the proper way. [180]

Oliver went on to detail his position in regard to his conscientious objection, referring to his role as a lay preacher, and handed over three testimonials from local clergy. None of this cut much ice with the court martial however, and Oliver was sentenced to two years in Wakefield Prison. We know a little of Oliver's later war experiences, and something of what underscored his stance, from letters which he wrote to the newspapers on the Isle of Man. One in the *Isle of Man Examiner* of 12 May 1917 read:

> *... perhaps you will allow me to state the facts. I am not a free man. I live at Wakefield Prison, which, in consideration of the feelings of conscientious objectors, is now called a work centre. I am under sentence of two years imprisonment with hard labour, which sentence is still running on, and does not expire until 1ˢᵗ March, 1918. My employment is in the prison hospital, where our patients are conscientious objectors only, and for whom, of course, I am willing to do anything. In this place alone I have seen at least three who will be called upon to make the supreme sacrifice in the struggle for freedom of conscience. A number of others (not patients) were sentenced to death but have now got ten years imprisonment instead, and yet we are not downhearted, but shall go right through to the end.* [181]

Oliver objected to the war on religious grounds but there were others who based their objections on political conviction. One such was Harold Lilley, an unemployed grocer's assistant of Castletown. Lilley stated that he was not religious, but was agnostic. He told a tribunal that he was an International Socialist, and objected to war on moral, social and humanitarian grounds, stating:

> *...as a humanitarian ... I believe in the sanctity of personal life and individuality, and I deny the right of any Government to compel me to kill my brother man.* [182]

Whilst in a letter to a newspaper he highlighted the treatment that conscientious objectors could expect:

> *... the right of freedom of conscience ... in times of war inevitably becomes a subject*

Harold Lilley, a Socialist conscientious objector from Castletown, who was imprisoned for refusing to join the army. (MS 12840)

for ridicule and misrepresentation. Such as espouse such a cause and hold such convictions are deemed to be actuated by no other motive but cowardice, and a desire to shirk the sacrifices demanded of others [but] the sacrifice to a sensitive and highly-strung disposition is more than they can ever realise. They are held up to public ridicule and contempt, have to bear the bitter knowledge of the estrangement of friends and loved ones ... The International Socialist and humanitarian who objects to warfare is actuated by the same motive as the soldier. They both desire to prevent the atrocities which are the usual concomitants of warfare. The Internationalist seeks to eliminate the causes which make war possible, so that the effort at prevention by the soldier shall never be needed. [183]

Across Britain as a whole, political appeals were outnumbered by those based on religious belief by as much as three to one, and in the Isle of Man the ratio seems to have been even higher. Political objectors as a rule received scant recognition from tribunals, and Lilley's case was no exception. He would however have undoubtedly derived moral support from the stance of a fellow Castletonian, James Ernest Radcliffe of Athol Terrace, who stated both religious and political objections to military service. Radcliffe had worked in a mine in Montana before the war, where he had formed friendships with citizens of what were now considered enemy countries – Germans, Austrians and Bulgarians. He believed that Internationalism was a far superior creed to mere nationalism, and he stated that war was inconsistent with the teachings of Christ. Asked if he would undertake RAMC work, Radcliffe stated that he

could not distinguish between fighting and assisting those who fought. When he was asked what work of national importance he was prepared to do, he stated that he would help a farmer who was shorthanded, but not if that meant releasing another man for the army. He must however have accepted some form of compromise, because Elijah Oliver and Harold Lilley were apparently the only two absolutists among the Manx COs; the latter also spent two years in prison as a result of his stance against conscription.

Quakers, Seventh Day Adventists and Plymouth Brethren were all pacifist sects. William Clucas Hardy was a Manx member of the Plymouth Brethren, and was called up in 1916. He also elected to serve with the Non-Combatant Corps. The war however cost him his life as surely as if he had died on a battlefield, for he contracted a fatal case of measles in an army camp in 1917.

The debate on conscientious objection raged in the newspapers of the Isle of Man as earnestly as in any other part of the British Isles. A few people could see the paradox that if the country did not uphold the right of these men to dissent from the generally held view of the war, then what grounds did it have to say it was fighting in the cause of personal freedom. To crush the conscientious objectors would be to give away any claim to the moral high ground over Germany, and even the Military Service Act itself allowed provision for the existence of conscientious objectors. Most others however had no truck with these perceived shirkers whatsoever. The conscientious objectors were deeply unpopular. In the view of one member of the Island's most celebrated literary family, W.Ralph Hall Caine, published in the *Isle of Man Examiner*:

The so-called conscientious objector is lacking in either sense or imagination – the sense to see that all peace is founded on our capacity for war and the imagination sufficient to realise that nowhere in the world is the non-fighter tolerated. Why, even the policeman in the street may at any moment call upon me in the King's name to help him against any murderous ruffian, and require me to risk my life in the interests of public security and peace.

No conscientious objector is entitled to the protection of force – directly expressed or merely implied – unless he is willing to contribute his quota of service. The logic of that fact is irresistible. But the conscientious objector says, "I object."

...The "soft sams" have no foothold anywhere, and the view of the great majority of people that I meet is that "conscience" is merely an expression of decadence. [184]

Archdeacon John Kewley also held robust views on this, though he appears to have objected to all who sought exemption on whatever grounds. Writing from Andreas Rectory on 16 June 1917 to the sister of a deceased soldier he states:

We are deeply grieved to learn the sad news conveyed by your letter received tonight. We know how deeply you will feel the loss of brave John, but you have the comfort of knowing that he died at the post of duty, that he laid down his life for his friends and his country. This is the greatest honour any man can have.

In your sorrow you will feel justly proud of him, as we all feel proud, for he has conferred honour on the family.

His memory will remain ever sweet and I am sure that you would rather have him entered his well earned eternal rest in this way than to have him with you as a shirker and coward escaping his duty like some I am sorry to say in the Isle of Man who will be despised to the end of their days. [185]

One MHK, in a debate about alcohol licensing, risked re-opening old divisions by attributing the existence of the 'soft sams' to excessive tea drinking – clearly linking the anti-conscription movement with the temperance crusade, which was so prevalent among the strong Manx Methodist community, and which had previously clashed with the licensed trade. A Methodist minister went even further, and earned himself three months imprisonment in Victoria Road prison for language likely to inhibit recruiting; the exact text of what the Reverend George Peet, a circuit minister stationed in Peel, had said in a sermon to a congregation in Castletown varied from newspaper to newspaper, but broadly he stated that he would rather go to hell with the conscientious objectors (who had more religion in their little fingers than some soldiers had in their entire body) than go to heaven with the womanising, drinking and profane soldiery that he had encountered in Peel. He countered the belief that soldiers who died on the battlefield would automatically go to heaven in spite of their previous sins, and stated that he hoped a lot more would end up on the German barbed wire if it jolted people at home out of their sinful ways. This was too much for the Manx authorities and Peet found himself before the High Bailiff. His congregation were broadly supportive of him and his motives, although they repudiated what he had said. One correspondent, Essie Callister, in the *Peel City Guardian*, was more scathing and wrote in an open letter:

Dear Mr Peet, After listening to your views on the COs this morning, I feel compelled to write to you to let you know that although you fire away ad lib from the pulpit, your congregation have still the conscience to think and act according to their own light. How is it you can find nothing to admire about the 'Tommy'? You have nothing for him but blame. According to you he has not a redeeming feature. You invariably refer to him as a 'drunken brute.' Where do the Conscientious Objectors come in? Are they all teetotal? I think not.

One should have more sympathy for them if true to their convictions, they came forward and said "We are cowards, we cannot fight." Then we would pity them as we could helpless children … You praise the seeming martyrdom of these 'cowards only' – the privations they endure – saying nothing of the thousands of the same crowd who revel in freedom of movement, able to go to their homes each night and dine in luxury … Are we to sit in silence and listen to these men being praised and presented with the 'flower of a blameless life' while our beloved brother soldiers and sailors are spilling their blood to save the hides of such as these? …. You say these COs are the most deeply religious men of our day – the finest, most clever and most good. Have not the flower of all the world not donned the khaki and blue in this most terrible war for Right; … If the 'Conchys' think that they are privileged to lie quiet and let the evil Hun ride unmolested through our country, devastating and doing just as they please …You admire the CO for seemingly having the courage of his convictions. When will you learn that it is better at times to smother one's conscience in order to pursue one's duty, as our Saviour did when he was nailed to the cross, although he prayed that if it was possible this "cup might pass" from him He said "Father, not my will, but Thine be done."[186]

The full extent of conscientious objection on the Isle of Man demands further investigation. However cursory examination of the tribunals for exemptions from military service in Douglas in 1917 reveal that the overwhelming majority of requests were made on the grounds of the individual's role in agriculture or industry rather than on grounds of conscience. Indeed, these two areas of the economy would become the major battlegrounds of the home front during the second half of the war.

In both sectors, ordinary workers were feeling the pressures of soaring costs of living. The rises in duty on sugar and tobacco proposed by Lord Raglan occurred against a background of living costs that were already rising. The effect of the war on prices was almost immediate – everything went up. As early as February 1915 a meeting of Peel Commissioners noted that the war was pushing up the price of basic commodities, and that the poor were suffering disproportionately as a result. In October 1915 it was reported that bread prices were soaring above pre-war levels, and flour was fetching between thirteen and fifteen shillings a sack more than it had done in 1913. A sixty year old Jurby farmer's widow, Eleanor Callister, recorded in a journal the steady increases in prices of daily commodities such as butter, oats and coal, adding:

Everything else dear in proportion through this great war. [187]

Indeed she was probably among the ones who suffered most from the rise in prices, those on fixed incomes. Some idea of the hardship now being felt on the home front comes from union leader Alfred Teare, who wrote in his memoirs that by 1917, the cost of living on the Isle of Man had risen 78% above what it had been in 1914. At the same time the only increase in wages for most

Alfred Teare, the founder of a branch of the Workers' Union on the Isle of Man. By 1918 he was 'the most powerful man' on the Island. (PG 3280)

workers had been a paltry shilling a week, taking the pre-war average wage of £1 a week up to twenty-one shillings a week, or an increase of just 5%.

As this was happening, there was actually a labour shortage on the Isle of Man; in January 1915 Ramsey Town Commissioners reported that the town surveyor had difficulty in obtaining men for harbour work, there was not a single able-bodied man on the books of the Poor Law Guardians, and employment in the building and related trades was at its usual level. The chief reason that wages had not kept up, in circumstances of rising prices and a shortage of labour, was the glaring absence of unionisation in the Manx workforce. Teare would do much to change this when he began a branch of the Workers' Union in the Island in 1917. The Workers' Union had been founded in England in 1889 specifically to bring together the mass of unskilled workers into a general union, the strength of which would lie in the sheer weight of its numbers. It was the first general union to be nationally recognised, and its leaders were among the union chiefs who met munitions minister David Lloyd George at the Treasury Conference in March 1915, at which the British Government had tried to tie the unions more firmly into the war effort by offering various concessions. The Workers' Union had a number of features which meant it would be successful in the Isle of Man during the First World War. As its historian Richard Hyman has written,

> *Its organising zeal often reached groups of workers who possessed none of the bargaining power of inherent solidarity of a factory proletariat ... The most striking development was in the Isle of Man ... a group of Douglas workers led by Alf Teare, a printing worker, opened a branch of the union*

Councillor George Titt, of Manchester. A leading figure in the Workers' Union, he played a significant role in unionising the Manx workforce. (Courtesy of Manchester City Council)

and by the end of 1918 it held well over a thousand members; branches had also been formed elsewhere on the Island and all local industries were covered. [188]

The structure of the union was more flexible than others, making it easier to open new districts or appoint new organisers, and by contrast with its more cautious rivals, the Workers' Union was committed to expansion, believing that there was no section of the working class which was not capable of unionisation. Thus it was that Manchester councillor George Titt, a divisional organiser of the Workers' Union, became involved with the setting up of branches on the Isle of Man. He himself noted in the union minute book that the Island was particularly suited to the Workers' Union model because there was:

No industry ... of sufficiently large dimension to warrant the formation of sectional unions. [189]

Such Manx industry as existed was mobilised for war work much like that in England; in addition to Gelling's foundry in Douglas, which during the war was turned over to shell production (and which, Bertram Sargeaunt tells us, ran day and night) Quiggin's rope works, also in Douglas, supplied hawsers to the Admiralty. Prior to the First World War, the most significant Manx industry was undoubtedly the lead and zinc mine at Laxey, and during the war its output must have become of crucial importance due to the massive increase in output of armaments and munitions in the UK. The authentic voice of the Laxey miner in the First World War comes from Bobby Kelly, interviewed in 1980 about his memories of working conditions. Kelly worked for just one year on the arduous Washing Floors, before being promoted, firstly to work on the steam engines 'Ant' and 'Bee'. This to him was heaven – twelve shillings a week, and a change to shift working of only eight hours per day. Later he moved on to underground working:

> *I got on a pitch with a lot of older men than me ... and I was the young fellow, and I remember I used to do all the blasting for them, because I was the youngest of the thing, you know, and when you were, what you call sinking a sump .. you'd be down there, lighting your fuses, maybe six fuses at a time with your candle, and the way you fired your thing in them days was you split the point of your fuse and you stuck a little bit of dynamite in it, in each one, and then you lit your longest fuse first, and went round on them all like that. These fellows on top would know how much time you had taken, and they'd shout, "Come on, come on." Then you'd have to put one leg in the tub, and hold to the chain till they wound you up to get to the top.* [190]

The reality of life for miners at this time was that it was dangerous and harsh, with little in the way of social security aside from that which they paid for themselves, through their Oddfellows or Rechabite lodges. Kelly continues:

> *I remember the day I got hurt ... there was a chap in the mines the [previous] night, and he broke his leg, and he got brought out. This day, I had a feeling, I didn't want to go to work ... Anyway, I went, but I weren't long at work till I was brought up in the dead box .. I just went down in this hole, when a lump of rock slipped off the hanging, and fell and caught me leg ... Well I was off, oh I was off for months, and the Captain of the Mines come to see me*

> *and he said, "You know Robert," he said, "We can't give you no compensation. Can't give you anything." He said, "You're a member of that club," and he said, "that'll have to keep you."* [191]

In 1914 a significant number of Laxey miners had joined the Colours. By 1917 however, grumblings of discontent were growing among the remaining workforce over the question of wages, in the face of escalating living costs. This was a particular grievance in view of the fact that wartime demand for metals had now (temporarily as it turned out) halted the slide in the fortunes of the company, which during the war paid its first dividend to its shareholders for some years. This upturn in fortunes came despite the fact that production was actually down as a result of the war. Captain John Roberts of the Laxey Mine appeared before a tribunal in 1918 to argue against the compulsory enlistment of eight of his men who had been called up for military service. Roberts stated that hitherto the company had done all it could to encourage men to enlist, and seventy-five of its employees were serving in the army, the navy or on munitions work. He stated that before the war 215 men were employed in the mine. Now that figure was about 160. Roberts further stated that the production of lead, zinc and copper in 1914 was 1937 tons, and that in 1917 it was 1043 tons, the difference being purely down to the reduction in manpower experienced by the mine and not by any depletion of the richness of the seam [192]. The profits however were not trickling downwards. One correspondent in the *Isle of Man Times* of 7 April 1917 wrote:

> *According to your report of a recent meeting of the Laxey Village Commissioners a motion was carried unanimously*

Bobby Kelly, of Laxey. He worked as a lead miner in the Great Laxey mine throughout the First World War. (Courtesy of Stuart Kelly)

to consider the wages paid to clerk and out of doors manager on account of the great advance in the cost of living. The manager and secretary of the Laxey Mines are commissioners and both were present. It would be very interesting to know how both gentlemen can reconcile his vote on that occasion with the wages paid on the Laxey washing floors, when married men receive the really magnificent wage of 17s per week. Think of it, Bread 10d for 4lb loaf, sugar 5d per lb, tea 2s 4d, bacon 1s 8d, potatoes unobtainable, yet men are asked to keep a family on 17s a week. But why worry, lead is £32 per ton. [193]

The following week another worker replied, disparaging the miners for their lack of militancy:

I quite agree ... with regard to poor wages paid in Laxey at present, but I see no hope for improvement in the future when we have men in our midst ... who are content to go on working for a starvation wage and can only manage to raise a grumble when a fellow worker gets his wages raised to a bare living. Certainly get the wages increased by all means ... but do not try to save your own pocket to the extent of a few pence per year at the expense of a fellow worker. [194]

Discontent was coming to a head and in October 1917 upwards of a hundred men signed up to a newly formed Laxey branch of the Workers' Union, at a packed meeting at the Working Mens' Institute. David Boreland, a baker from the village, was voted into the chair. Discontent rumbled on into 1918, when in April of that year T. E. Lewin, secretary of the branch, addressed a letter to the management:

At a fully representative meeting of the Laxey Branch of the Worker's Union, the following resolution was carried unanimously "That notice for the cessation of work to be tendered to the manager of Great Laxey Ltd to expire on 20th inst failing a satisfactory reply to the demands made on behalf of the men by this branch of the Worker's Union." Trusting for an early and favourable reply and that such steps will not be necessary. [195]

The Directors of the mine, in a letter dated 17 April 1918 replied:

In reply to yours of the 8th inst we regret to have to state that the financial position of the Great Laxey Mine is very little better than when we issued our statement on 29th November, 1917 in reply to a communication dated 14th November from the Worker's Union.

We now have the Balance Sheet from 1st April 1917 to 31st March 1918 before us which shows that the workers employed during this period had received £11537 0s 8d in wages against a balance profit of £237 17s 6d which even the Worker's Union must admit is a very poor return on the proprietors' invested capital of £60,000. Under the existing circumstances you will see the impossibility of any further advance in wages. [196]

Matters were at an impasse and the *Isle of Man Times* of 27 April 1918 reported that the workers had been on strike since the previous Saturday, that the Laxey Wheel had ceased turning and that as a consequence the lower levels of the mine were flooding. Within days, word had been received from London that the Ministry of Munitions was prepared to intervene in the dispute to resolve matters. The stakes were raised as negotiations with the Ministry on behalf of the miners were now undertaken by George Titt.

This was typical of the situation across Britain at this time. There was a general labour shortage as more and more men were called up for the army, as well as soaring demand for output from factories to feed the war effort. This situation emboldened the workers against their employers. Across Britain generally, industrial workers who for years had borne the brunt of the almost unrestrained capitalism of the Victorian and Edwardian eras, suddenly found themselves in a position of strength. From having to endure pitiful wages, summary dismissal without notice, inadequate and insanitary housing and a lack of basic medical care, they now found they were crucial to war production and the Westminster government was prepared to bend over backwards to appease them and keep them at their lathes or work benches. The result was a massive increase in union militancy as the workers sought to wring every possible concession out of the employers. The Isle of Man was no exception to this trend, and the First World War brought dramatic advances in unionism in the Island. William Clucas, chairman of Peel Commissioners and a noted radical, observed in a speech during the Glenfaba by-election in January 1917:

> War has elevated labour to a supreme position in the sense that the nation has discovered that it depends on the amount of service and sacrifice which labour can offer in the workshops, on the farm and on the battlefield.... [197]

The speed of the development of the Workers' Union on the Isle of Man was dramatic, and its ambitions quickly developed from improvement of workers' terms and conditions towards political aspirations, particularly constitutional reform. George Titt, speaking at an open air meeting in Douglas in November 1917, told the assembled members of:

> The power that was theirs if they used it aright in the political sphere. [198]

The mine management however were adept at putting their case forward in the press, and Mine Captain Roberts stated in April 1918 that wages were considerably higher than as stated by the union:

> In Monday's Daily Times it is stated that the average wage paid to the miners is 25s per week which is not correct. The actual figures for the month of March are in an average of 100 men including boys, 35s per head. The average wage for all employees, 167 in the mine (excluding officials) underground and on surface is 27s 4d per week. [199]

Meanwhile, with the Laxey Wheel no longer turning, nature was taking its course and the mine was flooding. F.J.Robertshaw the chairman of Great Laxey Mines wrote in response to a request for a meeting from George Titt:

> Seeing that the Workers' Union have in a very arbitrary manner closed down the mine, it seems rather late in the day to ask us to meet in the matter. Had you taken this course six months ago, I feel trouble would have been averted. In fact Capt Roberts was most anxious to meet you; and had you called at the mines office, he had been

instructed by me to give you the true facts of the position.

I may inform you, notwithstanding the disrespectful manner in which you and the miners treated the directors and management when we were at the mine in November, I am and have for some time past been in communication with the Ministry of Munitions trying to get a grant for the workers and I am now on my way to personally urge the matter and seeing that the workers have had £11537 0s 2d in wages for the 12 month period 31st March, against a balance profit of £237 17s 6d on the proprietors invested capital of £60,000 (written down to £7500 and £22500 for unwatering the mine), the dept will see the impossibility of the company granting any further advances and am hopeful of success. [200]

At the beginning of May 1918 a telegram was received by Lewin, the Laxey branch secretary, from Titt, stating that the Ministry of Munitions had ordered all men concerned with the wheel and pumps of the Laxey Mine to return to work immediately, and the remainder of the men employed in the mine to return as soon as possible. The decision of the ministry as to wages was held over pending a reply from the local secretary that all the men had returned to work. It was however expected that the men would be in full work on the following Monday.

A celebration was held in Laxey to thank George Titt for his efforts in securing an increase in wages for the men. Presentations were made and speeches given.

In August 1918 the work force received further good news, in that they were to receive a further nine shillings a week as a result of an award by the Coal Commissioners (the body which ran the coal industry, then under government control, and which set prices). This award was to come directly from the British Government and it brought the total weekly subsidy received by the miners from Westminster since the 1918 dispute to fifteen shillings a week. This of course was on top of the miners' ordinary wage. To set this into context, the ordinary private soldier in the British Army in France was receiving one shilling a day. Proficiency pay might top this up to a shilling and a half or perhaps two shillings but the man in the trenches was still a long way behind the industrial worker in terms of pay. This was a cause of much bitterness among the front line troops. The feeling lingered for years among ex-servicemen, that those who stayed at home in essential industries – the workers, not just the bosses – had lined their pockets during the war by holding the country to ransom through strikes, when those in the trenches could not go on strike without facing a court martial and a firing squad.

Of course the prosperity of the Laxey miners was entirely artificial. The mine, which had not really paid its way for years, and which had been near to collapse in 1914, had been propped up by the inflated wartime demand for metals, and the wages of the men were in turn being supported by the direct intervention of the British Government.

On 28 June 1919 the *Examiner* reported that from that date, the Westminster subsidy to the mine would cease. At a meeting of the employees, it was unanimously decided not to work for pre-war rates of pay, as these would not meet the increased cost of living brought about by the war. The men went on strike in July and held out for nearly four months – the mine was closed from 28 June to 25 November before a compromise was reached at the end of that year and the men drifted back to work.

However the effect on the mine during this period had been disastrous – it had flooded up to the 235 fathom level, and cost of pumping it out would have run to thousands of pounds.

In spite of the short term advances in terms and conditions secured by the miners during the war, this had been a blip in an otherwise downwards long-term trend. The war had given the mines a stay of execution, but that was all. Bobby Kelly in later life was nostalgic for the pre-war years, remembering:

> *That fellow ... Councillor Titt – he was going to do wonders for us, and he got us all sacked. We were doing alright, we weren't grumbling about our wages, well it was under the Great Laxey Mines. They couldn't afford to pay the money that he was fighting for. He came over telling us ... he'd get all this money, and we weren't getting paid, and it was getting on the end of the war then. You see ... We were, we were doing alright. Under the conditions we thought we were alright. We weren't earning a bad wage sometimes.* (201)

Aside from tourism, the other two of the three main planks of the Manx economy in this era were farming, and fishing. In the latter part of 1915 a committee of Tynwald looked into the Herring industry on the Island. It transpired that one of the largest pre-war markets for herrings had been Germany; in spite of the war, some ten to twelve thousand barrels had been packed in Manx kipper houses in 1915, but that figure would never have been reached without catches landed by Scottish and English boats. The report concluded that most Manx boats were now crewed by old men, with the implication being that most of the young men were away at the war.

Like Manx industry, Manx agriculture flourished during the war. It could be argued however that just as with industry, the apparent prosperity resulting from the war was not sustainable. A Tynwald report of 1915 indicated that agriculture was the only sector of the Manx economy which had not been adversely affected by the conflict. Orders were made under the Defence of the Realm Regulations prohibiting the export from the Island, except under Government Office permit, of potatoes, livestock, meat, eggs, oats and other essential articles. Yet in spite of this, and of the extra mouths which it had to feed during the war, namely the internees, it was still possible, Bertram Sargeaunt stated, for the Isle of Man to export on average 8000 tons of oats to England each year. According to Sargeaunt, Manx oats became famous during the war. All surplus turnips and livestock not required for the island population were also exported to England. Several million eggs were exported, as were considerable quantities of straw and hay.

There was certainly an increased demand for foodstuffs, and livestock in particular was at a premium in the early part of the war. Early in 1915 there was large scale export of cattle and sheep. Whilst this pushed up the price of beef and mutton to Manx consumers it undoubtedly increased farm incomes. Because of the shortages in Great Britain, English buyers were scouring the British Isles for supplies and some turned up at Douglas market. They outbid the local buyers by 1d and 1 1/2d per pound for the two types of meat. This in turn meant that the farming sector aroused the wrath of the visiting industry. The latter suggested that the shortfall in domestic revenue should now be made up by a tax raid on the war profits being made by the farmers. Samuel Norris noted:

> All agricultural produce had considerably increased in value, and those engaged in agriculture, as owners or tenant-farmers, were prospering greatly. The landed class, as distinct from the propertied classes, was enriched by the war ... for property owners in the towns on the other hand – and especially in Douglas – and for people of fixed incomes, the times had become very hard. [202]

Reaping with horses at Joughin's farm, Ballacrebbin, Andreas on 18 August 1915. (Manx National Heritage)

Manx farmers were keen to ensure that they received at the very least the same rates for their wool, oats, hay etc from the military authorities as were being paid for the same items in England. To this end, a deputation was sent to discuss the matter with the Lieutenant Governor. The *Examiner Annual* for 1917 continued:

> While the war has spelled hardship and even ruin for some people in the Island, it has undoubtedly enriched in substantial fashion the farmers of agricultural land. Prices of agricultural produce have gone up enormously — oats have sold at 32s 6d per boll, and potatoes at £12 per ton, prices never even approached in height within living memory. Cattle, sheep, and pigs, too, have yielded the farmers huge profits, and altogether what is now the leading industry of the Island has made tremendous advances because of Germany's effort to materialise a dream of world power. [203]

Another major Manx export to the United Kingdom was pit props and other timber required for English coal mines. This material had previously been sourced from Scandinavia but imports from across the North Sea had been largely stopped by the U-boat menace. As a result of over-harvesting, the plantations of the Isle of Man were largely denuded by the war's end.

The average size of a holding on the Isle of Man remained almost static during the war years from 52 acres in 1914 to 52.2 acres in 1920. However the method of use of that land changed dramatically during the war. There were 22,526 acres given over to cereal crops in 1914, but by 1920 that had risen to 54,596 acres. During the same period the head of cattle in the Island remained almost static at 21,000. It is intriguing to note that whilst it is a generally accepted fact that in England the requisitioning of horses by the army depleted the equine population of the countryside and accelerated the mechanisation of agriculture, that was not the case in the Isle of Man. T.A.Brew remembered that such mechanisation as did occur, happened late in the war, and then on only a few farms:

...when I was a boy about the year 1916, I would then be 10 years old. I remember several times men cutting corn with reapers, as I was only young my job was making bands. The older and stronger people done the lifting and tying ... It was when I was going to school that I seen the first tractor, this must have been about the year 1918, the War was on and production was at its peak, those tractors were very awkward, the ploughs used with them were clumsy, the larger tractors were very much like steam engines, and seemed to run very badly. Corletts, Ballamona, had these tractors, and the larger one was used for threshing. They tied it to a tree to keep it from creeping up toward the mill with the strain, it used to give great loud cracks out of it, which we could hear ... more than a mile away, like guns going off. The tractor was not reckoned suitable for our small fields and we seen these first tractors and ploughs sold for a song. It was not until the 1939 War that people again took an interest in the tractor.... [204]

Certainly some horses were commandeered from farms in the early stages of the war; Catherine Craine writes of the despair of a farmer in Ballaugh whose best horse was requisitioned, and also of a widowed woman who out of patriotism offered her only horse to the war effort. There was also undoubtedly some degree of mechanisation of Manx agriculture during the war, with increasing use of steam for threshing. However the number of horses in use on the land had actually risen during the war, from 5978 in 1914 to 6248 in 1920 (these are horses defined as solely for use in agriculture). This cannot be attributed to horses returning from war service, for these beasts were generally sold to Belgian knackers' yards at the close of hostilities (much to the dismay of the men who had worked alongside them). It probably stems instead from steps taken in September 1917 through an Order in Council to allow the Lieutenant Governor to prohibit the export of agricultural horses, and thus conserve those needed for use on the land. Alfred Teare likewise states that:

Farm labour was so cheap that it paid a farmer to send a man, horse and cart to Douglas or other quaysides and take their place in the queue to get their load of coal which was being imported by the Farmer's Club, which sold the coal at cost to members.

Mechanisation was almost non-existent, and the work on a farm was very arduous, with long hours. Harvest time meant extra work, and one of the first efforts to improve labour conditions was an application for 'harvest money'. [205]

Any discussion of the impact of the First World War upon agriculture inevitably involves consideration of conscription, because from 1916 onwards the two were inextricably linked. One of the arguments in favour of conscription was that it would ensure that labour was used most effectively; by ensuring that key workers remained in munitions plants, whilst unskilled agricultural labourers for example were drafted into the army. However these were already a scarce commodity on the Island. An interesting statistic appeared in the *Isle of Man Examiner* in April 1916, during the conscription debate. It stated that the total number of males in the Isle of Man engaged in agriculture between the ages of twenty and forty-five was 2167, employed over 92,000 acres. It further stated that the percentages of men of military age per 100 acres was as follows:

England and Wales 3.6%   Ireland 6.8%
Scotland 3.1%   Isle of Man 2.3%

So it could be argued that the Isle of Man was less able to spare its agrarian population than any other part of the British Isles, for it employed fewer men on the land than any of its neighbours. At a meeting of the Agricultural Society in January 1916, Mr T.E.Kneen stated that it was impossible to get a person to dock turnips, whilst Mr W.F.Cowell at the same meeting stated that:

> *The shortage of labour was serious in the island. Horses were standing in the stable, and not a man to take them out; work was getting behind.* [206]

Conscription would naturally affect agricultural workers more than industrial labourers, because the latter were vital for the production of munitions. If there was a labour shortage in the countryside, the farmers would just have to make the best of it. None the less they fought their corner, arguing against the call up of those most needed in their sector – the skilled engineers of the agricultural world, the blacksmiths. In a letter to the Government Secretary on 30 December 1916, John Kermode, the President of the Farmers' Club of the Isle of Man wrote:

> *This club is of opinion that Mr Prothero the new president of the Board of Agriculture hit the mark when he said that victory in this terrible war may be won on the cornfields and potato lands of Great Britain and thinks therefore that farmers ought to be given all facilities for doing their important duties. For this reason the club thinks that the dozen or so young blacksmiths in the Island would do much more towards the achievement of victory in their present occupations than if sent to the army, because farmers cannot do their work unless their implements and machines are kept in repair, and there are many things which a blacksmith cannot do without skilled assistance. These things include the mounting of ploughs, laying socks, laying big grubbers and sprung cart wheels, things which are essential to agriculture.* [207]

Samuel Norris by contrast alleges that in 1917 it was all too easy for some members of the agricultural sector to secure exemptions:

> *The military tribunals, on which were several members of the Insular Legislature, were now, under conscription, hearing appeals for exemption. It was a matter of some complaint that exemptions were too easily secured by farmers for their sons and others alleged to be on work of national importance here at home. Out of seventeen hundred men who had applied for exemption, not more than ten per cent were passed into the Army.* [208]

Threshing with steam at Larkhill Farm, Abbeylands, Onchan in 1917; a Clayton & Shuttleworth threshing engine. (PG 8063/7)

Another observer, writing to the *Isle of Man Examiner*, stated that though the members of the local tribunals were overwhelmingly agricultural in background, they had actually failed to defend agriculture by allowing so many men to be conscripted off the land, and that agricultural production was down as a result. The same correspondent went on to claim that the tribunals were not consistent, because there were some farms where almost all the hands had gone and others where many labourers were still employed. Widespread discontent was caused by these inconsistencies, and the assertion that landowners were able to secure exemptions for their sons, whilst ordinary labourers were called up [209].

In July 1916 the Isle of Man Agricultural Society obtained agreement from the manager of the Labour Exchange, that if a farmer who had one of his men in training in the army wished for his services for a fortnight or so for the harvest, he could approach the Exchange and the man might be granted leave, on what was termed 'agricultural furlough'. It was reported that a soldier named Cregeen from Baldrine had secured a remarkably generous four weeks of leave in July and August for this purpose. In March the following year the Exchange successfully requested that a dozen Manx ploughmen who were at the time serving in England with the King's Liverpool Regiment be temporarily returned for agricultural furlough on the Island. The southern branch of the society also secured agreement from the boards of Education that if sufficient farmers wanted the help, then schools would close early for the summer, with holidays being split into two three week periods to enable children to help with turnip thinning and other agricultural duties.

One correspondent, describing himself as a 'Countryman', stated in the *Isle of Man Times* in December 1916 that much of the shortfall in agricultural labour had been made up by the mobilisation of the Island's youth:

> *We know of many cases in the Island where youths of from 17 to 19 have been the sole horseman on one-team farms, and that youths of 15 and 16 have done all horsework on such farms in odd cases … I think still that the youths who got up from 14, 15 and 16, to 16, 17 and 18 during the two years of the war to be very useful auxiliary horsemen and ploughmen, and would greatly outnumber those who had fell out of use during the same period, and also the horsemen taken by conscription.* [210]

The same correspondent went on to claim, in contrast to Teare and Brew, that the shortage of casual labour in the countryside had been fully met by improved machinery. It seems hard to avoid the conclusion however that there was a general shortage of farm labour by 1917.

By that year, use of prisoners from the internment camps as labour on farms was widespread. The farmer paid the camp commandant 4 ½ d per hour for each man, of which 1 ½ d went to the man himself as wages and 3d went to Government Office towards his upkeep. For a seven hour day this equates to 2/7 per day. For a six day week an internee cost about 15/6, whereas a Manx labourer earned around 24 shillings a week, so the internees represented cheap labour. Not only were farmers enjoying record prices for their produce, they were producing it more cheaply than ever!

In 1926 Tynwald established a committee to report on the state of agriculture on the Isle of Man in the wake of the war. The pre-amble to the report stated that the committee:

> *[was] appointed as a result of the depression in agriculture, which has been acutely felt in the Isle of Man. Before the War, the Manx farmer's profit was small compared with the capital invested in his business, but on the whole his position was not worse than that of the English farmer, for the costs of production and selling prices were very similar to those on the mainland, and were fairly stable. The War has entirely changed this, and at the moment production costs are out of all proportion to the selling prices of farm produce. Assuming that before the War there was a small profit accruing to the farmer ... figures show that such profit must in most cases have disappeared altogether.* [211]

So if farm incomes had risen in the short term, and farmers had enjoyed record profits during the war itself, the longer term consequences of the war were far more detrimental towards the agricultural sector. Once government orders for meat and cereals had ceased with the coming of peace, prices had collapsed, whilst all other costs which had been driven up during the war remained high. At the same time the Manx farmers had lost the cheap labour source provided by the internees. The report stated that the following articles (which were the main produce of Manx farms) had increased on average over pre-war prices:

Barley 32%
Oats 33%
Fat cattle 48%
Fat sheep 55%
Hay 3%
Potatoes 51%
Milk 73%

However, at the same time the increase in the cost of living in January 1925 as against the same figure for 1914 was given as 80%. The report went on to comment on the continuous decrease in the number of men employed on farms:

> *This is not peculiar to the Isle of Man; it is taking place in England and all the continental countries, but as the Isle of Man is so largely dependent on agriculture, it is a much more serious question for us. It has been urged by witnesses before us that during the last few years the country districts have been denuded of the best type of worker.* [212]

Alfred Teare recounts how at a Michaelmas fair shortly after the First World War, Charlie Gill of Ballaugh, a well known orator, and farmworkers' union representative, addressed the assembled crowd of farm workers:

> *He took as his text the Bible story of the years of plenty and the lean years, how the surplus of the years of plenty was stored in granaries against lean years, and when they came, according to the Bible story, there was plenty for everyone.*
>
> *Charlie went on to describe the bumper years the farmers had during the war years, and how they had stored the surpluses (profits) in the granary at the corner of Athol Street (meaning of course the bank), but now*

Charlie Gill of Ballaugh, the farmworkers' organiser. (PG 13705)

that the lean years had come, a different attitude to that of the Bible story was being adopted, and the farmers were refusing to distribute the surpluses amongst those who had by their labour helped to create them. [(213)]

Family tradition has it that J.D.Clucas MHK was responsible during the First World War for the introduction of Suffolk sheep and Aberdeen Angus cattle to the Island, in order to improve Manx herds. Certainly Clucas farmed a considerable amount of land and he was interested in new techniques in agriculture. However the last Manx farmer to plough his land using oxen did so in

1911, so old methods in agriculture were already dying out even before the First World War. A good anecdotal source for the effects of the war upon agriculture and rural ways of life is George Quayle's *Legends of a Lifetime*. Quayle was born in 1895 and spent all his life on the land, mostly in Lezayre (in 1916, his father had obtained exemption for him from military service, on the grounds that he was his only horseman). Although a good portion of his book is given over to folktales, and the author does not consider the First World War important enough a subject to devote a chapter to in its own right, it is intriguing to note the number of times in which he refers to the war in passing (almost subconsciously) as a full stop, denoting the ending of a practice or tradition. For instance he states that:

...another old custom that continued until the beginning of the First World War [was] blowing horns for a wedding. [(214)]

On another occasion he tells us that:

...there were even houses in the parish where it was forbidden to read a newspaper on a Sunday, and this as lately as 1919. [(215)]

The passing away of his father's labourer Old Billie Quirk, aged eighty, in 1917 is taken as symbolic of the death of old ways in which the countryside was managed and cared for, Billie having been one of the stalwarts on an upland farm at Sky Hill. Quayle laments the dereliction of the upland farms which he states has been caused by the younger generation deserting them (implicitly as a result of the war), and the elderly residents left behind being less and less able to maintain the walls and gates. The author also notes the replacement of traditional intensive human labour in the countryside with machinery, and goes on to describe the way in which the old practice of repairing roads with stone died out:

> Up to the First World War the Highway Board had no machinery to make the roads ... the Highway Board (before the days of state pensions) would pay an old pensioner five shillings a week ... old Tom Cleator, then nearly 80, broke up those stones with a hammer ...It's hard to believe this was as recent as 1915. [216]

Whilst some traditions died out, it is interesting to note that certain folk tales or superstitions actually underwent a revival during the First World War. Sightings of the ghostly 'death coach', a supernatural indicator of forthcoming bereavement, were reported in the countryside again after an absence of many years. One family, the Quayles of Peel, were aghast when, at dinner, the portrait of a family member serving in France inexplicably fell from the wall. The soldier, Gordon Quayle of the Black Watch, was killed the same month. Walter Gill in his *Second Manx Scrapbook* discusses premonitions of death in general and adds:

> Of a less common type is a dream-vision of a young soldier's death in France during the late war. It was seen by an elder relative and friend of his, from whom I had the particulars. She woke suddenly in the middle of the night and sprang up with a vigorous clap of the hands, exclaiming, "That's the shot that killed C.H.!" In her dream she had heard it and had seen him fall backwards from the top of a ridge. When she came in to breakfast the others present greeted her with a general hand-clapping, and chaffed her about her nocturnal performance. But it was learned afterwards that C.H. had been sniped that night while leading his men out to an attack or a raid, and had fallen backwards into the trench. He died next day. [217]

Gill offered another example of this phenomenon:

> From a friend of many years standing, the widow of a former Speaker of the House of Keys [believed to be widow of John Robert Kerruish], I have the following account of a visionary message from a battle-field. One afternoon while walking home from a visit, she saw, on reaching the stile to the East of the Crossags Farm, near Ramsey, a form which she knew to be that of her stepson, coming towards her, but still a considerable distance away. When they drew near to each other she realised with horror that he had no head. He then vanished. She went home feeling depressed and unwell, and fearing that some misfortune had befallen him. Soon afterwards a letter came with the news that he had been wounded. Some weeks later, when she visited him in hospital, he told her that while he was in the company of five other men a shell which killed the others outright had flung him some distance away and buried him, causing severe injuries to his head. When this was happening the thought of her flashed through his mind, and she seemed to be present. [218]

Today it is almost impossible to imagine the stress and anxiety caused on a daily basis by the knowledge that a dearly beloved son, husband or brother was on active service and in imminent danger. Many at home could hardly bring themselves to read the growing casualty lists, and the mere sight of the Post Office telegram boy was enough to instil panic. Lancelot Quayle, the father of Gordon Quayle mentioned above, wrote movingly of the loss of his only son; what sustained him in his grief was pride, and also a deep religious conviction that he and Gordon would be re-united in the hereafter:

> It is nearly an impossibility for a man to be long in this war without being wounded or killed. And after the continual suspense it seems that even the dread news of 'killed in action' brings to overstrained human nature a sense of relief and relaxation. This may be strange but it is true. Our greatest agony I believe was giving him up at first ... the motive power of his going was the sense that his country called him and his was no craven coward spirit – to put personal safety before the call of duty which in his case was clearly the call of God ... but we also had a sacrifice to make, and we did not falter either, and we know what it is to give our only begotten son ... in our deep sorrow we have been helped by the rivers of sympathy which have flowed to us from hosts of good people ... I thank God that in his infinite mercy he ... gave to Emily and me the tremendous honour of possessing (if only for a short time) such a true, brave, honest & affectionate son as Gordon whose memory we honour & revere. [219]

In spite of their internal differences, most people of the Isle of Man remained proud of their part in the war, even though this came at a terrible cost. The Manx cultural and language magazine *Mannin* stated in 1917:

> *Manxmen continue to shed their blood in the sacred cause of homeland. Since the last issue of Mannin, at least fifteen Manx sailors have perished in the loss of vessels of H.M. Navy, and many, alas! many Manx soldiers have died on the battlefield particularly since the commencement of the new offensive. Shortly before the publication of this issue, it was computed that since the outbreak of war four hundred and twenty-seven officers and men of Manx birth or blood have been killed in action or have died of wounds, while fifty-nine others have succumbed to disease or accident, and twenty-seven have been reported missing. In addition, fifty are detained in enemy internment camps, and no less than five hundred and eighty-five have been wounded. Seventy-three officers and men and two nurses have received military decorations, or have otherwise been specially mentioned for conspicuous gallantry or meritorious service.* [220]

The words were those of Sophia Morrison, the Manx cultural activist, folklore collector and author. The secretary to the Manx Language Society, Yn Cheshaght Ghailckagh, from 1901 until her death, Morrison was one of the key players in the period of the Manx national revival at the end of the nineteenth and beginning of the twentieth centuries, and was active in the pan-Celtic movement. Yet she saw herself as a Manx patriot second, and a subject of the British Empire first. In her view, the sacrifice made by the Isle of Man was its duty as part of that Empire.

The role of Manx women in general in the early part of the war was very much defined in terms of sacrifice. Women were told that it was their duty to sacrifice their husbands, brothers and sweethearts to the war, and their main role at this point was perceived as being simply to toured the south of England for a year, singing at camp concerts and in hospitals and convalescent homes, gaining the affection of wounded Tommies. Prior to the war, at the age of fourteen, she had won the first prize in the open soprano solo class at the Manx Music Festival, and it was said that she possessed one of the loveliest soprano voices the Isle of Man ever produced. Likewise, Effie Fayle, 'Manxland's sweet contralto' performed patriotic songs at the Grand Theatre in Douglas on a nightly basis in 1915, including *For the Red, White and Blue*, a song dedicated to the Manx heroes at the front. Clearly, in spite of the war, there was still a lively nightlife to be sampled in Douglas if one wished to look for it, and the Grand Theatre picture dome was drawing in crowds of visitors nightly.

By the end of 1915, the first faltering steps were being taken towards mobilising Manx women towards a more active contribution to the war effort. In September a hundred Manx girls left for Rochdale for instruction in weaving. Initial reports suggested that they had proved themselves very adept. In January of 1916 the Manx Industries Association, under the guidance of the Revered Charles Copeland-Smith, a Methodist Minister stationed in Douglas, set up operations in the Derby Castle. It held contracts from the War Office and Admiralty for socks and shirts and was already employing 1000 people, most of whom were suffering as a result of the collapse of the boarding house trade, many of them women. Copeland-Smith himself stated that he had encountered opposition to his work from the upper echelons of society, though he maintained that his factories sought to provide a safety net for those out of work, rather than poaching them from elsewhere:

Sophia Morrison, who died aged 56 in 1917. Her vision of Manx nationalism was firmly rooted within the British Empire. (PG 6693)

encourage their men folk to enlist. Other women were to contribute to the war effort more directly by boosting morale. During the early part of the war, May Clague

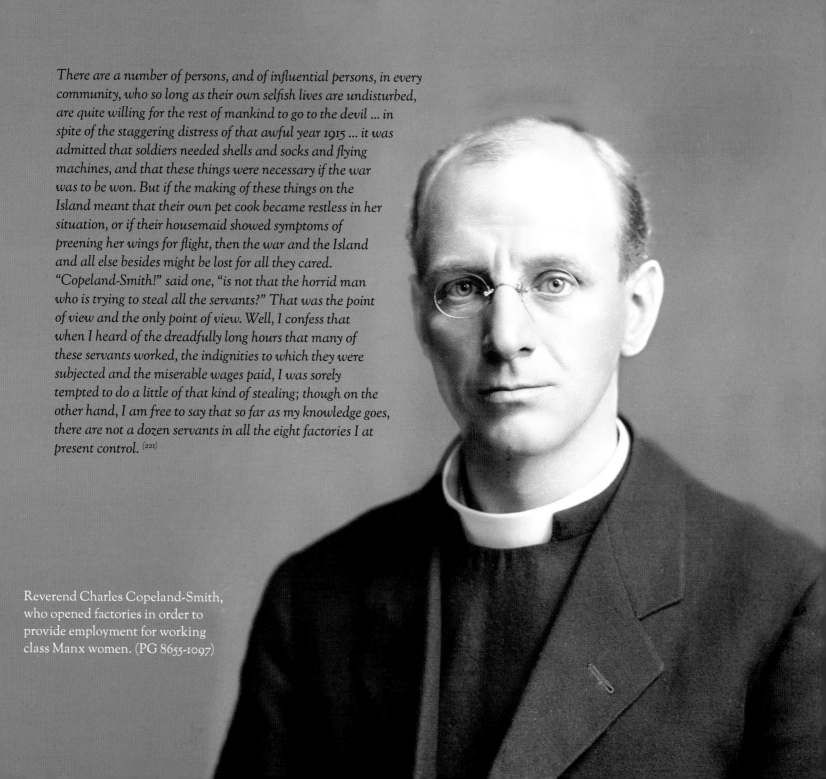

There are a number of persons, and of influential persons, in every community, who so long as their own selfish lives are undisturbed, are quite willing for the rest of mankind to go to the devil ... in spite of the staggering distress of that awful year 1915 ... it was admitted that soldiers needed shells and socks and flying machines, and that these things were necessary if the war was to be won. But if the making of these things on the Island meant that their own pet cook became restless in her situation, or if their housemaid showed symptoms of preening her wings for flight, then the war and the Island and all else besides might be lost for all they cared. "Copeland-Smith!" said one, "is not that the horrid man who is trying to steal all the servants?" That was the point of view and the only point of view. Well, I confess that when I heard of the dreadfully long hours that many of these servants worked, the indignities to which they were subjected and the miserable wages paid, I was sorely tempted to do a little of that kind of stealing; though on the other hand, I am free to say that so far as my knowledge goes, there are not a dozen servants in all the eight factories I at present control. [221]

Reverend Charles Copeland-Smith, who opened factories in order to provide employment for working class Manx women. (PG 8655-1097)

Alfred Teare noted the social benefit of Copeland-Smith's industries in the absence of any form of welfare provision:

Many a female boarding house or apartment–house keeper had reason to be grateful to the reverend gentleman for his help, as it provided, in many instances, their only means of subsistence. [222]

Later Vickers of Barrow-in-Furness took over the Palace and Derby Castle ballrooms and turned them into hangars for the production of airship components. As the

A Parseval airship under construction by Vickers at the Palace ballroom, Douglas. (PG 13751-1)

requirement for space increased, Laxey Glen Restaurant and Onchan Head Pavilion were also used. This work was of crucial importance as the airships under construction – Parseval, Zeppelin and the Sea Scout models – were vital in combating the U–boat menace in Home waters. Duggie Lewis started work for the firm as an apprentice at Easter 1916 and remembered:

There were 60-80 women working in the Palace ballroom and there was a Miss Kelly (later Mrs Lewin) working as a tracer in the drawing office. [223]

All the girls employed had to be under twenty-four years of age. After getting a job, they were sent to Barrow for a month to be trained. One of the women, sadly now unidentified, remembered:

We stayed in a hostel [in Barrow] and went to the factory every morning …. [back in the Isle of Man] we cut out and stitched the balloons and put tapes on. The girls at Derby Castle had to get inside the balloons to stick the skins on, and they had electric light bulbs on extending flex so that they could see what they were doing. [224]

Industrialisation was coming to the Isle of Man, whether it was wanted or not, and the *Examiner* commented:

The boarding house industry is not the noblest work that women can be engaged in by any means, but it does not blast its womenkind like the factory. But if the factory must come, then the Factory Act must be extended, and all measures necessary for the women's protection created and put in force. [225]

The newspaper noted warily that a number of English companies were considering setting up an arm in the Isle of Man, but they must not think that they could take advantage of the Island's economic distress by paying lower wages than they would in England for the same kind of work. If the Isle of Man was to be industrialised, then the Isle of Man Government should take the lead in enabling it. As there was less reliance upon coal in industry now, the Isle of Man's previous disadvantage in this area was less important.

In 1915 Emett's outfitters of Douglas began the production of their own socks and gloves, partly in response to difficulties in receiving supplies from their usual sources, but also for philanthropic motives in providing local employment. For this reason they tried to avoid direct competition with Manx Industries Association, and focused increasingly upon the production of woollen gloves. The business expanded rapidly, occupying several premises, and by late 1916 exporting to England, Canada, the United States and elsewhere. By this stage they employed over 150 girls. A journalist who visited the firm that autumn reported:

I am fully convinced that this firm has done good work for the Island in its hour of need. The opportunity has been unique, and, perhaps, without these peculiar times, created by the war, the industry could not have been established. Mr Emett sees no reason why the work done now should not be carried on permanently. There is every

Nora Hammonds, aged 19, who worked on airship production at Vickers in Douglas. (PG 13728)

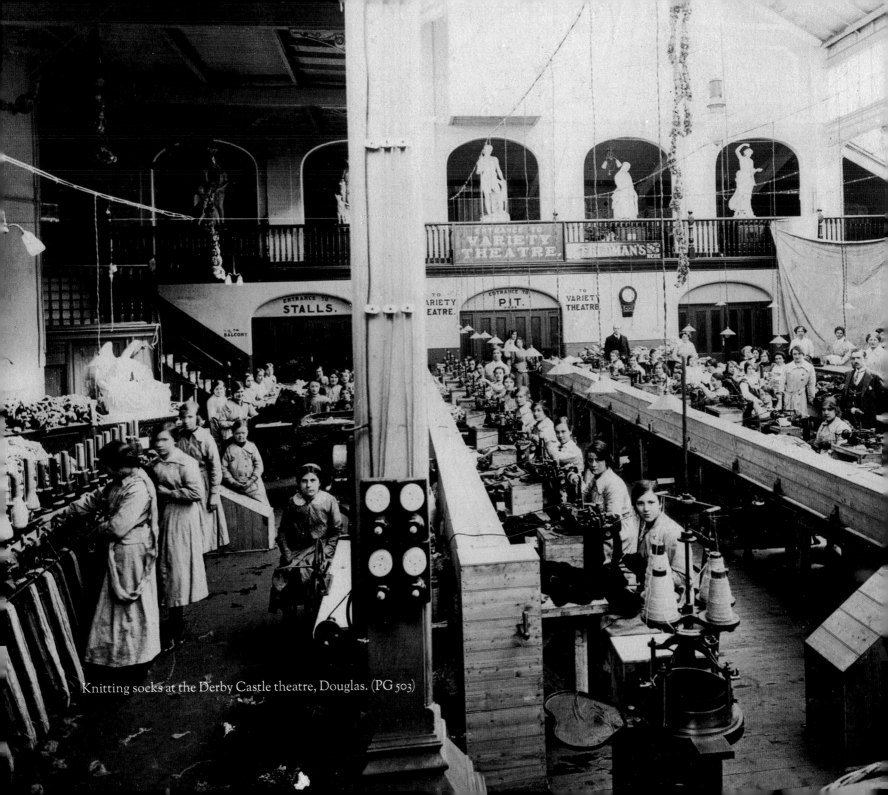

Knitting socks at the Derby Castle theatre, Douglas. (PG 503)

reason to believe that such will be the case. "Of course, everything depends upon the girls themselves," said Mr Emett. They are learning a new trade, and they will not be able to keep this trade without a fight. We have proved in many ways that we are able to manufacture for ourselves goods which hitherto came almost entirely from Germany. Why not gloves also? The work done so far reflects great credit on the girls of Manxland. They evidently enjoy their work, and there seems little fear of any who have tasted the joys of a days work well done, and finished by 6pm, going back to the old hours which prevailed before the war. [226]

Here again, the workforce was soon quite effectively unionised. Alfred Teare once again noted:

The organising of the girls employed in the glove industry was considerably helped by girls who took on the task of shop stewards and collectors. Names which come to mind in this respect are Grace Radcliffe (whose father was employed in the 'Times' office) Fanny Kewley and Lillian Morrison ...The negotiation of agreements was, however, a more difficult job. As the knitting of gloves was split up into several operations, and the earnings were on a piece-rate basis, it took some calculating what was a fair rate in order to give the operative a fair return for her labour. Comparable rates were fixed with those of English and Scottish firms. [227]

Miss J.Kelly of Douglas, a member of the Women's Land Army in England. (PG 8655-2618)

However the *Isle of Man Examiner* astutely observed in an article in April 1917 entitled 'The War of the Genders' that allowing women into industry was not merely allowing them to compete with (and perhaps underbid) male workers for wages. More than this, it threatened the very concept of marriage itself, and would lead to what it described as 'racial disease'. Women having discovered the wage slavery of factories would no longer wish to enter the unpaid slavery of marriage, with all its domestic drudgery, the piece argued [228]. Nevertheless the mass mobilisation of women across the British Isles allowed the British Government to square the manpower circle, by keeping an army of several million men supplied with reinforcements, without seriously weakening agriculture and industry, the two pillars upon which the war effort rested.

The question remains as to how far women in the Isle of Man were directly affected by the war. Clearly more women were in the workplace, but these were probably from the class of women who had always worked. It was also noted that women on the Isle of Man could not be induced to work on the land. They would undertake indoor work on farms, such as in the dairy, but for cultural reasons would not plough. In the *Isle of Man Times* of 3 June 1916 a farmer called Mr Lay was reported as saying:

> *It was found impossible to get women to work on the land. Their work was within doors, and you could not get them to take a pair of horses to plough.* [229]

Alice Gibb, of the Grove, near Ramsey. She worked at the Chilwell munitions factory, near Nottingham. (MS 09412)

Whilst in the *Examiner* of 10 June 1916 a farmer called Sayle stated that he had two daughters and:

They have never worked on the land. You can't get women to do work like that. [230]

Significantly, no branch of the Women's Land Army was established on the Island during the First World War. It is also important to observe that the Isle of Man differed from the UK in that the increased numbers of women in industry were not there because there was a shortage of men in a pre-existing industrial base, but rather, an industrial base had been artificially created in order to provide employment for women who would otherwise be facing financial hardship.

Rather more unusual were the experiences of middle class women and girls. Alice Gibb, for example, had never worked before the war; the Gibb family, of the Grove near Ramsey were sufficiently wealthy for the female members to pursue those Victorian feminine crafts of needlework and embroidery. She, along with her sister Janet, was educated by a governess, and might well have followed in the footsteps of her mother and maiden aunt by leading the life not of a recluse, for the Gibbs were great travellers, but of one who is largely sheltered from the realities of life as endured by other classes. As it was, in 1916 Alice became a supervisor at Chilwell munitions works near Nottingham, and she also seems to have had a spell as a matron in a hostel for girls working in the factory. The work was physically demanding, with long shifts in often unpleasant surroundings. It also brought Alice into direct contact with the working class women of Nottingham, perhaps the first time this had happened

to any great extent in her life. It was a curious parallel with the experience of upper middle class males on the Western Front. She wrote to her sister from Beeston:

Our caravan is rather sweet [with] a very good stove but the nights are awfully cold we have each bought a grey blanket 7/6. Hugs one, so ought to feel better. The bunks are real sprung mattresses very comfortable & I did the whole place down with sheep dip. Today I came to work at 5am & Miss Nicholls did the house arriving at 8.30. After I go to the clean shell store there will be no more luxuries of that sort ... this last month has been really play work. I am sorry to go back to night shifts but have insisted that I shall only go for a month's trial.... [231]

In 1916 Gladys Christian, the daughter of a Douglas bank manager, was a trainee teacher at the Maria Grey Training College in London. She also experienced war work in England, albeit of a different nature. She wrote of a journey by train to Norfolk where she and fellow students were to undertake agricultural work. The journey at first had more than a touch of a holiday feel about it, in spite of the uniform:

We wore khaki armlets, and these together with our general appearance, were enough to convince anyone that our goal was 'the land' ... our first weekend was spent in exploring and admiring, but we were all glad when Monday morning arrived and 'work.' So we all clothed ourselves in our varied working outfit, and were escorted to the fruit fields by the manager ... At the fields we were introduced to our fellow-workers, who eyed us and our garments with some curiosity – we wore short

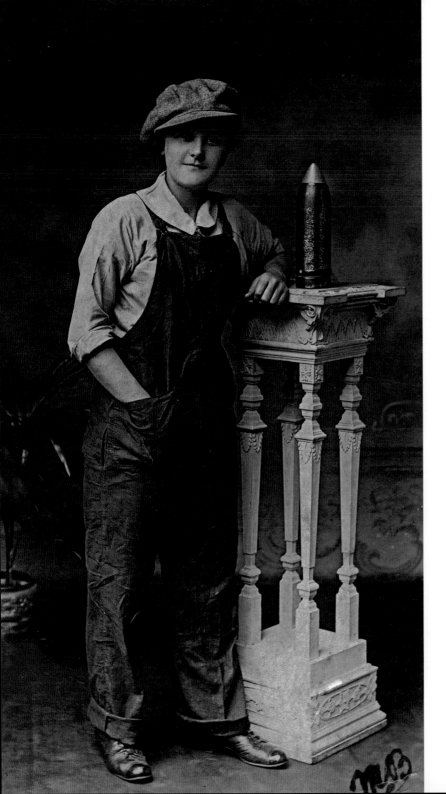

overalls, boots and shady hats, some even had leggings, riding breeches and smocks – and we also met two overseers who turned out to be awfully decent men. Well, we were next given two seven pound cans each, and set to work at two to a row of raspberries. At first we thought the work quite easy, and wondered why we weren't always fruit pickers; but soon our backs began to be troublesome, and when the sun came out our opinions changed ... we used to work till 8pm, and then crawled home to a bath, a hot meal, and bed. (232)

Some sense of the reality of war however was injected into the situation by two Zeppelin raids, of which Gladys wrote:

It was really a peculiar sensation to lie in bed and hear 'the thing' buzzing overhead, while the whole house shook and the windows rattled when the bombs fell. I leaned through the windows both times, but could see nothing because of the fog. The second night we were all made to crawl down some deep, dark stairs to the ground floor, and huddled for two hours in a dark room, but after much grumbling we were allowed to return to our beds. (233)

Mary Brew came from a more modest background. The daughter of a Douglas barber, her war work in England also brought her within range of the Zeppelins. After the war she remembered:

Mary Brew, of Douglas, a munitions worker at Coventry Ordnance Works; she endured Zeppelin raids as well as the dangers of working with high explosives. (PG 13708-2)

Three sisters and myself left Douglas during the first months of the Great War, our destination being Coventry to work on munitions. There was no work of that kind being done in Douglas. We soon found out there was really a war on. We started work at 6am and continued to 6pm, worked one week night shifts and one week day shifts with 1½ hours off per shift for meals. The wages were 2½d per hour (weekly wage 13s 1d days, 16s 9d nights) Sundays included. The Coventry Ordnance Works were under Government control, and the girls had to keep their jobs or otherwise be out of work for six weeks. The control was taken off in 1916, and wages went up to £1 4s and £1 10s. The Zeppelins always paid their terrifying visits while we were on night shift. Lights would go out, and girls would faint by the dozen. The persons to be pitied on those occasions were the nurses, who were always in attendance. It was a nightmare those four years of war ...[234]

Even without air raids, munitions work was dangerous enough. There were frequent explosions, and the chemicals often affected the girls' skin, though on the whole 'munitionettes' as they were called were proud of their role in the war.

Single women on the Isle of Man had held the vote since 1881, so the war did not bring to them the obvious political reward of emancipation, as it did to the women of the United Kingdom. Whilst the political and social advancement of women in the Isle of Man was undoubtedly spurred on by the war, the pace of change was not as rapid as that in the United Kingdom. Marion Shimmin, the first female MHK, was not elected until 1933, in contrast with the situation at Westminster where Nancy Astor was the first female MP to take her seat, in

1919. Annie Bridson meanwhile came from a more modest section of society. She was born at 17 Drinkwater Street in Douglas, and was brought up at 14 Oxford Street. Her father was a mariner and young Annie attended Tynwald Street and Hanover Street schools. Teacher training was one of the few career opportunities available to bright working class girls at this time and Annie went on to study at Ripon Teacher Training College. At the outbreak of the war she returned to the Island to teach at Hanover Street School. The war encouraged her political activism and she joined the Isle of Man Teachers' Association, the Manx branch of the National Union of Teachers. In March 1918 she became a member of a more radical group, the Douglas Class Teachers' Association, and attended the founding conference of the Manx Labour Party. She would go on after the war to become the first woman president of the party, and eventually a member of the House of Keys, though this would not be until after the Second World War.

As previously discussed, numbers of Manx women served afloat in war zones as members of the Merchant service, earning medals in the process. Other Manx women served as nurses. Annie Warren Gill was born at the Curate's Cottage, Rushen Abbey. She took up nursing as a profession in the 1890s and was an army nurse in the Boer War of 1899-1902. She reached the peak of her career during the First World War, when as matron of Edinburgh Royal Infirmary she was senior matron of the entire Scottish nursing service. At the end of the war she was created a CBE. Mildred Moore went out to Serbia as matron with the British Red Cross to care for wounded Serbian soldiers. She took out with her sixteen nurses, and was in charge of a large hospital in Serbia. She returned to the United Kingdom in July 1915, and after nursing for a short time in a military hospital she went to France, where she became a Senior Sister in a British Red Cross Hospital. Esther Jane Bridson was trained at the Royal Southern Hospital, and became matron of Noble's Hospital in 1905. She continued as matron until her retirement in December 1922, and nursed civilians, war wounded soldiers, and German and Austrian internees at Noble's for the duration of the war. Afterwards she was awarded the medal of St John, in recognition of her service in running the hospital during four years of conflict.

Dolly Rogers began her nursing training before the war. In 1915 the theatre sister at Noble's, Miss Stewart, joined the Army nursing service and Dolly Rogers was appointed in her place – an appointment she was to hold for the next thirty years. She too tried to offer her services for overseas nursing, but was rejected on medical grounds. Nonetheless she was kept extremely busy as Noble's became a military hospital in part. Sister Stewart, her predecessor, was placed in charge of a hospital ship at Malta, and later in the war was in charge of a hospital near the French lines. Other nurses from Noble's served in war hospitals in England and further afield. A list prepared in 1917 by the matron, Esther Bridson, is impressive:

> *...16 have either joined Queen Alexandra's Imperial Military Nursing Service or the Territorial Force Nursing Service. The following are some of the names:- Queen Alexandra's Imperial Military Nursing Service: Sister Stuart is in France; Sister Fayle, in France; Sister Cowin, in Salonika; Nurse Joughin and Nurse Paterson are in Egypt; Nurse M. Simpson, in Winchester; Nurse Fraser, in St Albans; Nurse Kermode in Dartford (called up this week); Nurse Murray is in Devonshire Red Cross Hospital, Buxton; and Nurses I. Simpson, H.S. Benson, and M. Timby are Territorial Force Nurses at the 1st Western General Hospital. Nurse K. Rothwell has just been appointed Staff Nurse, and is shortly to begin duty at the Samaritan Hospital, London.* [235]

The long hours and mental trauma of dealing with a seemingly endless stream of men broken in body and mind must have taken its toll on these women. In January 1917 the *Isle of Man Examiner* reported that Miss A.Proctor, formerly matron of the Ramsey Cottage Hospital, who had been on the staff of a large hospital on the Western Front, was invalided home due to the severe strain of the work. A year later the influenza epidemic ravaged hospitals, and their overworked nurses, as the English commentator Vera Brittain recounted in her memoirs. Nurse Alice Mona Mylchreest, Quartermaster at Basford House Red Cross Hospital near Manchester, and Commandant of the 82nd Detachment East Lancashire Red Cross, died of peritonitis whilst on a visit to her family in Peel, on 1 September 1918. She was just thirty years of age when she passed away. After leaving boarding school, she had attended the Manchester School of Art, and had commenced her services with the Red Cross Society in September 1914. One month after the death of Alice Mylchreest, on 9 October, Nurse Sara Walker of Hammersmith Military Hospital died of an ovarian tumour at the residence of her parents at Castletown. Nurse Walker was even younger at twenty-nine years of age, and had been two years in the service. One has to question if these medical conditions were inoperable, or had overwork prevented the two young nurses from seeking treatment in a timely way? It certainly seems likely that fatigue would have masked their symptoms in the early stages.

Annie Knox, sister of Archibald Knox, served with the Territorial Force Nursing Service. In 1917 she was mentioned in dispatches, as well as being decorated with the award of the Royal Red Cross. Her confidential report from No 1 Stationary Hospital at Rouen stated:

> *[she] has had charge of a heavy surgical division. As Acting Surgical Sister she had charge of acute surgical hut. She is a very good surgical nurse. Thoroughly to be relied on; hard working & has proved a very satisfactory Sister.* [236]

Elizabeth Taggart, from Ridgeway Street in Douglas, became a nurse in Manchester, where she met and fell in love with her fiancé. When he was killed in action at Passchendaele in 1917, she resolved to throw herself with even greater vigour into war work. She took a job as a welder in the Manchester factory of aircraft producer AVRO, it was pioneering work and a position which she held until the end of hostilities. That same year, in summarising the work of Noble's Hospital nurses, the Receiver General J.T. Cowell paid tribute to young Manx women in general who had responded in Britain's hour of need in no lesser way than young men had done:

> *I am one of those who believe that one of the outstanding features of this great and terrible war, with all its results*

Mary Elizabeth Faragher (right) of Douglas worked at the Vickers armaments works at Barrow-in-Furness, operating a five ton crane. (PG 13748)

Civilians packing Christmas parcels for troops at Barrack Street mission in Douglas, during the Great War. (PG 11524)

which we mourn, will be the manner in which the women of this country have come to the front. How splendidly they have fulfilled the mission which many were afraid would not be fulfilled to the extent it has been. But I make bold to say that where women have had a chance, in no position in which they have been placed at the call of the country, have they failed to render splendid service. But in no way, I believe, without exception, in no way have the women of the country, and especially the young women, so nobly fulfilled the purpose of life as they have done in nursing the sick and wounded during the war. It will be one of the brightest pages in the history of this country how nobly our women have responded to the call to alleviate suffering and how ready they have been to take their places at the call of their country. [237]

An example of the way in which the war touched those of all ages comes from the pen of Ada Cain, a member of the St Matthew's Girl Guides, who wrote an account of her patrol's summer camp at Port St Mary in 1916. Many of the activities reinforced a sense of duty, patriotism and the idea of conforming to authority. She wrote:

While we were playing the vicar came round and told us he was going to take us to the village church, St Mary's. When we heard this, we tidied ourselves, and, when we were ready, we formed up in patrols. It was too early to go to church, so we went down to one of the piers to see the fishing boats. On the way down, we saw the Union Jack flying, and as we passed it we saluted it. We did the same thing when we returned. Whenever we see the Union Jack flying we are supposed to salute it. [238]

For another Douglas child, war work came in the form of packing Christmas gifts for soldiers. Anne Bannister, who was aged seven in 1917, remembered:

We were kept busy preparing parcels for the trenches. At our church (St Andrews) and doubtless all the others, helpers got together khaki mittens and mufflers, chocolates, needle cases, and loads of Black Cat cigarettes. We raised money by having concerts where somebody was sure to render 'Tipperary' or 'Keep the Home Fires Burning' ... I had to leave Miss Gelling's private school as our shop wasn't making enough money to pay the fees. I went for a while to Murrays Road and then to Park Road. I can't remember much about food shortages. So either we didn't fare too badly or the older people cushioned us youngsters against any deprivation. I still managed to get sweets with my Saturday penny, anyway and didn't do too badly for Christmas presents. [239]

The Christmas of 1917 was one of the quietest ever remembered in the Isle of Man. The *Examiner* newspaper noted that there was a marked absence of the usual feasting. In the churches there were the customary services, and at night the cinemas were open. These did good business, because the weather was unusually clement for the time of year. The 'Hunt the Wren' boys carried on the Boxing Day tradition, and hot food was distributed to 450 poor people. There was a pantomime (Dick Whittington) at the Villa Marina, given by the children of St Thomas' school, and earlier in the week 1000 children of Manx soldiers and sailors were entertained by Mr J.Goldie-Taubman at the Nunnery. At Ramsey, it was recorded that there was no dried fruit available for cakes or Christmas

puddings; oranges were available but were so expensive as to be prohibitive. New Year was also quiet at Ramsey with no brass band or choir in the streets. Douglas was more musical with a number of choirs and brass bands in evidence, but the tunes they played were of doleful character. The *Examiner* records that:

> The people generally were quiet. Perchance the exorbitant price of spirituous [sic] refreshments was a factor in the remarkable sobriety of the crowds on the first day of 1918. (240)

One intriguing effect of the war upon the Manx homeland concerns crime. Generally speaking there was a decrease in petty criminality; the *Isle of Man Examiner* reported in April 1917 that crime had fallen year on year up to that point, whilst the Norris Modern Press *Manx Yearbook* states that across the whole Island in 1918 the number of offences for which proceedings were taken was 485, slightly less than half the pre-war level. Whilst there is evidence in newspapers and police records of drunkenness during the war, and soldiers in particular were frequently arrested for being inebriated on licensed premises, this was nothing new. Douglas for as long as it had been a holiday resort had an undercurrent of drunken rowdyism, and in fact in Douglas the arrest rate for this type of offence was something like four times higher before 1914.

However at the same time there was actually a rise in

The first women police constables appointed by the Isle of Man constabulary, Mrs Louisa Cannell and Miss Margaret Lewin, in 1917. (MS 09310) some types of crime, most notably prostitution. Evidence from the surviving Douglas police records, for example lock-up books and charge books, points to an increase in offences involving prostitution or soliciting by young (and sometimes not so young) women from less than 1% of all crimes before the war to 7% by 1917. The reasons for this increase are not entirely clear. Whilst it could be attributable to different recording methods or a more hard line, less tolerant approach to policing the streets, this seems unlikely.

Stronger contenders are firstly increased hardship (indeed hardship verging on destitution in some cases) which was forced on the lowest strata of society by the collapse in the visiting trade, and the loss of associated seasonal work; and secondly the transformation of the Island brought about by two massive internment camps and their attendant soldiery. Police and prison records testify to the calibre of the men the military authorities were using to guard their camps, and quite clearly the best and brightest were being deployed on the battlefields of France. It would not be unfair to describe some of those sent to guard aliens at Douglas and Knockaloe as 'old lags'. Among the worst and most reprehensible men the army had, one almost gets the feeling they were sent to the Isle of Man to give the remainder of the army some respite from their activities, and they were as much prisoners here as those they guarded. The range of their criminality as documented in prison records is breathtaking, ranging from theft (from prisoners and from each other), drunkenness, attempted murder, and sexual offences. Wherever such soldiers are posted in large numbers, camp followers appear, and the Isle of Man in the First World War was probably no exception

to this rule. One of the few women to receive a custodial sentence for this type of activity did so in June 1918, not for the offence itself but ironically because she posed a threat to the efficiency of that very soldier. A twenty-one year old from Tynwald Street, she was arrested together with another prostitute whilst soliciting on Victoria Road at 10.30pm, presumably within close proximity of Douglas Camp. Whilst her cohort merely received a fine for her troubles, this lady was instead charged that, 'whilst suffering from venereal disease in a communicable form, did solicit or invite members of His Majesty's Forces to have intercourse with her.' She received six months imprisonment with hard labour.

It can be no coincidence that the Isle of Man's first women police officers were recruited during the latter half of the First World War, when Mrs Louisa Cannell and Miss Margaret Lewin were appointed not as Specials but as regular police constables. They were sworn in on 29 October 1917, and were followed on 1 July 1918 by Elizabeth Eleanor Kermeen. Significantly, no further female officers were recruited by the Isle of Man Constabulary until July 1940. Mrs Cannell had previously held the position of Probation of Offenders Officer for Women in Douglas and the south of the Island for a number of years, and she was asked to consider joining the police force, a request which she accepted. It might also be added that both she and Miss Lewin were staunch members of the Salvation Army. The fact that female officers were required at this time was probably less to do with a shortage of male officers, and more as a result of the increase in female criminality as the war went on.

The diary of the Acting Chief Constable,

Superintendent Quilliam, for the middle part of 1918 illustrates the state of the home front by this stage. Aside from instances of theft of sheep and potatoes, much of early July is taken up with descriptions of the major strike and demonstrations which took place over bread prices. During the summer of 1917 the British Government sanctioned the subsidising of flour and bread to an extent which allowed a loaf to be sold at ninepence until such time as the subsidy should be revoked, and this example was followed by the government of the Isle of Man in modified form. The Manx subsidy was granted to cover a period of six months, commencing on 26 November 1917. In the ordinary course of events, the specified period would have expired on 26 May, but the Lieutenant-Governor made arrangements to allow the loaf to be sold at ninepence until 30 June. The bread subsidy was inextricably linked with the question of income tax, in that the Island could not afford to continue with it unless direct taxation was introduced. However, a disagreement ensued between Raglan and the House of Keys over who should have control over the monies raised. The Lieutenant Governor had warned the Keys eight months earlier that renewal of the bread subsidy would be conditional upon the passage of the bill and resolution of the dispute, but still no agreement was reached. With time running out, on the Friday prior to the end of the extension, 27 June, Lord Raglan in the course of the annual financial statement to Tynwald unilaterally announced that the subsidy would terminate at the end of the month. It was this announcement which precipitated the protest from the Manx people – a protest which took the form of the most severe disruption of trade and industry ever experienced in the Island up to that point.

When the news of the coming increase in the price of the loaf was made public, the reaction of the by now well organised Manx labour force was swift. The master bakers stated that they could not produce bread at ninepence a loaf without the subsidy, and it was clear that the workers were not going to accept the increase without a fight. At the instigation of the officials of the Isle of Man District of the Workers' Union, representatives of the various trade unions were summoned to meet at Douglas on Saturday 29 June, and it was decided unanimously that unless steps were taken to ensure the continuation of the ninepenny loaf, a general strike should result. The union men notified the government of the decision, and also decided that public meetings should be held in various parts of the Island with a view to enlisting public support for the demand for the subsidised loaf. Superintendent Quilliam wrote on 4 July:

> *The strike has commenced. The official of the Seamans and Firemans Union attended the 2 steamers in the harbour and at his request the crews came ashore willingly. The trams are stopped as are also all the principal places of business, including newspaper offices. Several small places were opened, but pickets went round followed by groups of boys and women, all of one mind & demanded the workers therein to come out which they did. Captain Moughtin HK acted defiantly at the outset and several hundreds of persons behaving in a threatening manner collected round his place; there were 4 constables there under Inspector Duke & Sergeant Cringle, but they were helpless against such a crowd which surged onwards and at this time several missiles were thrown and the Captain's windows broken and there appeared to be a*

determined effort to get hold of the Captain & duck him in the harbour. It took the police all their time to save him and his daughters which they did by escorting them to the police station. To avoid further interference I ordered a car and they drove to the house of a relative but he declined to pay for it. The police seeing the temper and numbers of strikers advised shops to close and kept the crowd from committing damage. No other way was possible under all the circumstances. The only remedy by force was to apply for a Military Force and this I could not recommend because the crowds were orderly excepting when defied. I had several talks with the Government Secretary, closed all business premises, resisted calling out Military and urged that a solution be found and that House of Keys be summoned to reconsider the matter. I also recommended that Tynwald be adjourned. Governor agreed to adjournment. [241]

Captain Robert Moughtin was a curiosity; a working class mariner with Tory views (he had opposed the introduction of Old Age Pensions before the war) who sat in the Keys for South Douglas, a working class constituency. His obituary in *Manx Quarterly* stated:

At one time the popular idol in South Douglas, his attitude in connection with what is known as the bread strike of July, 1918, undoubtedly brought him into utter detestation with his quondam admirers. The proprietors of most of the places of business in Douglas prudently complied with the suggestion of the Labour organisations of the town that the establishments should be closed pending the result of the agitation for the restoration of the flour subsidy. But Capt. Moughtin, who was independence personified, opened his

coal yard, and for a long time stood in the gateway, passively, and at times orally, defying the mob which demanded the closing of the gates. In the end the yard was attacked, and notwithstanding the protective efforts of a number of police constables and strike leaders, the Captain was somewhat roughly handled. It is highly probable that his experience on the occasion had a detrimental effect upon his health, though he was at business again in the course of two or three days. [242]

The General Strike of 1918 was possibly the worst instance of labour unrest ever to occur in the Isle of Man. It affected virtually the entire workforce of the Island. It included not just the crews on the Steam Packet vessels which refused to sail, but also the Isle of Man railway, which was effectively paralysed. The reason for this outburst of discontent lay not just with the nine penny loaf, though that ostensibly was the issue which triggered it. Instead the strike reflected a whole range of grievances which had built up among the Island's workforce; grievances over the questions of old age pensions, and workmen's compensation, over which the workforce had been treated with contempt again and again.

Commenting on the strike in a report, George Titt noted:

Perhaps the most important feature was the splendid fight put up in the form of a general strike by the whole of our members to retain the 9d loaf in July 1918. The feature of this fight was that the members of our Union were fighting not a sectional fight for their own personal benefit, because as members of the Workers' Union they could have used their organisation to increase their own wages to meet any

Captain Robert Moughtin MHK, who in 1918 defied the strikers by opening his coal yard. (PG 8655-3296)

increase in the cost of living, but as true citizens they recognised that thousands of other people were unable to increase their earnings to meet any increase in the price of bread, and therefore they took the social view, and decided that a fight must be put up on behalf of those who were less able to take care of themselves. This spirit is one that we hope will grow in volume among all sections of the working class in future, and I am proud to place on record the unselfish action of our members in the Island.... [243]

In 1918 Raglan was forced to cancel the Tynwald Day ceremony as a result of the General Strike. For an autocrat who had previously wielded such power, it must have been a deep humiliation. Less than twelve months later, Raglan would tender his resignation as Lieutenant Governor. In November of that year, the war finally drew to a close. Telegrams posted in Douglas carried the news to excited crowds. Pubs threw open their doors, but, newspapers noted, there was very little drunkenness. This was partly due to the poor quality of wartime beer, but also the feeling of the bulk of the population was muted. There was some display of flags, and in Peel an American flag was hoisted, sent by an ex-patriot Manxman in anticipation of the moment the Kaiser was defeated, but as J. Goldsmith, chairman of the Eastern District Education Board, told the members:

As a community we have suffered heavily. I have been told of one terrace in this town where half the houses were unable to display bunting on Monday week. Why? Because into those houses had come the Angel of Death, and hearts were too sore for rejoicing. If any evidence on that subject is needed, just walk through our cemeteries.

The names of four brothers upon one stone in Braddan Cemetery show the cruel nature of the struggle. Such a record is enough to make angels weep. [244]

The columnist 'Occidental', writing in the *Peel City Guardian*, observed that:

...feelings are mixed ... There is joy in anticipation of the return of the boys, and much deep joy; and we are glad that the war cloud has rolled away; but I have already come across instances of sadness, accentuated by thoughts of 'the boys who will never return.' I don't go in much for the offering of palliative suggestions in such cases; they are generally useless. Silent sympathy is often the most acceptable offering. Many will find it hard to adjust though to the coming changes – they had settled into the prevalence of a state of war. The aliens in the camps no doubt feel queer, wondering what is to be done with them. It will be anything but pleasant for the men who may have lived in England for many years if they are forced to reside in an unsettled Germany. The men who have lucrative posts at the camps will have to contemplate losing their jobs at an early date, and the Manx Government will have to look for its revenue from other sources than the camps. "Allotments" will be revised and to some that will not be altogether a joy. Settling back will be a big job. [245]

The famous Manx novelist, Hall Caine, speaking at an Armistice Day ceremony in Douglas, stated that:

Liberty has nearly been wrecked during the last four years. We have seen it as we see ships outside sometimes beset in tumultuous seas, with the black cormorant of Autocracy screeching and squirming above it. [246]

On the face of it the reference was to the despotism of the Kaiser, which had been averted, but it could equally well have been an allusion to the behaviour of the Lieutenant Governor. He continued:

Sorrow sits at many a poor Manx fireside, and will never rise until we ourselves have risen. Some of the bravest and best – the favourite boy and the hope of young Manx manhood – have gone from us forever, and we shall realise that more and more as the time goes by. It makes my heart bleed to think of the Manx mothers, and the Manx fathers too, whose pride of life is gone. But to such who are watering their pillows with their tears, I would say - you have one great consolation: Your loss is the world's gain. You have given your sons for the greatest battle for Liberty and Freedom that the world has ever fought.... [247]

One of the long term effects of the First World War upon the Isle of Man was the realisation that its economy, so heavily reliant upon summer visitors, had been found to be woefully exposed when that trade had collapsed due to the war. Many of the Island's leaders were left with a resolve that the economy must diversify, if it were to survive. More than this, Tynwald, so long emasculated, was determined that it would never again be dominated by a figure such as Raglan. When he resigned in 1919, he had not even the courtesy to inform Tynwald, so little did he regard that august court. Nevertheless concessions and reforms had been won, notably control of finance by Tynwald achieved in 1919, and the task of the post-war years was to consolidate these.

HMS *King Orry* leads German battleships in to surrender in the Firth of Forth, November 1918, a painting by Arthur Burgess. (L20221)

Chapter Five

Garnering the Harvest

Internationally, the artistic and literary response to the First World War has undoubtedly been one of the most enduring legacies of that conflict. The poetry which was born of the anguish experienced by that generation which served in the war has entered the canon of British literature, more so than poetry inspired by any other conflict before or since. Poets like Wilfred Owen and Siegfried Sassoon stand alongside the likes of Byron and Wordsworth in our national consciousness. Only slightly behind the poetry comes the huge and influential body of prose bequeathed to us by the 1914 generation. Works by Robert Graves, Siegfried Sassoon, Henry Williamson and a host of others provide us with a rich landscape of text which will still be studied generations hence.

The response of the artistic community was also similarly inspired by the war. There were official war artists who documented the fighting, and of course a huge quantity of monumental art was produced in the aftermath of the conflict. These responses were not solely 'English' in their nature. The Irish painter Sir William Orpen captured the desolation of the battlefield in his work, and was made an official war artist. Francis Ledwidge was an Irish nationalist, but also a war poet whose work has been increasingly recognised in recent years. In Scotland, the work of Cyril Morton Horne and Charles Hamilton Sorley has been published to critical acclaim.

In the Isle of Man, much of the Manx cultural revival took place against the backdrop of the First World War, with people such as Mona Douglas leading a renewed interest in language, song and dance. Indeed, even though at times her interpretations of Manx history and folklore have been controversial, it is impossible to discuss the Manx cultural landscape of the twentieth century without reference to Mona Douglas. She was born (according to one of her accounts) on a Steam Packet vessel in 1898, though her birth was registered in Liverpool. Already a published poet by 1915, she stepped into the shoes of Sophia Morrison upon her untimely death in 1917. At the Welsh National Eisteddfod that year, Mona Douglas was inducted into the Gorsedd of Bards of Great Britain, with the Bardic title Mona Manaw. One of her most prized possessions for the remainder of her life was the green silk sash she was awarded by the Bards at this event. In her unpublished autobiography she played down the significance of the First World War, stating that cultural developments were suspended for its duration, but her cherishing of this object means there can be no doubt that the war provided the context for one of the defining moments of her career. Later, she spent time in Dublin during the Black and Tan era, and was profoundly influenced by these events, which were in their turn one of the outcomes of the war. Her September 1914 poem, *How the*

Mona Douglas, who emerged as a poet during the First World War, and subsequently became a leading light of the Manx nationalist movement. (MS 9545)

Manx go to War, was rather jingoistic and pro-war, the first verse reading:

> *There's 'prentice boys from Douglas,*
> *And fisher lads from Peel.*
> *There's boys from out the Corrany,*
> *And up past Laxey Wheel.*
> *Oh the boys of Ellan Vannin,*
> *That were reared beside the sea,*
> *Have come out to fight the Kaiser*
> *And his men from Germany!* [248]

However the poetry as well as the political ideas of Mona Douglas clearly developed and became more nationalistic as the war progressed. *Manx Song and Maiden Song* published in 1915 was somewhat naïve, and largely composed of sentimental work; much of its content comprised odes to the beauty of the Manx landscape, or the wistful longings of those forced by economic needs to wander far from the Isle of Man. Yet 1916's *The Manx Call to Arms* was a much more strident statement of nationalist aspiration:

> *Honour calls! And can we falter?*
> *We, the sons of Gorry's band,*
> *Who, in many and ancient battle*
> *Firmly took their stand*
> *Where the war-rose reddest bloomed,*
> *Where the sword-cloud thickest loomed;*
> *Glory-winning, or death-doomed!*
> *Ellan Vannin calls! Though England*
> *Rule us, we are yet half free;*
> *Holding scatheless through the ages*

Laws and liberty.
Gorry's Tynwald! Still it stands –
Guarded now by alien hands,
Yet held steadfast 'mid the lands.
Freedom calls! And we are ready
Each his summons to obey:
Mann sends forth her sons with gladness
To the watch, the fray.
Ere our Freedom can be won
There is fighting to be done –
And wherever rings the war-cry we arise
and follow on! (249)

The message here seems to be that wholehearted Manx participation in the war may yield the prize of greater independence afterwards. The widely vaunted idea that Britain was fighting for the rights of small nations for self-determination encouraged nationalist movements across the British Empire to similar aspirations. Indeed, in 1917's *To My Country*, Douglas was even more explicit in this sentiment. The poem is among the most overtly political of her works, and the third verse in particular is significant:

You who have slept unnumbered years,
Oppressed, despoiled for foreign gain,
Your very dreams made dim with tears,
Your old, wild spirit numb with pain:
Awake! And burst your bonds, and see –
You who have slept so long, so long –
How you may yet again be free
Will you but struggle and be strong.
Over the nations far and wide –

Listen! – the horns of Freedom blow;
O far away the unseen tide
Is turning, swinging to the flow!
Wake! Strive, and in your striving find
A long-lost utterance of the soul,
A quickening radiance in your mind,
A vision of the utmost goal.
What matters the unequal fight? –
Your wakening soul can scorn defeat:
Freedom shall crown your brow with light,
And weave her glory round your feet. (250)

Unlike the Manx nationalists of a previous generation, such as Sophia Morrison, whose national aspirations were framed firmly by a vision of the Isle of Man as part of the British Empire, Mona Douglas felt no such constraints. Indeed her inspiration was nationalist Ireland, which since 1916 had battled to be free of that empire. In 1919 she published *A Dhooragh*, which contains the poem *The Awakening*:

Dark the east with war and woe;
Red clouds glow and spread afar –
What is that to us but pain
For men slain in England's War?
England cannot reach our heart;
Far apart from her we stand,
While we give as gave the dead
Blood to shed at her command.
But across the sea at last
Comes a blast that thrills and stirs,
Waking dreams in prisoned lands,
Breaking bands and barriers.

We have heard a cry, a cry;
In our sky has dawned a light;
Land has cried to land in chains –
Through our pains come strength and sight.
From the west there shines a light
In our night of darkest need:
Through the darkness answering gleams
Leap as dreams from souls that bleed.
Kinsmen of the shining west!
Your unrest wild hearts have shared:
Soon from our land, too, shall rise,
Through wild skies, a singing bird. [251]

The potency of this rallying cry in support of what was an armed insurrection against British rule in a sovereign British territory, and which amounted at the time to treason, was powerful. Indeed it is questionable whether Mona Douglas could actually have published it whilst the war was still on, which perhaps accounts for the date of 1919.

It should not be forgotten however that Mona Douglas represented just one strand of opinion in the Isle of Man at this time. A poem by James B.Morton Barnes of Foxdale, published in September 1914 entitled *Something Ought To Be Done*, expresses something of a Christian Socialist ideal, and whilst not exactly anti-war suggests that the conflict is a distraction from pressing social reforms. The last verse runs:

Something ought to be done, my boys,
Our country to defend,
We want not war and cannons' noise,

But something that will end
The cause of all the din and strife,
And banish all despair,
That, like a surgeon with his knife,
Roots out the fell disease,
Let's cast away the things that tease,
And give a chance to life
To bud and blossom, bloom more fair;
So let us inwardly make peace,
Then battle, crime and greed will cease;
Hesitate no more, but run,
For surely something ought to be done. [252]

The same month, an equally reflective poem entitled *Tho' Battles are Won* was published by Beatrice Eyre of Laxey:

When we talk of the glorious battles
Our well-beloved nation has won.
Do our thoughts dwell at all on the carnage,
On the terrible crimes that are done?
Do we think of the wives, now lone widows,
Who weep tho' the battles are won,
Of the mothers, whose brave sons have vanished
For ever, and left them alone?
Do we think of the bright little orphans
Whom 'Daddy' will fondle no more?
He has laid down his life for his country.
And sleeps on a far distant shore. [253]

Whilst Josephine Kermode ('Cushag'), not to be outdone, published *What a Manx Boy Did*, the inspiration for which may have come from a previous conflict, for the poem has interesting parallels with the story of Bugler Dunne, the Manx boy hero of the Boer War:

Came a shot from Ambush near
And hit poor Juan-y-jaggad-Keear,
Laid him low in pain and fear,
And Juan bogh was crying.
In the darkness lying,
Juan bogh was crying;
Lying low in pain and fear,
Poor Juan bogh was crying!
Then upon his bugle, he
Went playing on right merrilee:
Played them on to victory
Did Juan beg of Mannin!
Juan beg of Mannin,
Deed on Ellan Vannin!
Played them on to victory
Did Juan beg of Mannin! [254]

Josephine Kermode, the Manx poet known as 'Cushag'. (PGN 05429)

More 'mainstream' verse is to be found in the work of Frederick Bishop Kermode. *Mannin* volume 9 of 1917 carried a poem by him, reprinted from the *Isle of Man Times* of 21 April 1917. A son of the rector of Ballaugh, and brother of both Josephine Kermode and P.M.C.Kermode later of the Manx Museum, Frederick was educated at King William's College. During the Great War, in his mid-sixties, he was headmaster of schools at Eastbourne and Brighton. Not having experienced combat himself, the poem perhaps lacks the punch of the work of Owen or Sassoon, but may instead be regarded as a good reflection of the perspective of a civilian, coming to terms with death on an industrial scale. Entitled *Gardens* it reads in part:

Somewhere in France
Was another garden - a lonely rood
In the broken heart of a mangled wood,
And all around
Upon every mound
Were little white crosses with names thereon,
In the pale white sunshine cold and wan;
No man might see the Gardener there,
Yet I found the marks of His loving care.
I bent me down those names to spell
Dear English names that we knew so well-
And I whispered the words with bated breath,

Of the gardener old, 'There is no death'!
And I bared my head and looked at the sun,
And I gave God thanks for every one;
For I knew that the happy dead would rise
To flower in the garden of Paradise. [255]

Likewise, another poem written from the perspective of the bereaved is entitled, *My Faith in God*. The verses below are extracts from the poem, which was written by Mrs Alberta Moore of Arbory Street Methodist Church, Castletown, when she heard of the death of her son in France:

My heart was full of sorrow
The severest in my life
I knew that on the morrow
Might begin the awful strife.
The morrow came, and with it
The tempter who did sneer
And try to shake my faith in God
In vain did he appear.
Three more days passed, and with them
Came anxious thought, and worry
And then the sudden startling news
My boy had gone to glory. [256]

An interesting poem dealing with similar issues, but written in the Anglo-Manx dialect, was published in 1916. Entitled *The Widow*, it commemorates those Manx sailors lost aboard HMS *Ramsey* and HMS *Goliath*. Published under a *nom de plume*, 'Nancy Bell' the author was Miss A.I.Caine:

I hadn' the heart for to tell her,
So I tuk her the paper instead –
When she seen his ship's name in the headline,
"My man'll be drownded," she said
"My gough, but the swimmy me head's gone,
Could I ax ya to read it for me?
Jus' wait till I purron the kettle,
The childer is wantin' their tea.
"An' hundhreds of sailors aboord her,
An' jus' these ones saved? Mercy me!
An' think of the lil childher prayin'
'Ternal Father' and 'Glory to Thee.'
"An' couldn' the Lord stop all this fightin',
Or not lerrit start? – O me head!
Aw, Jim, how I wish I was with ya!
The good it'd be to be dead!"
The paper slipped urrov me fingers,
I gorrup and went out by the gate –
An' I seen the whole skutch of the childher,
An' wondhered who'd get them their mate. [257]

There are some similarities to other dialect works such as *Our Tommy*, by Josephine Kermode published in September 1914:

Our Tommy to the war has gone
And left his ease behind him.
He'll bang the Kaiser to the wall
Wherever he will find him.
But, dear my heart, the time is long,
And dark the cloud that's o'er us;
Yet we for all will show the way,
To face the days before us.

> *When Tommy left good-bye at home,*
> *His voice with pride was ringing: –*
> *"There's wives and childher there beyond*
> *That need the help we're bringing."* [258]

For her part, Kermode was equally as concerned with animal casualties as human ones, penning in 1917 *The Blue Cross*:

> *Do you hear the cry, the piteous cry*
> *From the shell-struck earth to the flaming sky –*
> *"Oh think of us that suffering lie,*
> *Your faithful wounded Horses!"*
> *There's the hero's Cross for the valiant brave,*
> *There's the Holy Rood o'er the soldier's grave,*
> *There's the Red Cross Aid your men to save –*
> *And what for the wounded Horses?*
> *O a penny here, and a penny there,*
> *And the silver groat that you can spare,*
> *For the Blue Cross Boys whose skill and care,*
> *Are saving the wounded Horses.* [259]

A final offering from the Home Front comes in the form of a piece of what can only be described as doggerel, which was composed by William Gell (author of *Mannin Veg Veen* and other similar items of verse) and which appeared as *Duke Street and Market Place Douglas, Past and Reminiscent* in 1918. Mostly comical in nature, it does however contain some intriguing verses:

> *And here recurs to memory Tommy Tate,*
> *Who aimed to render service to the State;*
> *His shop with draperies was all alive,*

> *With gorgeous crinolines a perfect hive;*
> *How often I admired his stalwart figure,*
> *As fine a man as ever pulled a trigger;*
> *He quickly rose a step above the ranks,*
> *A corporal in our premier "Loyal Manx"!*
> *When knowing wiseacres would sniff the air*
> *And bid less favoured ones for war prepare,*
> *With apprehension quick to action grown*
> *(The sleek "objector" then was quite unknown),*
> *In countless thousands Britain's loyal sons*
> *Came forth with eagerness to man the guns...*
>
> *The memory of Joe Coupe still with me lingers;*
> *With twine and paper seeming intertwined,*
> *His manual prowess still recurs to mind.*
> *(A worthy son of his hard by, quite fit,*
> *In this great war for right had done 'his bit';*
> *For shirking slackers quite a good example,*
> *Of whom our streets still show a sorry sample).* [260]

These were clearly references to the ongoing internal strife between those who were serving, and those who through conscience or exemption were perceived as not to have done so.

In 1914 a *Book of Manx songs* was published, for troops at the front, the cost being met by Walter Gill, of Prenton, near Birkenhead. Gill, who was in later life the author of the *Manx Scrapbook*, served in the war as a private soldier. Despite this, none of the songs reflected the current conflict, indeed some were of considerable age. From among others who served on the front line, some powerful poetry survives. Private R.H.Ennett, a Manx soldier, composed *Killed in Mesopotamia* about a comrade who lost his life in that theatre, another Manxman by the name of Private W.B.Radcliffe:

He was a boy, no more than that –
A boy, so young and fair,
A simple-hearted laddie,
With neither thought nor care.
He boasted of no feats nor strength,
He had no claims to fame,
But he heard the call to battle,
And obeyed. Did you do the same?
He left his home, his friends, his work,
All that his soul held dear;
He gave them up for duty,
He had no thought of fear;
Nor did he cast a backward look
Of sorrow or regret –
He had heard the call to battle,
And obeyed. Did you do that?
The toll of battle now is paid,
The grave has claimed its own –
Those soldiers brave and gallant,
These heroes, every one;
Amongst the dead, so quiet, so still,
A soldier laddie lay;
He had heard the call to battle,
And obeyed. What do you say?
They buried him at evening time,
With military honours,
This gallant Manx laddie,
Who died for us and ours.
A simple little cross they raised,
This epitaph it bore –

"He heard the call to battle,
And obeyed. Could he do more?" [261]

The Reverend Horace Mylchreest, a minister from Union Mills serving as a Chaplain to the Forces in France, composed the following verse in August 1916, whilst attached to a casualty clearing station. He like Ennett could have been under no illusion about the reality of war, and his poem perhaps represents the difficulties faced by a man of God struggling to come to terms with wanton destruction carried out in the name of that God:

There's a sheltered spot where the willows grow,
And the Poplars stand so high;
Where magpies chatter and the old black crow
Caws alone his mournful cry.
There are wheatfields near, and the poppies red
Dot the gold with crimson blots;
There's a silent stream with a reed-strewn bed
O'erhung with forget-me-nots.
But shadows are cast where the poplars grow,
And the willows hang to weep;
Where the poppies show, with a blood-red glow,
'Mid stalks where death's angels reap.
There are changes here in this vale of peace,
Where wood-pigeons coo so low;
And far thunder peals make life's music cease –
Save the dirge of one black crow.
With a blasting breath spread the clouds of hell;
The pall of hatred and strife.
On the wings of night grim heralds foretell
The struggle 'twixt death and life.
From mankind divine, from God's own elect

Is garnered the harvest of ill,
First fruits of the grain, foul passions eject
Lusts' bias of man's free will.
In thy mercy look, O Father of all.
On Thy suffering flock distressed.
Bid the discord cease, make Thy people call
For chords of eternal rest.
Forgive us dear Lord; make us own Thy sway;
Purge our hearts from hatred's dross;
Lead us on the way to eternal day;
Thy way! Thy Life! Thy cross! (262)

The dark humour of the First World War British soldier is well known, and his use of laughter as a method of lightening the burden of life in constant danger is demonstrated in publications such as the *Wipers Times* or Bruce Bairnsfather's *Fragments from France*, which often highlighted the absurdities of the situation in which front-line soldiers found themselves. In 1916 two Manx soldiers composed an amusing piece of verse along similar lines. A parody of a popular music hall song, it never the less captures the reality of front-line service. It was called *Sing Me to Sleep*, and part of it reads:

Sing me to sleep, where bullets fall,
Let me forget the war and all;
Damp is my dug-out, cold are my feet,
Nothing but bully and biscuits to eat.
Sing me to sleep where bombs explode
And shrapnel shells are a la mode;
Over the sandbags helmets you'll find,
Corpses in front of you, corpses behind.
Far from La Guerre I'm longing to be,

Where German snipers can't pot at me;
Think of me crouching, where the worms creep
Waiting for someone to put me to sleep (263)

In the field of prose, the Isle of Man's greatest writer of the late nineteenth and early twentieth centuries was undoubtedly Thomas Henry Hall Caine. Almost forgotten today, in his heyday Hall Caine was probably the most famous novelist in the English language. Born in 1853, he was a creature of the Victorian age, and like Archibald Knox was too old to see front line service. However he turned his efforts towards support for the war and in 1914, he produced a charity book, in support of the exiled King Albert of Belgium. King Albert in turn rewarded Hall Caine by creating him an Officer of the Order of Leopold. Caine tried to involve America in the war by writing articles, mainly for *The New York Times* and in 1915 he gave a series of lectures in the USA, but these were not well received. He wrote a series of articles for *The Daily Telegraph* about how the war was affecting 'ordinary' people, and these were published in 1915 as a book entitled *The Drama of 365 Days: Scenes in the Great War*. The *Isle of Man Examiner* reviewed the book, commenting favourably upon his withering pen portraits of the Kaiser and others.

In 1916 Hall Caine was invited to work with Lord Robert Cecil at the Foreign Office, towards the creation of the League of Nations after the end of the war. The same year Caine wrote a small book entitled *Our Girls: Their Work for the War Effort* to show that women were also playing an active part in the war. He was also involved in producing a propaganda film to assist the war effort but the war ended before the film could be

completed. Towards the end of 1917 Caine was offered a
baronetcy but he declined it and instead he accepted a
knighthood as a KBE, in recognition of his propaganda
work on behalf of the British government. He insisted
on being called, not 'Sir Thomas Hall Caine' but 'Sir
Hall Caine'. It is interesting to note that one of Hall
Caine's last works, *The Woman of Knockaloe* was set
against the backdrop of internment on the Isle of Man,
but it was simply that – just a backdrop. Hall Caine dealt
with none of the real issues or strains which internment
had produced, nor offered any solutions to the crises
which the war had caused on the Isle of Man, and the
novel was simply a love story along the same lines as
many of his previous works. Hall Caine fell out of
favour with the British public after the First World War
– he was perceived as a 'Victorian author' and his ideas
were considered outdated.

A lesser known writer, born at Durham but of Manx
descent, was Jessie Douglas Kerruish. Having published
in 1916 *Tales and Legends of the Isle of Man*, in 1917 she
followed this with a novel set in the Ottoman Empire
Miss Haroun al-Raschid. However, Kerruish's best-known
and most celebrated work was undoubtedly her macabre
novel *The Undying Monster: A Tale of the Fifth Dimension*.
The story was first published in 1922, and tells of the
uncovering of a hereditary family curse unraveled by a
psychic detective. It is tempting to speculate that this
story was inspired by the surge in interest in spiritualism
and clairvoyants, among those seeking to contact lost

**Thomas Henry Hall Caine. The best-selling novelist was
knighted at the end of the war for his propaganda work on
behalf of the British Government. (1954-5806)**

relatives in the wake of the war.

Another female writer was Emma Burgess, author of *Muriel Cannell – A Manx Story of War Time*. In the novel, the eponymous heroine, an independent young woman, must choose between two suitors, one a civilian whom she loves, the other in the army, whom she does not. Perhaps the story was a metaphor for the choices facing the Manx people. For Burgess, the war was an opportunity for the Isle of Man to find its soul. She believed that in relying on the tourist trade for so many years, morality had been sacrificed in the name of profit, stating:

> *Our love for our Motherland could not save her from distress in this time of war and upheaval. We have deplored this distress, and bewailed our financial ruin, but there is another side to it. Distress is not necessarily disaster. This temporary cessation of the visiting industry may truly be a blessing in disguise.* (264)

In her view the war had shown Manx people that they had a choice, between what was easy, and what was right and morally correct.

After the war, all of the published literature about the Island's experience centered upon internment. Two important memoirs were Cohen-Portheim's *Time Stood Still* and Stoffa's *Round the World To Freedom*, quoted in Chapter Three. The one Manx war writer who might well have made a name for himself, were it not for the misfortune of circumstance, was John McCauley. Born in 1895 in Queen Street, Douglas, McCauley was educated at Hanover Street Elementary School. He was working at Gelling's Foundry when the First World War broke out. He was persuaded by a foreman to enlist and joined a

Special Reserve battalion of the Border Regiment. By January 1915 he was in the front line in France. Despite his lack of formal education, McCauley had tremendous enthusiasm and ambition, and learned several new words from the dictionary each day. He began writing his war memoirs, based upon his wartime diaries, in the early 1930s and work colleagues at the foundry persuaded him to send them to the *Isle of Man Examiner*. The newspaper published them, anonymously at first, but such was the demand to know the identity of the author that eventually it was revealed to be McCauley. In the 1930s McCauley was an active member of the Labour movement and it was at one annual conference that he met Ernest Bevin. In 1933 Bevin tried to help McCauley to find a publisher, but without success. It was at the height of the war memoir 'craze' and two publishers replied to Bevin along the lines that although McCauley's material was good, the market for war memoirs was simply flooded. If he had been more persistent, it is possible that McCauley's book would have been published and would have stood alongside the greats of 1930s literature – *All Quiet on the Western Front*, *Goodbye to All That*, and *Memoirs of a Foxhunting Man*. One of the opening paragraphs of McCauley's memoir runs as follows:

> *The World War was a fortnight old when my employer came up to me in the workshop and said, "Well, John, England is at war, you know; she badly needs young men like you today." He knew that I had served in the special reserve before the outbreak of war. Perhaps that knowledge gave him the courage to ask me to go, for after all, it needs a little courage to ask a young man to go out and face death, even for his country's sake. My only reflections then were:*

"How romantic it will be, what can war be like?" I might just be in time to see the end if I join up at once.

My imagination was running away with me. I could see the soldiers of the different countries dumped into three or four fields to fight it out. If I didn't join up quickly the war would be over, and I would miss this wonderful spectacle.

Then again, I could see myself crouched behind a hedge with a rifle in my hands searching for a target. It never occurred to me that the enemy would be looking for targets, too. The spirit of adventure impelled me, as it did millions of boys and young men like me all over the world in those days, and I told my employer I was willing to go.

How pleased he was. Perhaps he thought he had done his bit. My decision seemed to give pleasure to my workmates, too. Why it was so, I never could tell, but they shook me by the hand, clapped me on the back, and wished me good luck and a safe return. I too began to feel quite pleased with myself. I was already getting elated at the promise of the great adventure. There was a grim awakening in store for me. [265]

John McCauley, of Douglas. Although simply educated, his war memoir makes dramatic reading. (PG 7058/3)

McCauley's work has featured in recent documentaries both on Channel 4 and on BBC TV. Beyond this, Manx war literature is sparse. There were no other war novels, and few other war memoirs – certainly none that were published.

Turning to drama, the Peel playwright Christopher Shimmin, with the help of Sophia Morrison, staged a number of plays during the war. Although most had been written prior to 1914, the conflict added a new dimension to some, such as *Luss ny Graih* a comedy written in the Anglo-Manx dialect. The title translates as *The Love Herb* and the play is set in a village post office, where the postmistress dreams of finding romance. Performed by the Peel Players in December 1914, funds from six of the seven performances were donated to war relief charities. In the post-war years, ex-serviceman T.A.Quayle scripted a humorous play entitled *Bullets, Billets & Blighty*, full of soldiers' dark humour. The preface stated that it was dedicated to the Douglas Branch of the Royal British Legion in memory of the unquenchable spirit of those who served. Although the play reads like a precursor to *Blackadder Goes Forth*, there is a serious moment when a sentry on night duty is visited by an ethereal figure, who tells him:

> The Spirit of your fallen comrades is proud to welcome those other sons of Mother England whose sense of honour has led them to forsake everything that is dear to them. From all corners of the earth, wherever men of British blood found themselves, they came. From the distant Dominions of the Commonwealth, from the ruling Princes of India, from the sorely tried people of Ireland, from dear little Ellan Vannin, came the ringing message that the nations of the Empire would stand together. This very ground, now desolated, even as it has been desolated many times in history, is sacred ground. Drenched in the blood of those sons of Britain who have died for noble ideals. Their bodies are dead, but their glorious spirit still lives. [266]

From a Manx perspective, none of the most significant visual artists of the first two decades of the twentieth century experienced the war directly. The Isle of Man's greatest artist, Archibald Knox, was too old for combatant service. He did however leave a valuable account of how the war impinged upon his creativity, writing in 1919:

> I have done hardly any serious work during all the five years: the first two summers I tried sketching in the neighbourhood in the evening when work was over but it was always a failure: chiefly the dampness: that at least was the obvious reason of failure; but I was so unsettled and nervous: I tried designing and that suited me better. But I did not produce much that was of value. I spent the evenings of about six months on 'The Deer's Cry' but it will be I think mostly wasted; designing in celtic form so many forms of [which] keep coming in sight – that unless one is ready to work them out at the time they are lost: I have a good number of pages in outline but it will take a serious study of each one to find out what colour scheme I had intended.... [267]

The Deer's Cry is arguably one of Knox's most significant works, and at the very least the war provided the context for its creation. The poem is a lorica or prayer of protection often recited before battle, so perhaps the conflict was also more directly an inspiration for the work. Knox also produced a wide range of memorial art in the years following the close of hostilities, but he drew inspiration for this work from the Celtic heritage of the Isle of Man, and the landscape at home which was familiar to him, rather than the landscape of shell holes and barbed wire which haunted the memories of so many who had served. Knox's memorial crosses owe more to those of the Celts and Vikings a thousand years previously than to the neo-classicism, replete with Greco-Roman columns, which was on the march across Britain in the early 1920s. His near contemporary, John Holland, was approaching the end of his artistic career, and despite goading those he believed to have German ancestry produced nothing himself which might be considered 'war art' or which was influenced by a response to the war. William Hoggatt was of a younger generation, aged thirty four when the First World War began. At the time he was a teacher at King William's College. Possibly for reasons of poor eyesight he does not appear to have undertaken any combatant service in the war. His artistic career continued unaffected by the conflict, and several times during its course there were exhibitions of his work. Even more so than Knox, Hoggatt's style remained stubbornly uninfluenced by the events of the Great War. It drew from him no artist response whatsoever.

John E. Aitken of Port St Mary was a thirty-five year old artist, specialising in maritime scenes. He was called up for military service in March 1916 but told the tribunal that he had strong conscientious objections to the taking of human life, since he would feel himself personally responsible, even if acting under orders, stating:

> I would not kill. I am utterly opposed to killing. I do not feel that it is right ...I would rather be killed than to kill a man. I am quite willing to work, but not to kill. [268]

He said that he would gladly join the Royal Army Medical Corps or undertake other non-combatant work. He was granted a conditional exemption by the tribunal, but on the evidence of his notebooks it appears that by the latter stages of the war, Aitken was in neutral Holland. Save for a watercolour of an armed trawler patrol, which was still very much in keeping with his pre-war work, Aitken also produced nothing which was directly inspired by the conflict.

This lack of response to the war was not however solely confined to Holland and Hoggatt. Across the spectrum of early twentieth century artists working in the Isle of Man, there was a strange reluctance to confront the war and its realities. On the Island from 1915 to 1918 there was hardship, food shortages, political unrest and the billeting of thousands of enemy aliens, yet none of this do they reflect in their work. As a case in point, John Henry Yeend-King was a fabulously talented artist in the opinion of many people, yet his depiction of a Manx farmstead in 1915 was little altered from works being produced thirty or more years earlier. In Yeend-King's case, it might well be argued that the death of his son from war wounds in April of that year could justifiably lead him to seek solace in escapist art, but what might be termed 'social realism' was obviously missing from the work of many other Manx artists. By contrast, the numerous artists working within the internment camps chose to depict camp life in great detail, indeed their work is almost defined by its sense of realism. Perhaps the most important of these internee artists was George Kenner, who primarily depicted scenes of camp life, though there were other significant artists at work, notably Fritz von Kamptz who excelled at portraiture.

All of the internee-produced work was intended for internal or private consumption. The only piece of Manx public or semi-public art depicting a scene from the war was actually painted by an Australian. Arthur Burgess's *Surrender of the German Fleet* depicts the Isle of Man Steam Packet Company vessel *King Orry* leading the German High Seas Fleet into internment in 1918. The work was in fact commissioned by the Steam Packet Company to hang in its board room. Quite reasonably the directors of the company wanted a public statement of the highly significant part its ships had played in the war. The almost propagandist nature of Burgess's commission is reflected in the fact that the painting leaves the casual viewer with the impression that *King Orry* led the entire German Fleet into surrender. In truth she led only one of several columns of German ships. This was none the less a great honour, as she was the only merchant vessel so nominated and all the other flotilla leaders were Royal Navy ships.

Of course a great paradox of the First World War is the question of what might have been. What even greater talent was squandered on its battlefields, talent which might have enriched future generations? In the field of visual arts it might well be argued that in the Isle of Man the idea of the 'lost generation' finds its best evidence in the fact that there was little in the way of significant new artistic expression until the post Second World War era. Indeed, it could further be argued that the artists of the Isle of Man remained locked in their nostalgic view of the Manx countryside and coastal scenes, views in most cases little altered from their nineteenth century counterparts.

In the 1930s on the Isle of Man the most significant person in the visual arts who had been directly affected by the war was not actually Manx-born. Dusty Miller, the cartoonist for the *Isle of Man Times*, and author of *It's a Fact*, which he illustrated himself, was deeply affected by his experiences in the conflict. Born in Liverpool, Miller had been a Post Office telegram boy prior to 1914. He saw service in the war with the Post Office Rifles and was gassed, this leading to the removal of a damaged kidney later in life. After the war he joined the Liverpool City Police, and came to the Isle of Man in the 1920s when he married a Manx girl. Many of Miller's cartoons grew darker and more reflective around Armistice Day, and particularly so after the outbreak of war in 1939.

Overall the cultural response of the Manx people to the war was a varied one. Much of the literature associated with the war has now faded into obscurity, and

This sketch by Dusty Miller shows the ghosts of 1914-18 coming to the assistance of the soldier of 1939. (2005-0069/55)

the art work though important remains familiar largely to those with a specialist knowledge of, or interest in, the subject. However the Knox-designed war memorials, particularly those at Onchan, and in Regent Street Post Office in Douglas, remain an everyday part of the landscape, and retain a relevance to generations born many years after the First World War. It is these which perhaps represent the Isle of Man's most enduring creative legacy of the conflict.

Lieutenant Governor William Fry presenting medals to veterans, around 1920. (PG 13708)

Chapter Six

Epilogue

In the wake of the First World War, trouble flared in Russia, the Middle East, and in Ireland where nationalists including Sinn Fein were battling the forces of the Crown in a bloody and bitter confrontation. When a proposal for the Isle of Man to contribute £250,000 towards the costs of the war incurred by the British Government met with hostility in Tynwald, Ambrose Qualtrough MHK questioned which war the funds were actually going towards:

> I don't know whether it is the war with Russia, or whether it is the war with Turkey, or the war going on with our brother Celts in Ireland [but] I am not going to be a party to it ... it is only to help the Black and Tans in Ireland. [269]

However if the sympathies of Qualtrough and, as we have already seen, Mona Douglas, lay with the republicans in Ireland, there were still plenty of young men on the Isle of Man who were quite prepared to help the Black and Tans. At least ten young Manxmen joined the Royal Irish Constabulary between 1920 and 1921, and one was wounded in a clash with the IRA. They were part of a wider phenomenon which saw young men across the British Isles who were too young for the war, or who had just missed it, eager to find excitement either in Ireland, with the Palestine Gendarmerie or in other post-war flashpoints.

Among those who had served in the war and who had seen action, there was much bitterness in later years towards those who they perceived had not. In Manx society in particular the stresses and divisions caused by the war spread through the years which followed like ripples on a pond. The debate over conscientious objection was still rumbling in the newspapers even after the war had ended, with some, including MHK Gerald Bridson, calling for the conscientious objectors to be deprived of the vote. Elijah Oliver again wrote to the *Isle of Man Examiner*, this time to say that:

> The legislation disenfranchising the objectors was passed without proper knowledge of the facts. The peculiar results are (1) that objectors who, for various reasons were never 'called up' can freely exercise their vote. (2) that any imprisoned objector, repenting from the error of his ways, and joining the army, must lose his vote, and (3) hundreds of objectors from the mainland can come to live over here and exercise their full rights of citizenship, for the simple reason that they have committed no offence in the Isle of Man. I have one of these latter cases in mind at the moment, and it is no wonder that Mr R.B.Moore called such legislation "war panicky legislation," now to be regretted. [270]

Oliver went on to observe that even if the Manx Labour Party was too timid to parade its own previous anti-war stance in front of the post-war voter, it nonetheless had the courage to oppose this piece of legislation.

Nevertheless the divisions caused by the war remained high in the consciousness of many who had lived through it. In 1941, during the Second World War, an anonymous correspondent in the *Isle of Man Examiner* wrote:

> *White feathers for certain stay-at-home young men are proposed. I remember something of the kind during the last war, but something more drastic than white feathers is required. We all know the public has a short memory; take our City Fathers for instance. A few of them were young men twenty-five years ago, trembling in their shoes as they appealed for exemption from military service, but they succeeded in dodging the war. Now we have them posing as our leading citizens; they will even take part in patriotic movements, so long as the other fellow does the fighting.* [271]

William McLean had written in a similar vein to the *Isle of Man Times*:

> *These men of the army of yesterday gave much in defence of their country, whilst conscientious objectors in one guise or another (no names), stayed at home, and others fled to Ireland until after the war.* [272]

Whilst the war was in progress, among those actually fighting there was little dissent from the view that their cause was just, and that the Kaiser and German militarism represented a menace to the British way of life. This was certainly true in the Isle of Man. In the post-war years however, and more particularly in the 1930s as ex-servicemen suffered the humiliation of unemployment, and as a new war loomed large upon the horizon, those views became discredited. Port St Mary minister Reverend J.H.W.Haswell, an ex-serviceman himself, told his congregation on Armistice Sunday in 1935:

> *I believe that one supreme truth has been dearly won for us by our illustrious dead – that war is utterly futile – that it does not achieve the results claimed for it, that it never has, never can, and never will produce peace, liberty and justice ... it leaves behind it an aftermath of misery, hatred, and desire for revenge.* [273]

The only positive aspect which he identified in the war was the spirit of self-sacrifice which it had engendered. Bitterness grew over the treatment of ex-servicemen in the depression-ridden interwar years, and the absence of a 'land fit for heroes' (the expression used by British Prime Minister David Lloyd George at the end of the war) added fuel to this fire. In 1938 McLean wrote to the *Isle of Man Times* of his anger at his rejection for employment in favour of younger men who had not served in the war, commenting:

> *I feel [bitter] ... at times, and so do thousands more unemployed ex-servicemen, but what is the use? I know we deserve better treatment, and I believe we will get it when the roll is called up yonder.* [274]

In a November 1939 edition of the same newspaper we find an ex-serviceman writing angrily that so many of his ex-comrades are dependent on the proceeds of poppy sales instead of being in gainful employment:

> *[The poppy] fund was originally formed to help ex-servicemen when they were sick or to start them in small businesses, but in recent years it has become a means of subsidising the dole: and twenty years after the so-called Great War, with a greater one in progress, the Manx Government are content to allow the men who fought for their country in her time of need to depend on charity for that little extra help that the Poppy Fund is able to give for six or eight weeks every winter. When will our Government waken up to the realisation of its responsibility to the men who are prematurely aged through their war services, and spare them the disgrace of accepting this charity year by year through sheer necessity?* [(275)]

Whilst in the same edition McLean again wrote that the memory of his wartime comrades should not be used to prop up discredited notions of the righteous nature of the war:

> *Do we wish to remember them? Yes, always; but in the quietude of our homes with our memories of their comradeship. We have no desire to see those poppies again on sale in the streets. Let the past die as the past of previous wars have faded, and which are now only dim memories. Let us forget that we ever took part in the last war, for it only brings bitter regrets.* [(276)]

The shabby treatment of disabled veterans was a particularly vexed point among ex-servicemen in the post-war years. Robert Oates, who lost part of his leg at

PC Edward Brew, of the Royal Irish Constabulary. Manxman Brew joined in 1921 as the force recruited outside of Ireland, following the mass resignation of local constables. (PG 8642)

La Bassée in 1914 was in the 1930s receiving 24 shillings per week disability pension together with 4 shillings fourpence pension as a time-expired Regular soldier. He was also able to eke out a meagre living labouring in the river at Union Mills, as well as working as a joiner and as a night watchman, and on this as a widower he raised four children. It was a graphic example indeed of life in the post war 'land fit for heroes'. Alfred Teare in his *Reminiscences* gives a stark illustration of the short memories that many in positions of power had, when it came to war-wounded, during the inter-war years:

I was responsible for introducing a Bill into the Keys providing for employment for disabled persons, many of whom had suffered disablement because of war service ... One of the clauses in the Bill was the compulsion on employers to employ three per cent disabled persons on their staffs. The "thanks" for what these men had suffered in a war to protect his property was expressed in his opposition to the Bill when ... Mr R.Q.Hampton said: "The passing of the Bill will mean an addition of five per cent to the wages bill of the firms, without any guarantee that they will get anything like value for it." [277]

At least two Manx servicemen were totally blinded in the war and were cared for by the St Dunstan's charity, William Christian of Douglas, and Edgar Taggart of Castletown, who was badly wounded and lost his sight in 1917. T.H.Colebourne lost the sight of one eye in France, but went on to establish and build up a successful radio and television retail business in Douglas between the wars. The Disabled Soldiers' Fund was set up in the Isle of Man to assist injured ex-servicemen return to civilian life, precisely by starting up such businesses. Douglas Henry Creer, a horseman, had joined the army in February 1916. Wounded in the head and leg in July of that year, he had spent nineteen months in hospital before discharge. Able to walk only with difficulty, he could not return to his former occupation. He was granted £50 by the fund specifically to set up a newsagent's and tobacconist's on Prospect Hill.

Indeed there is ample evidence that those injured or maimed in the war strove to overcome their difficulties and to live as normal a life as possible. One amputee, William Caren, who had lost a leg in the opening battles of the war, was still able to go fishing. In one tragi-comic incident his prosthetic leg was almost the cause of his demise, when his boat having capsized he was thrown into the sea and the leg began to fill with water, threatening to drag him under. Fortunately he was able to hold it above the waves until help arrived. Daniel Faragher lost his leg on the Somme in 1916; he nevertheless lived to be 81. Prior to the war he had been a painter and decorator. He could not return to his

A collecting box for the St Dunstan's charity, in the form of cartoon character 'Old Bill'. This one was used in Douglas. (1986-0077)

pre-war occupation, as with one leg he was unable to climb ladders, and so he retrained as a boot repairer. His father's greenhouse at the rear of the family home, 34 Farrant Street in Douglas, became his first workshop. His daughter later recalled that in spite of his disability her father remained cheerful all of his life, only becoming unhappy when his stump caused him pain. She recalled a particular incident when he attended hospital in Liverpool around 1970, where children suffering from Thalidomide disabilities were fitted for artificial limbs. He said that those people who complained about their lot should see how those children got on with life with a smile. He himself was fitted for an artificial leg at Roehampton War Hospital around 1920, it stayed in the house all his life but he could not wear it because of the discomfort it caused. He got around instead on crutches, and his daughter remembered that he was particularly fast and mobile.

It is something of a myth that Ballamona mental hospital was filled with shell shocked ex-servicemen in the 1920s. Preserved casebooks show that there were undoubtedly some ex-servicemen being treated at the hospital in those years. Indeed in one case from 1919, an ex-soldier from Ramsey is explicitly stated to have a history of shell shock, and his medical notes describe his delusions whilst on the ward:

> [He] is of the opinion that he is [being shot at] by the Germans and about to go over the top. [278]

Disabled veteran Daniel Faragher, seen in the 1970s. In spite of the loss of a leg on the Somme, Faragher lived into his 80s.
(PG 13596/4)

However in many other cases, there were clearly pre-existing mental health issues present, though that is certainly not to deny the fact that many men on the Isle of Man grappled for years afterwards with the lingering effects of what they had experienced or witnessed in the war. In February 1933 a Douglas ex-serviceman named Johnson – a married man with five children – tried to commit suicide by gassing himself in his oven. He had been a prisoner in Germany during the war, and now found himself in ill health and out of work. At his subsequent trial for attempted suicide, the man burst into tears and sobbed through the whole proceedings, declaring:

> *The position to me seems hopeless. I am fighting against the tide.* [279]

In this instance the High Bailiff was sympathetic, and tried to obtain medical treatment for the man. It took a lot longer however for there to be general acceptance of the fact that ex-servicemen could suffer long term mental after-effects of their experiences, despite being apparently in perfect physical health. As late as 1944 so called 'war-neurosis' sufferers were brought to the attention of the Legislative Council by Deemster Farrant on behalf of the British Legion, who stated that:

> *These were ... cases in which there was no visible disease, but where by some peculiar upsetting of the nervous condition as the result of war service the sufferer became incapable of earning his living. If he was given a job he might carry on for some time then suddenly cease to be capable of going on with it.* [280]

Circumstances for disabled veterans began to improve after the Second World War. In 1951, in the first of a new scheme on the Isle of Man, Robert Pritchard of Linden Grove, Douglas, a former member of the Royal Field Artillery who had been seriously wounded at Guillemont on the Somme in 1916, was presented with a brand new Morris Minor car specially adapted with hand controls. The car was provided by the British Government's Department of War Pensions, to enable him to get more easily to his place of work, the offices of the Douglas Corporation Electricity Department, and also to facilitate his leisure activities, for Pritchard was also a keen scoutmaster. Among the people who had served abroad, the greatest legacy of the war was undoubtedly the sense of comradeship which it bred, which endured until all but the last of them had passed away. There is ample evidence for this in the frequent re-unions of the Manx Service Company, which occurred regularly until the 1980s.

Among Manx nationalists such as Mona Douglas, the war was a defining epoch and for her at least the fracture between England on the one hand, and what was to become the Irish Republic on the other, had a profound influence. Indeed for her it helped to shape a vision of the future in which the Manx took their place in a pan-Celtic brotherhood, free from the sometimes malign influence of England. In the early 1920s under the title *Manx Nationalists in the New Age* she wrote of this vision:

> *Many thinkers and writers have placed the responsibility for this ... state of affairs with the great war out of which we are just emerging; and doubtless the war has played its part in leading up to the changes that are upon us. But it was only a part. War or no war, these changes had to*

come sooner or later; for the cause of them lies deeper than war or peace, and was at work, not in one nation merely, nor in three or four, but in every place where there were visionaries to dream and strive, minds to think, and hearts to suffer and be glad, long before the war began. But the war and the many happenings in its train and the changed conditions of life have brought these things into greater prominence, and made the beliefs of the few articulate, and the impulse of the many more obvious, and the light of the approaching new age clear for all to see; and in this new light that is pouring in on us all our ancient and cherished ideas and habits and beliefs and aims have to undergo a very close scrutiny indeed. [281]

She continued:

Nationalism in the past – and not Manx nationalism only – has been too material; too much concerned with ideas of suspicion and hatred of other nations, and with armies and navies and flag-waving. But the new nationalism that is coming with the new age, the nationalism of which I stand ... as an ... unworthy exponent, will make love, not hate, its central idea, and love and trust will permeate it through and through. Armies and navies will not be necessary, because the security of the nation will rest not on war and the acquisition of power or territory, but on the love and thought and work of our people for their own country. [282]

Whilst her vision was never realised in its fullest extent, there can be no doubt that those nationalist activists like her, whilst remaining on the fringes, still managed to influence mainstream political agendas. Who can argue that since the First World War the Isle of Man's relationship with its larger neighbour has altered out of all recognition? Though it would not be officially adopted as the flag of the Isle of Man until 1931, the three legs on a red background, previously confined to merchant vessels, began increasingly to be used in place of the Union Flag from about 1915. Just as with Australia, Canada and New Zealand, participation in the war led to a growing sense of awareness of a separate national identity.

For ordinary working people on the Isle of Man, the war transformed a society whose patterns of life and customs were in many ways unchanged over centuries, into one which began to resemble the society we know today. T.A. Brew, a miller from Sulby who grew up during the war and was just too young for service in it, describes the complete sea-change in attitudes which resulted from it:

....Education did not only come from reading. The war years between 1914 and 18 made men travel, they visited places which they had never heard of, they seen things which they had only heard about, they seen the power of the Motor, the Tractor, these were only coming to the Island at that time and were the toys of the rich. Up to this time all men on farm work had been paid so much per year, and it was a good man who got 20 to 25 pounds per year, most got from six to twelve. There was men who earned a weekly wage, these were the men who trimmed and cleaned the roads, I don't know how much per week they got, but they were all crofters, so it couldn't have been much, anyway, the difference between their wages and the farm worker wasn't great enough to cause discontent.

It was after the 1914/18 war that men at these jobs

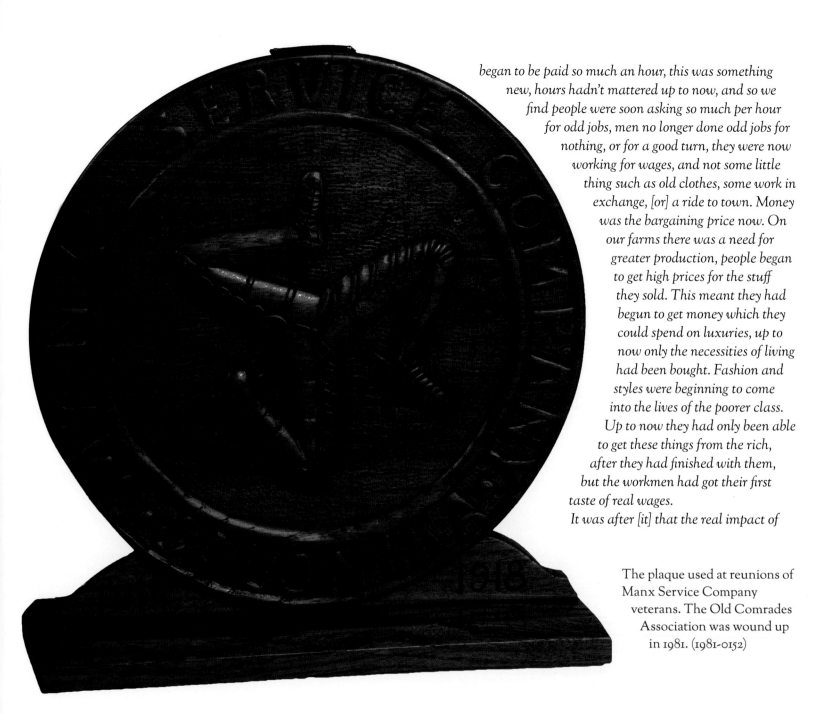

began to be paid so much an hour, this was something new, hours hadn't mattered up to now, and so we find people were soon asking so much per hour for odd jobs, men no longer done odd jobs for nothing, or for a good turn, they were now working for wages, and not some little thing such as old clothes, some work in exchange, [or] a ride to town. Money was the bargaining price now. On our farms there was a need for greater production, people began to get high prices for the stuff they sold. This meant they had begun to get money which they could spend on luxuries, up to now only the necessities of living had been bought. Fashion and styles were beginning to come into the lives of the poorer class. Up to now they had only been able to get these things from the rich, after they had finished with them, but the workmen had got their first taste of real wages.

It was after [it] that the real impact of

The plaque used at reunions of Manx Service Company veterans. The Old Comrades Association was wound up in 1981. (1981-0152) *the war was felt in the Island, men were no longer willing to work for a few pounds per year, they had seen Employers getting big money, and now they wanted a share of it. They had done their duty for their country, it was now up to their country to do its duty to them, and so we find the beginning of that time when the Government began to be employers of large numbers of men, at good wages, light work, and short hours. Working for a toff was no longer looked on as being an honour, the poor had been the slaves of the rich, the workman had been the slave of the employer.* [283]

Above all, the feeling grew among those in the lower strata of society, that having given their all for the state, they had a right to expect more than charity to look after them, as had been the case in the nineteenth century. The state, they felt, was obligated to them. As early as November 1918, a man named Cowin from Maughold was advocating the creation of what would become the Welfare State, even if it would not be until the aftermath of another war that this would be realised:

In the name of God, our manhood and womanhood, let the men who have suffered, bled and died in the great European inferno, and moistened the fields of France and Flanders with their blood, let them and their dependants be given a sufficient State pension to decently maintain them, as they have a right to be maintained, and if there are cases of special hardship, then let there be additional State allowance unstained by the least tint of charity. [284]

The First World War was a cataclysmic event, the watershed between the old world and the new, and this was as true for the Isle of Man as it was for Imperial Russia (though the Isle of Man avoided the bloodshed). It would be no exaggeration to state that the modern Isle of Man was born out of the ordeal of the First World War. The Island's constitutional and political framework was dragged kicking and screaming into the twentieth century. It was in the field of politics that the legacy of the First World War was perhaps most in evidence. Tynwald in the 1920s was packed with those who had earned their stripes on the battlefields at home rather than on the battlefields of France: men like Christopher Shimmin, Ambrose Qualtrough, Alfred Teare and William Clucas, who through the Manx Labour Party and the trade unions had challenged Lord Raglan and the prevailing political status quo. Though faced with recession and economic hardships in the 1920s, the Island had finally thrown off the yoke of an administrative system which had survived since the days of Atholl rule in the 1700s. Unlike the years prior to 1914, it now had both a growing sense of itself as a nation with its own destiny, and the ability to confront those hardships head on and ameliorate them as best it could.

Notes

Chapter One

1. *Isle of Man Weekly Times* 26.9.1914
2. *ibid*
3. *ibid*
4. *ibid*
5. *op cit* 3.10.14
6. *op cit* 7.11.1914
7. *op cit* 24.10.1914
8. *op cit* 31.10.1914
9. *Ramsey Courier* 2.10.1914
10. *Isle of Man Weekly Times* 24.10.1914
11. *op cit* 26.9.1914
12. *op cit* 31.10.1914
13. *op cit* 7.11.1914
14. *ibid*
15. *ibid*
16. *Mona's Herald* 13.1.1915
17. *ibid*
18. Manx National Heritage, Green papers MS 13001
19. Manx National Heritage, Killey papers MS 09832
20. *Isle of Man Examiner* 15.1.1916
21. *Isle of Man Weekly Times* 13.5.1916
22. Manx National Heritage, Ashley McGain letter 27.6.16 MS 12928
23. *Isle of Man Weekly Times* 15.7.1916
24. *Ramsey Courier* 18.8.1916
25. *op cit* 11.8.1916
26. Manx National Heritage, Folk Life Survey, J.R.Corlett C/154
27. The National Archives, Kew, Jefferson service papers WO 339/23677
28. *Isle of Man Weekly Times* 30.9.1916
29. *The Cushag* December 1916 p64
30. *Isle of Man Weekly Times* 11.11.1916
31. Manx National Heritage, Corlett papers MS 10987
32. *ibid*
33. *Isle of Man Weekly Times* 2.12.1916
34. Manx National Heritage, Corlett papers MS 10987
35. *Isle of Man Weekly Times* 9.6.1917
36. *Isle of Man Weekly Times* 1.9.1917
37. Manx Aviation Preservation Society archive MAPS367
38. *Isle of Man Weekly Times* 1.12.1917
39. Manx National Heritage, Gibb papers MS 09412
40. Manx National Heritage, McCauley papers MS 10129
41. Manx National Heritage, Frank Lace Clucas papers MS 11470
42. *Isle of Man Weekly Times* 31.7.1915
43. *op cit* 25.9.1915
44. *op cit* 4.9.1915
45. *Isle of Man Examiner* 11.5.1918
46. Manx National Heritage, Bertie Reid papers MS 13110
47. Manx National Heritage, Edward Holmes memoir MS 13125 (courtesy of Barry Quilliam)
48. The National Archives, Kew, Buckley service papers WO364/491
49. *Ramsey Courier* 11.10.1940
50. Manx National Heritage, Corlett papers MS 10987
51. *Mona's Herald* 1.4.1920

Chapter Two

52. *Isle of Man Weekly Times* 21.3.1964
53. *ibid*
54. *Isle of Man Examiner* 1.1.1916
55. *ibid*
56. *ibid*
57. *Mannin* Vol VI 1915
58. *Isle of Man Weekly Times* 15.5.1915
59. *Manx Star* 11.1.1980
60. *ibid*
61. *Isle of Man Weekly Times* 11.9.1915
62. *Ellan Vannin* vol 3 #9 December 1928
63. *Isle of Man Examiner* 19.8.1938
64. *Mona's Herald* 9.6.1915

65. The National Archives, Kew ADM101/335
66. S.W.Roskill, *The Royal Naval Air Service 1914-18* Navy Records Society 1969 p222
67. C.J.Blackburn *How the Manx Fleet Helped in the Great War* Douglas 1923 p46
68. *Mona's Herald* 18.8.1915
69. Blackburn *op cit* p48
70. Blackburn *op cit* p49
71. Blackburn *op cit* p23
72. Blackburn op cit p36
73. *Mona's Herald* 14.6.1916
74. *ibid*
75. Manx National Heritage, Harry Tylden Mosse recollections MS 13129
76. *Isle of Man Examiner* 3.10.1969
77. Blackburn *op cit* p41
78. William Wedgwood-Benn, *In the Sideshows* London 1919 p78
79. Wedgwood-Benn *op cit* p147
80. John Rushworth Jellicoe, *The Crisis of the Naval War*, London 1920 p81
81. Manx National Heritage, Quine memoirs MS 13119
82. Blackburn *op cit* p31
83. Blackburn *op cit* p33
84. Blackburn *op cit* p27
85. *The Cushag* Vol 12 No 39, March 1918
86. http://www.communigate.co.uk/ne/chesterlestreetheritage/page36.phtml
87. *Isle of Man Weekly Times* 4.3.1916
88. http://uboat.net/wwi/ships_hit/1208.html
89. *ibid*
90. Bertram Sargeaunt, *The Isle of Man in the Great War* Douglas 1922 p102
91. C.H.Cowley *Caves of Peel Hill* in IOMNHAS *Proceedings* Volume IV pp23-30
92. *Isle of Man Weekly Times* 17.11.1917
93. The National Archives, Kew ADM 137/1515 (additional research courtesy of Adrian Corkill)
94. Manx National Heritage, Patrick Cadogan letter MS 06573/2
95. Isle of Man Family History Society Journal May 1997
96. The National Archives, Kew ADM 137/1515 (additional research courtesy of Adrian Corkill)
97. Manx National Heritage, Harry Tylden Mosse recollections MS 13129

Chapter Three

98. *Isle of Man Weekly Times* 11.5.1935
99. *Isle of Man Examiner* 11.12.1936
100. *Isle of Man Weekly Times* 28.11.1914
101. Charles L Hartmann, *Kriegsgefangener auf Gibraltar und der Insel Man* Bern, 1918 p181
102. *op cit* p188
103. Frederic Dunbar-Kalckreuth, *Die Manner Insel* Leipzig 1940 p183
104. *op cit* p186
105. Maurice Jeger, *22 Monate in Englischer Kriegsgefangenschaft – Aus den Internierungs-lagern Shrewsbury, Handforth, Knockaloe, Douglas (Insel Man)* Vienna 1917 p67
106. Manx National Heritage, Schonwalder papers 10.11.15 MS 12028
107. *op cit* 24.11.1915
108. Paul Stoffa, *Round the World to Freedom* London 1933 p230
109. Paul Cohen-Portheim, *Time Stood Still* London 1932 p32
110. *op cit* p36
111. Manx National Heritage Schonwalder papers MS 12028 23.1.1916
112. *Manx Quarterly* V3 No17 October 1916 pp71-74
113. Manx National Heritage, J.T.Baily papers MS 10417
114. HMSO *Reports of visits of inspection made by officials of the United States Embassy to various internment camps in the United Kingdom*, London 1916, p21
115. Manx National Heritage, J.T.Baily papers MS 10417
116. Otto Schimming, *13 Monate hinter dem Stacheldraht* 1919 p15
117. Ottoman archives, Istanbul, HR.SYS. 2203/20
118. Herbert Bury, *Here and There in the War Area*, London, 1916 p143
119. Manx National Heritage, Rudolf Hartmann papers MS 12779
120. Manx National Heritage, Schonwalder papers MS 12028 18.8.1915
121. *op cit* 2.12.1915
122. *op cit* 3.6.1916
123. *op cit* 1.5.1916
124. *op cit* 1.10.1916
125. *Isle of Man Examiner* 29.5.1915
126. *ibid*
127. Manx National Heritage, Mary Faragher papers MS 13141

128. *Isle of Man Examiner* 16.3.1918
129. *Ramsey Courier* 8.3.1918
130. *Peel City Guardian* 9.11.1918
131. Manx National Heritage, Lilley papers MS 12840
132. *Knockaloe-Lager-Zeitung*, No 1, 7.10.1916
133. *Knockaloe-Lager-Zeitung*, No 9, 18.6.1917
134. *Lager-Echo*, No.1, 18.11.1916
135. *Knockaloe-Lager-Zeitung*, No 8, 25.5.1917
136. *Lager-Echo*, No 1, 18.11.1916
137. *Knockaloe-Lager-Zeitung*, No 19, 5.9.1918
138. *Knockaloe-Lager-Zeitung*, No 10, 4.7.1917
139. Manx National Heritage, Archibald Knox letter 26 October 1919, MS 09954/2
140. Manx National Heritage, Kenner memoirs MS 11425
141. *ibid*
142. *Knockaloe-Lager-Zeitung*, No 1, 7.10.1916
143. *Knockaloe-Lager-Zeitung*, No 1, 7.10.1916
144. *Knockaloe-Lager-Zeitung*, No 16, 6.2.1918
145. Cohen-Portheim, *op cit* p128
146. *Knockaloe-Lager-Zeitung*, No 10, 4.7.1917
147. *Lager-Echo*, No 6, 28.7.1917
148. *Knockaloe-Lager-Zeitung*, No 3, 22.12.1916
149. *Knockaloe-Lager-Zeitung*, No 15, 29.12.1917
150. *Lager-Echo*, No 4, 30.3.1916
151. *Knockaloe-Lager-Zeitung*, No 8, 25.5.1917
152. *Knockaloe-Lager-Zeitung*, No 13, 7.10.1917
153. *Der Querschnitt* volume 1, 1921
154. *Knockaloe-Lager-Zeitung*, No 1, 7.10.1916
155. *Lager-Echo*, No 8, 15.9.1917
156. *Knockaloe-Lager-Zeitung*, No 2, 18.11.1916
157. *Lager-Echo*, No 1, 18.11.1916
158. Isle of Man Public Record Office, Ballamona Hospital Casebook C17/1J
159. *Isle of Man Examiner* 24.1.1963
160. *Isle of Man Weekly Times* 17.1.1964
161. *Knockaloe-Lager-Zeitung*, No 18, 27.6.1918

Chapter Four

162. Manx National Heritage, Catherine Craine diary 13.8.1914, MS 09230
163. *Isle of Man Examiner* 5.12.1914
164. *op cit* 28.11.1914
165. *Manx Church Magazine* November 1915 p234
166. *Isle of Man Examiner* 13.2.1915
167. *op cit* 6.2.1915
168. Craine *op cit* 6.8.1914
169. *Isle of Man Examiner* 11.9.1915
170. Manx National Heritage, Sophia Morrison, letter 25.3.1915, MS 09495
171. Christopher Shimmin, *Outlines from Manx History* Peel 1916 p25
172. *Isle of Man Examiner* 12.8.1916
173. Samuel Norris, *Manx Memories and Movements* Douglas 1938 p281
174. Morrison, *op cit* 15.8.1916
175. Brown & Sons *Debates in the Manx Legislature* 19 March 1918 Vol 35 p289
176. *Isle of Man Weekly Times* 9.9.1916
177. *Isle of Man Examiner* 16.9.1916
178. *Isle of Man Examiner* 20.5.1916
179. *Ramsey Courier* 16.6.1916
180. *Isle of Man Examiner* 18.7.1916
181. *op cit* 12.5.1917
182. *op cit* 3.6.1916
183. *op cit* 18.3.1916
184. *op cit* 27.5.1916
185. Isle of Man Family History Society Journal, Volume vii no 1 (January 1985)
186. *Peel City Guardian* 26.1.1918
187. Manx National Heritage, Eleanor Callister notebook, MS 09735
188. Richard Hyman, *The Workers' Union*, Oxford 1971 p35
189. Modern Records Centre, University of Warwick, *Annual report of the Workers' Union* 1918. MSS.126/WU/4/1/13, p23
190. Manx National Heritage, Bobby Kelly interview, SA 0328
191. *ibid*
192. *Isle of Man Examiner* 23.3.1918
193. *Isle of Man Times* 7.4.1917
194. *op cit* 14.4.1917
195. *Isle of Man Examiner* 20.4.1918

196. *ibid*
197. *Isle of Man Weekly Times* 27.1.1917
198. *op cit* 1.12.1917
199. *op cit* 27.4.1918
200. *ibid*
201. Kelly *op cit*
202. Norris *op cit* p405
203. *Examiner Annual* 1917
204. Manx National Heritage, Folk Life Survey T.A.Brew BTA/C
205. Alfred Teare *Reminiscences of the Manx Labour Party* Douglas 1962 p51
206. *Isle of Man Examiner* 22.1.1916
207. Manx National Heritage, John Kermode letter 30.12.1916, M08291/83
208. Norris *op cit* p404
209. *Isle of Man Examiner* 24.2.1917
210. *Isle of Man Weekly Times* 16.12.1916
211. Brown & Sons, *Report of the Committee Appointed by Tynwald on Agriculture* Douglas 1926 p40
212. *ibid*
213. Teare *op cit* p32
214. George Quayle *Legends of a Lifetime* Wigan 1979 p2
215. Quayle *op cit* p80
216. Quayle *op cit* p88
217. W.Walter Gill *A Second Manx Scrapbook* Bristol 1932 p55
218. Gill *op cit* p91
219. Manx National Heritage, MS 13070
220. *Mannin* Vol V No9 p562
221. *Manx Quarterly* No 19 Volume IV
222. Teare *op cit* p58
223. *Isle of Man Weekly Times* 30.5.1978
224. *ibid*
225. *Isle of Man Examiner* 29.1.1916
226. *Isle of Man Weekly Times* 23.9.1916
227. Teare *op cit* p58
228. *Isle of Man Examiner* 28.4.1917
229. *Isle of Man Times* 3 June 1916
230. *Isle of Man Examiner* 10 June 1916
231. Manx National Heritage, Alice Gibb letter (undated) MS 09412
232. *The Cushag* December 1916
233. *ibid*

234. *Isle of Man Examiner* 11.12.1936
235. Manx National Heritage, Report of Noble's Hospital 1917, M 06271
236. The National Archives, London WO/399/12635
237. Manx National Heritage, Report of Noble's Hospital 1917, M 06271
238. *Isle of Man Weekly Times* 23.9.1916
239. *Isle of Man Courier* 24.10.1980
240. *Isle of Man Examiner* 5.1.1918
241. Manx National Heritage, diary of Acting Chief Constable Superintendent Quilliam MS 09310
242. *Manx Quarterly* No 21 1920
243. Modern Records Centre, University of Warwick, *Annual report of the Workers' Union* 1918. MSS.126/WU/4/1/13, p23
244. *Isle of Man Examiner* 23.11.1918
245. *Peel City Guardian* 16.11.1918
246. *Mona's Herald* 20.11.1918
247. *ibid*

Chapter Five

248. *Isle of Man Weekly Times* 26.9.1914
249. Manx National Heritage, M 05314
250. Mona Douglas *Mychurachan*, London 1917
251. Mona Douglas *A Dhooragh*, Douglas 1919
252. *Isle of Man Weekly Times* 26.9.1914
253. *Isle of Man Examiner* 5.9.1914
254. *Isle of Man Weekly Times* 12.9.1914
255. *Isle of Man Weekly Times* 21 April 1917
256. Manx Methodist Historical Society Newsletter No3 October 1985
257. *Isle of Man Weekly Times* 12.8.1916
258. *Isle of Man Weekly Times* 19.9.1914
259. Manx National Heritage, M 01086
260. William Gell, *Duke Street and Market Place Douglas: Past and Reminiscent* Douglas 1918 p12
261. *Isle of Man Weekly Times* 12.5.1917
262. *Isle of Man Examiner* 11.11.1916
263. *Isle of Man Weekly Times* 30.9.1916
264. *Mona's Herald* 12.7.1916
265. Manx National Heritage, McCauley papers MS 10129

266. Manx National Heritage, MS 02337
267. Manx National Heritage, Archibald Knox letter 26.10.1919 MS 09954/2
268. *Mona's Herald* 29.3.1916

Chapter Six

269. Brown & Sons *Debates in the Manx Legislature* 1920-1921 Vol 38 p642
270. *Isle of Man Examiner* 28.2.1920
271. *op cit* 7.11.1941
272. *op cit* 20.5.1939

273. *Isle of Man Examiner* 15.11.1935
274. *Isle of Man Weekly Times* 30.4.1938
275. *op cit* 4.11.1939
276. *ibid*
277. Teare *op cit* p71
278. Isle of Man Public Record Office, Ballamona Hospital Casebook C17/1J
279. *Mona's Herald* 7.2.1933
280. *Ramsey Courier* 29.9.1944
281. Manx National Heritage, Mona Douglas papers MS 09545
282. *ibid*
283. Manx National Heritage, Folk Life Survey T.A.Brew BTA/C
284. *Isle of Man Weekly Times* 28.11.1918

Bibliography

Belchem, John *A New History of the Isle of Man* Volume V, Liverpool, University of Liverpool Press, 2001

Blackburn, C.J.*How the Manx Fleet Helped in the Great War*, Douglas, Louis G.Meyer, 1923

Breitensträter, Hans *Meine Kampf*, Berlin, Eysler, 1923

Brown & Sons, *Debates in the Manx Legislature* Douglas, Brown & Sons

Brown & Sons, *Report of the Committee Appointed by Tynwald on Agriculture* Douglas, Brown & sons, 1926

Burns, Ian M. *Ben-My-Chree Woman of my Heart: Isle of Man Packet Steamer and Seaplane Carrier,* Leicester, Colin Huston, 2008

Bury, Herbert *Here and There in the War Area*, London, A.R.Mowbray, 1916

Cohen-Portheim, Paul *Time Stood Still*, London, Duckworth, 1932

Corkill, Adrian *Shipwrecks of the Isle of Man*, Stroud, Tempus Publishing Ltd, 2004

Cowley, C.H. *Caves of Peel Hill* in *IOMNHAS Proceedings* Volume 4 pp. 23-30, 1945

Cresswell, Yvonne *Living with the Wire*, Douglas, Manx National Heritage, 2010

Douglas, Mona *Manx Song and Maiden Song*, London, McDonald, 1915

Douglas, Mona *Mychurachan*, London, John long, 1917

Douglas, Mona *A Dhooragh*, Douglas, Clucas & Fargher, 1919

Dunbar-Kalckreuth, Frederic *Die Manner Insel*, Leipzig, Paul List Verlag, 1940

Gell, William *Duke Street and Market Place Douglas: Past and Reminiscent* Douglas, Broadbent, 1918

Gill, W.Walter *A Second Manx Scrapbook,* Bristol, Arrowsmith, 1932

HMSO, *Reports of visits of inspection made by officials of the United States Embassy to various internment camps in the United Kingdom,* London, Harrison & sons, 1916

Handscombe, David *King Orry 1913-1940,* Ramsey, Ferry Publications, 2006

Hartmann, Charles L *Kriegsgefangener auf Gibraltar und der Insel Man* Bern, P.Haupt, 1918

Hyman, Richard *The Workers' Union* Oxford, Clarendon Press, 1971

Jeger, Maurice *22 Monate in Englisher Kriegsgefangenschaft – Aus den Internierungs-lagern Shrewsbury, Handforth, Knockaloe, Douglas (Insel Man)* Vienna, Max Pöck, 1917

Jellicoe, John Rushworth *The Crisis of the Naval War* London, Cassell & Co, 1920

Liddle, P.H. *Men of Gallipoli* London, Allen Lane, 1976

Norris, Samuel *Manx Memories and Movements* Douglas, Norris Modern Press, 1938

Quayle, George *Legends of a Lifetime* Wigan, Douglas Printers, 1979

Roskill, S.W. *The Royal Naval Air Service 1914-18*, London, Navy Records Society, 1969

Sargeaunt, Bertram *The Isle of Man and the Great War* Douglas, Brown & Sons, 1922

Schimming, Otto *13 Monate hinter dem Stacheldraht*, sl., Missionsagentur, 1919

Shimmin, Christopher *Outlines from Manx History*, Peel, W.K.Palmer, 1916

Stoffa, Paul *Round the World to Freedom* London, Bodley Head, 1933

Teare, Alfred J *Reminiscences of the Manx Labour Party* Douglas, Island Development Company Limited, 1962

Wedgwood-Benn, William *In the Side Shows* London, Hodder & Stoughton, 1919

West, Margery *Island at War* Laxey, Western Books, 1986

Index

Numbers in bold refer to illustrations

IN LOVING MEMORY OF
P.TE JAMES QUILLIAM BRIDSON,
16264 13TH ROYAL SCOTTISH RGT.
BELOVED SON OF ROBERT & F.M. BRIDSON
WHO GAVE HIS LIFE FOR HIS COUNTRY
AT THE BATTLE OF ARRAS